FREEDOM'S EDGE

Freedom's Edge takes the reader directly into the heart of the debate over the relationship between religious freedom and LGBT and reproductive rights. The book explains these complex areas of law, and what is at stake in the battle to protect each of these rights. The book argues that religious freedom and sexual freedom share some common elements and that in most contexts it is possible to protect both. *Freedom's Edge* explains why this is so and provides a roadmap for finding common ground and maximizing freedoms on both sides. The book enables anyone with an interest in these issues to understand what the law actually teaches us about religious freedom, sexual freedom, and how they interact. This is important because what is often argued by partisans on both sides distorts the legal and cultural stakes and diminishes the possibility of compromise.

Frank S. Ravitch is Professor of Law and the Walter H. Stowers Chair in Law and Religion at the Michigan State University College of Law, and Director of the Kyoto, Japan Summer Program. He is the author of several books, including *Marketing Creation: The Law and Intelligent Design* (2011) and *Masters of Illusion: The Supreme Court and the Religion Clauses* (2007). He is the co-author, with the late Boris Bittker and Scott Idleman, of the first comprehensive treatise on U.S. law and religion in more than fifty years, *Religion and the State in American Law* (2015). Professor Ravitch has published numerous law review articles and book chapters addressing U.S. and Japanese constitutional law, law and religion, and civil rights law in leading journals. Moreover, he has written several *amicus* briefs addressing constitutional issues to the United States Supreme Court.

Freedom's Edge

RELIGIOUS FREEDOM, SEXUAL FREEDOM, AND THE FUTURE OF AMERICA

Frank S. Ravitch

Michigan State University College of Law

CAMBRIDGE
UNIVERSITY PRESS

CAMBRIDGE
UNIVERSITY PRESS

One Liberty Plaza, 20th Floor, New York NY 10006, USA

Cambridge University Press is part of the University of Cambridge.

It furthers the University's mission by disseminating knowledge in the pursuit of education, learning, and research at the highest international levels of excellence.

www.cambridge.org
Information on this title: www.cambridge.org/9781107158870

© Frank S. Ravitch 2016

First published 2016

Printed in the United States of America by Sheridan Books, Inc.

A catalog record for this publication is available from the British Library.

ISBN 978-1-107-15887-0 Hardback
ISBN 978-1-316-61155-5 Paperback

Cambridge University Press has no responsibility for the persistence or accuracy of URLs for external or third-party Internet Web sites referred to in this publication and does not guarantee that any content on such Web sites is, or will remain, accurate or appropriate.

This book is dedicated to my wife Chika, my daughters Elysha and Ariana, and my parents Carl and Arline.

This book is also dedicated to all people who seek to build bridges between communities rather than destroy bridges.

CONTENTS

PREFACE

I wrote this book because I can no longer sit back and watch as out-spoken opponents of religious freedom characterize any attempt to protect it as discrimination, and as opponents of sexual freedom char-acterize same-sex marriage as somehow eroding the fabric of America. Moderate voices are often drowned out by more radical ones on each side, and the media seems to prefer the radical voices. This makes sense since radical voices often make for a "sexier" headline or news story than do the nuanced positions of moderates. Yet, as a deeply religious person who strongly supports LGBT rights and reproductive freedom, I know I am not alone in supporting freedom on both fronts.

Two problems often arise in public discourse on religious free-dom, LGBT rights, and reproductive freedom. First is a lack of balance – not just in media reports but also in debates I often overhear in stores or restaurants. It seems that few people consider the possi-bility that we can have strong religious freedom laws *and* strong protection for both LGBT and reproductive rights. It is not that no voices are out there advocating for this but rather that those voices are not being heard as well as the voices of those screaming on one side or the other.

Second, few people besides law school professors and some in the broader legal community truly understand the law governing religious freedom, LGBT rights, and reproductive rights. And why should they? This law is highly complex, and those of us involved in the legal debates often use quite a bit of legalese as shorthand when we discuss these issues. This makes our discussions more understandable within the legal community, but it can mystify the law for laypeople who could

easily understand it if they did not have to sort through the meaning of
the vast array of terminology lawyers and courts use. If people do not
understand the law, it is hard for them to gain a well-informed position
on these issues because the issues are heavily connected to the law.

This book has two major goals. First, it aims to present the issues in
as balanced a way as possible so that readers understand that protections for religious freedom and for LGBT and reproductive freedom
are not necessarily antithetical – in fact, it is possible to have
both. Second, this book aims to explain the law in a way that those
who are not lawyers can understand it and also use it to help inform
their views on these issues.

In suggesting a balanced approach, I stress the areas of commonality between the issues, but I do not stray from the areas of conflict.
Where conflict is unavoidable I advocate compromise, which I realize
will be uncomfortable for people on both sides. I apologize for the
discomfort, but it is healthy discomfort because it requires us to challenge ourselves to expand our horizons and work to heal a sensitive area
in our remarkably polarized society. In this way, it is a bit like a doctor
apologizing for the discomfort caused by a test or procedure that may
save someone's health or life. The reality is that religious freedom is
currently at risk, as demonstrated by the recent defeats of state religious
freedom laws, and LGBT and reproductive rights are also at risk as
backlash continues to grow. A bit of discomfort while confronting these
issues may help us protect both.

These are hard issues, especially in our currently polarized society,
but the choices are to compromise or to harden positions on both sides,
thus increasing rage at the extremes and fanning the flames of the
culture wars until we lose one freedom or the other. If this book is
successful at achieving its goals, I expect people on both sides to be
challenged and perhaps the extremes on both sides to be enraged, but
my goal is to speak to the vast number of people in the middle, and to
those on either side who are willing to compromise to protect the
freedoms that matter to them.

I have decided that it is time to take what I know as a law professor –
focused on law and religion, as well as on constitutional law – and speak
to the public, rather than within my field where I am most comfortable.
Quite honestly, the task of doing so scares me because doing an

adequate job is onerous; yet I feel a deep need to do this because remaining silent only increases the chance that freedoms may be unnecessarily lost on both sides. As a moderate on these issues, I want to give some voice to the silent majority and can only ask you, the reader, to engage with these issues. I hope you gain something from reading this book. I fear that I am an inadequate messenger given the importance of this task, but I hope you will learn something from what I have written here.

ACKNOWLEDGMENTS

I owe a great debt to many of my colleagues both at Michigan State University and around the country for their support and comments. Most important, I am grateful to John Berger at Cambridge University Press for having faith in this project and for his tireless efforts to shepherd this book to press in a timely fashion. I would also like to thank Joanna Breeze, Karthik Orukaimani, and Brianda Reyes at Cambridge University Press for excellent production support. I also thank Linda Benson for her excellent copyediting and Morten Jensen at Cambridge University Press for his excellent marketing support.

I thank many colleagues for their input. First, I would like to thank the participants in the 2013 Annual Law and Religion Roundtable held at Stanford University, which is where the idea for this book was born. I also thank Brett Scharffs and Scott Idleman for their excellent comments as the project moved forward. Many thanks to my colleagues at Michigan State University College of Law who provided excellent comments on this paper when I workshopped it, and to the participants in the Florida International University Law Review's 2015 Law and Religion Symposium who also provided excellent comments on what would become Chapter 4 of this book. Finally, I want to thank the independent reviewers who reviewed the book proposal and sample chapters for Cambridge University Press. Their comments and criticisms were immensely helpful and their insights were essential in improving this book.

I would also like to thank Charles Ten Brink, Hildur Hanna, and the staff of the MSU law library for their consistently excellent support. Thanks also to David Loudon and Laura Bondank for excellent research assistance. Special thanks go to Allegra Smith who did an excellent job proofreading and providing helpful suggestions for this book. Of course, any errors are mine alone.

The term "acknowledgments" is not adequate to express my gratitude to my family for their constant love and support: my brilliant and supportive wife Chika, who supports my work even when I get stressed about finishing a project, and my incredible daughters Elysha and Ariana, whose energy, intelligence, and creativity are a constant example for me. They make life brighter every day. My parents Arline and Carl Ravitch are the best parents any child could ever hope for and without whom none of the things I have been fortunate enough to do would have ever been possible. They are a constant source of love, support, joy, and inspiration. My late Bubby and Pop-Pop, who even after their passing continue to inspire me and serve as examples of hard work, love, and kindness. My sisters Elizabeth and Sharon and their wonderful families are not only supportive but also wonderful people. Last, but not least, are my Uncle Gary and Aunt Mindy and Aunt Jackie and Uncle Ken and their wonderful families who are supportive of everything I do.

I have incorporated modified sections from two articles into this book:

Frank S. Ravitch, Be Careful What You Wish For: Why Hobby Lobby Weakens Religious Freedom, 2016 Byu L. Rev. 55 (2016).

Frank S. Ravitch, Essay: Complimentary or Competing Freedoms: Government Officials, Religious Freedom and LGBT Rights, 11 Fiu L. Rev. 163 (2016)(symposium).

1   A VIEW FROM THREE PLACES

October 10, 2010

Dr. Weisman's office was painted in calming tones, and Janet focused on a colorful work of abstract art hanging on the wall behind the doctor's desk.

"What do you think it means?" Janet asked, pointing to the picture. She and Michelle had been together for twenty years through good times and bad. Michelle loved art and Janet hoped the distraction might calm her.

Michelle looked carefully, "I'm not sure. It looks like . . . well, kind of like, music."

A moment later Dr. Weisman appeared and walked around to his desk. "You have a heck of an eye," Dr. Weisman said, looking at Michelle. "It's a reprint of a Kandinsky piece and some experts think it's an attempt to represent music on canvas." Michelle smiled.

Dr. Weisman's tone became more serious. "I have good news and bad news. But the good news is pretty good. It's not stage III."

Michelle and Janet sighed in relief. "So what is it?" Janet asked.

Dr. Weisman took a deep breath, "Michelle has stage II ovarian cancer." Janet held Michelle's hand as Michelle began to cry. Michelle's heart raced and she started to hyperventilate. Janet put her arm around Michelle, trying to calm her even though Janet wanted to burst into tears herself.

Dr. Weisman gave them some time to recover. When he next spoke, his voice was soothing. "I know this is not what you wanted, but it can be treated and it has not spread outside of the ovaries and uterus."

Michelle wiped her eyes. "Will I be okay?"

Dr. Weisman nodded, "The prognosis is good in most of these cases. We will need to operate, but since it hasn't spread very far we should be able to knock it out with surgery and several rounds of chemo. The chances of long-term survival are good, but we need to move as quickly as possible to make sure it doesn't spread farther."

Michelle seemed more at ease. Janet was ecstatic that the prognosis was good. Michelle would be okay. Nothing else mattered. It had only been a week or two, but it seemed like an eternity since the irregular test came back and then the follow-up showed signs of cancer. Janet and Michelle were powerless to do anything while they waited, but now they knew it was treatable. Yet Janet knew Michelle was terrified of chemo and still in shock from the newness of the situation. She wanted to make the fear go away, but she didn't know how. She held Michelle closer and she could feel Michelle relax a bit.

Janet relaxed a bit too. Then it hit her. Janet held her anger back as fear and desperation gripped her. She was powerless. Thankfully, at that moment Michelle excused herself to go to the restroom. Janet looked at Dr. Weisman and began to speak. "What about insurance? Michelle isn't covered. We have paid out of pocket for everything up to now."

She and Michelle had been devoted partners for twenty years, but since their state did not allow them to marry and Janet's employer, a mid-sized engineering firm, did not provide benefits for same-sex couples, Michelle could not be covered under Janet's policy. Michelle's job with a building supply company had been reduced to part time a year earlier and she lost her benefits, including health coverage. At first they thought Medicaid would provide coverage, but Michelle made too much to qualify for Medicaid, although just barely, so she remained uninsured. The desperate search for insurance coverage began long before Michelle learned she might have cancer, but after losing half her salary, any decent coverage was out of reach.

Dr. Weisman scratched his chin and thought for a few moments. "I can do the surgery for free. If you ever win the lottery you can pay me back," he said as he smiled. Then his expression turned somber. "But the hospital and drug costs will be significant."

"How much do we need?" Janet asked, her mind racing through every way in which they could raise the money.

"Just the hospital and drug costs will probably be more than $50,000 and could be as much as $175,000 depending on the amount of chemo Michelle needs and the recovery time," Dr. Weisman replied. Janet calculated that they could probably raise $15,000 from their own funds and friends and family, but even if they sold their house they would not have more than $25,000 total given their current mortgage and sagging housing prices.

The conversation stopped abruptly when they heard Michelle talking to a nurse in the hallway. Both Janet and Dr. Weisman knew that Michelle did not need extra stress. When Michelle returned to her seat, Janet turned to her and gave her a hug. "Thank God it's treatable," Janet said warmly; yet she knew that getting the treatment quickly would not be easy without insurance.

December 10, 2015

Mandy Rodriguez stared at the letter. Her mind raced in a thousand directions. She had overcome so much. What about her 4.0 GPA in the graduate counseling program? What about all of her volunteer work to help poor patients in need of clinical services in the program's counseling assistance program? The words on the page were inconceivable.

Dear Ms. Rodriguez:

I am sorry to inform you that you have been expelled from the counseling psychology program at Sycamore State University. The hearing committee voted unanimously to expel you due to your refusal to counsel clients in same-sex relationships about marriage issues in the mandatory counseling clinic. The committee found that you have no right to refuse such counseling based on your religion. Moreover, the committee found that your willingness to counsel gay or lesbian clients on any issues unrelated to marriage, and your willingness to refer clients in same-sex relationships who seek counseling regarding marriage issues, while positive steps, are inadequate to enable you to meet the clinical requirements for graduation. You must be willing to counsel any client on any issue regardless of sexual orientation.

Dean Francis Smith-Maquid

Mandy tried to hold back the tears. She had worked so hard, not just for herself but also for her five-year-old son, Andrew. She had escaped an abusive relationship and wanted to find a career where she could help people and support her son. Counseling psychology was perfect.

Mandy hadn't had any problems until Prof. Stinson's clinic. She was asked to counsel a same-sex couple regarding marital issues. Mandy referred the couple to another student in the clinic because she held a deep religious belief that marriage should be between a man and a woman. She had no problem counseling gay and lesbian clients about other issues, and in fact she had counseled a lesbian client whose ex-husband was abusive before and after the client came out.

Prof. Stinson was furious that Mandy referred the same-sex clients seeking marriage counseling to another student. Mandy recalled the conversation as a tear rolled down her cheek. Prof. Stinson said, "What is wrong with you! You have a duty to counsel everyone who comes through the door under our policies!"

Mandy was scared, but she was prepared for this. She responded to her professor, "I have counseled everyone who has come through the door until now, and I have no problem counseling gay and lesbian clients about any other issues, but my religious commitments do not allow me to counsel same-sex couples about marriage. I would be no good to them so I referred them to a student who could counsel them without objection. The other student gave me one of her client files involving spousal abuse so that my caseload was not reduced and her caseload was not increased."

"Do you honestly believe that same-sex marriage is such a sin that you can't counsel about it? This program is built for the twenty-first century, not the fifteenth!" Prof. Stinson huffed.

"Yes, I do, but it's nothing against gay people. It just has to do with my religious commitments and beliefs about marriage. If I help with that kind of relationship I would be facilitating the sin. I can't do that." Mandy was almost in tears.

"You can't refer a client just because it violates your views." Prof. Stinson said.

"I checked the policies and there is nothing preventing it, and there is a policy allowing referrals for patients who want to terminate their life because of the moral issues it raises for counselors. My issues come from religion, but they are still moral issues," Mandy said.

"I will be filing disciplinary charges against you," Prof. Stinson said.

Mandy remembered the sting she felt when Prof. Stinson said that. A week later, Professor Stinson filed charges against Mandy. Two weeks after the charges were filed, the department held a hearing. Mandy attended the hearing and testified. She had thought that the hearing went well. Even Prof. Stinson was respectful of her views. Maybe it was all a ruse to make her feel confident and not raise a complaint outside of the university. Mandy wasn't sure what to do. She was frozen.

"Mommy, why are you crying?" Andrew asked.

"It's okay, Andrew. Mommy was just reading a sad letter."

"From who? Why is it sad?" Andrew asked.

"From some people who don't know how to respect beliefs they disagree with."

"They must not be very nice."

"Well, that's not for us to decide, Andrew." Mandy hugged Andrew tightly, crying quietly so he wouldn't worry.

October 15, 2014

Amy looked at her pack of birth-control pills. She had been on them since her surgery to remove an ovarian cyst, just after she turned 25. Her mom, Betty, had ovarian cysts as well. Both aunts on Betty's side of the family had had ovarian cancer. Aunt Anna did not catch it before it was too late and died from it.

Amy remembered her initial visit with Dr. Brock after the surgery. Dr. Brock told her in no uncertain terms that she needed to take the pill to lower her risk of ovarian cysts and ovarian or uterine cancer. Amy was happy to have an edge in fighting her genetic predisposition, and it gave her even greater hope that she would be there to see her children and grandchildren grow up.

Amy looked at the pictures on her nightstand. There was one of her and Jim at the beach, and pictures of Abby and Max in their little jeans and t-shirts playing in the front yard. Amy allowed a smile as she thought about that day at the beach with Jim. It was the day they decided to adopt. They went to the beach to help relax after learning that Amy had fertility issues. When Jim found out, he joked that he was like a kid, so they didn't need to have kids. Amy did not buy his calm front. She heard the pain underneath his laughter, and she suggested they take a weekend at the beach near her parents' house. Amy also began researching adoption.

Now she could not imagine life without Abby and Max. That's what made the letter from her employer even more troubling. Amy was angry, but what could she do?

Jim had lost his job a few months earlier. They were able to scrape by on Amy's salary while Jim looked for work. They had always been a two-salary family, with both Amy and Jim adjusting their schedules to make sure Abby and Max were taken care of. The letter she held would cost them at least $700 a year, and given that they were already in debt and just scraping by, Amy didn't know what to do. The letter read:

Dear valued Slangtontech employee:

Slangtontech is proud of each of our 7,000 employees. We are writing to inform you of a change in our benefits program that may affect some of you. In light of the United States Supreme Court's recent ruling in *Burwell v. Hobby Lobby*, we will no longer cover contraceptive care. We are a self-insured and closely held company.

John and Ellen Slangton and their family respect all employees, but their religious commitments prevent them from covering contraceptive care. Slangtontech has reluctantly covered contraceptive care since 2010 under the state's mandatory contraceptive coverage law, and since 2014 under the Federal Affordable Care Act. Doing so has caused the Slangtons great pain. We believe that the recent decision by the United States Supreme Court in *Hobby Lobby* allows us to stop covering these items under the Affordable Care Act, and we also believe our state constitution will be interpreted in the same manner so that we need not cover contraceptives despite the state's mandatory contraceptive coverage law.

No other benefits will be affected. We wish you and yours a grace-filled year.

Slangontech, Inc.

Amy knew without looking how much her pills would cost. The doctor told her she needed to be on Yasmin 28 for a variety of reasons, including that two other pills she had tried caused her to have migraines. She had been taking the generic version, but even the generic cost $60 per month, and that was without any price increases; *$720 a year*, she thought. She could cut back on food and not buy the kids much for Christmas, but even that might not cover it. Or, she thought, she could go off the pill until whenever Jim got a job. Dr. Brock was clear that she needed to stay on the pill, but would a few months without it hurt? She knew the answer. Dr. Brock was clear that going off the pill for any period of time put her at risk for ovarian cysts, and that the longer she stayed off the pill the greater her risk of ovarian or uterine cancer. But what else could she do?

September 23, 2014
Jonathan Stein sat in his room. He felt nauseous, and the feeling would not go away. Ever since he spoke with Mr. Winston and Coach Fenton, he couldn't sleep or eat. Now, his parents were at school pleading his case to the principal. It wasn't fair. He never had these problems at his old school district. He didn't mind moving to his new school until all this started. He liked having a nice big yard and a smaller school, but now he felt like an outcast with a scarlet J, for "Jew," on his chest. All of this because he needed to miss two days of school for Rosh Hashanah, the second most important Jewish holiday of the year.

Between Coach Fenton's threat to bench Jonathan, who was a starting linebacker for the school's football team, if he missed two practices for "some Jew holiday," and Mr. Winston's refusal to allow him to take a makeup for a test that would greatly affect his grade in chemistry because, "I don't give makeup tests unless there is a medical reason," Jonathan felt like his life was falling apart. He was only in the eleventh grade, but he had a serious chance at a college scholarship for football or academics. Being benched would keep college scouts from seeing him play, and a low mark in chemistry would decrease his GPA. He couldn't afford either. His parents didn't have a lot of money, and he knew a scholarship would be needed if he wanted to have a brighter future.

Jonathan heard the front door open and hope returned. He went downstairs and saw his mom crying in the kitchen. His dad looked dumbfounded. Jonathan's dad saw Jonathan and said, "Jon, come and sit down." Jonathan sat at the kitchen table. His dad continued, "Jon, I don't know how to reason with these people. The principal said that it is up to the teacher whether to allow a makeup test. He has talked to Mr. Winston, but Mr. Winston won't budge. The principal disciplined Coach Fenton for the way he spoke to you, but he can't make him change his mind about benching you if you miss practice without being injured."

Jonathan's mind raced and he remembered eighth-grade civics. "What about the Constitution? Don't we have a right to be who we are?" Jonathan's mom looked dejected. "We brought that up and the principal said these are general policies that apply to all students the same so they don't have to give you an exception. He said if the state had something called a religious freedom law, he would be able to help, but there is no religious freedom law here so it is up to the teachers."

Jonathan wanted to cry. He noticed that his dad was close to tears too. "It's my fault," his dad said. "We should have never moved here. I should have never taken the new job."

"But it's a great job and until this everything has been good here." Jonathan's mom said. "Who could have known about this? There is no way you could have known."

"Jon, I don't know what to tell you. We will support you whatever you choose to do about Rosh Hashanah. We can't force a decision on you," Jonathan's dad said in a soft voice.

"I don't really have a choice," Jonathan accepted his fate. "We have observed Rosh Hashanah for more than two thousand years. Even during the worst times people found a way. I'm not going to stop just because Mr. Winston and Coach Fenton are so ignorant."

Jon's mom and dad smiled with pride, but inside their hearts ached because they knew this would hurt Jon's chances of getting a college scholarship, whether academic or for football.

I INTRODUCTION

We are in the midst of a supposed war between sexual freedom[*] and religious freedom. If you watch the news, spend time in the

---

[*] The term "sexual freedom" is under inclusive. Clearly, LGBT and reproductive rights are about far more than sex. They are about fundamental questions of one's ability to be free and control one's destiny. LGBT rights are about being who you are without discrimination

blogosphere, or listen to activists and politicians, you will hear examples of discrimination against one side or the other. It seems, at least in most media accounts, that the conflict between religious freedom and LGBT rights is insurmountable. Yet, there is a fundamental problem with this supposed conflict, namely, that in many cases it is not real. Religious freedom, LGBT rights, and reproductive freedom can coexist – at least in many contexts – even if some on one side or the other of the culture wars are uncomfortable with this fact.

Yet, the visceral attacks on the Supreme Court's recent decision to protect same-sex marriage and the equally visceral attacks on proposed state religious freedom laws in Michigan, New Mexico, Kentucky, Georgia, Indiana, and other states demonstrate that factions on both sides are adept at attacking laws and policies with which they disagree. Unfortunately, when one observes these attacks it becomes clear that many of those attacking have a complete inability, or perhaps lack of desire, to find common ground or put themselves in the shoes of those with whom they disagree. This sometimes brings public discourse on the relationship between religious and sexual freedoms down to the lowest common denominator, which is an affront to those who seek to move America forward without leaving millions of Americans behind.

Immoderate factions on both sides have had a disproportionately large role in framing the issues in the court of public opinion. The media, it should be no surprise, has often latched onto more radical voices and given the impression that those voices speak for one side or the other. Make no mistake; much of the problem here is based on perception and the framing of issues rather than on an inherent tension between religious freedom and sexual freedom. By the time you finish reading this book, you will understand how these important freedoms can coexist in many contexts, and how in those situations where common ground cannot be found, informed choices can be made that will allow the remaining walls between religious freedom and sexual freedom to stand without increasing

---

in the most fundamental aspects of life, and reproductive rights are about the freedom to control your body and determine your own future. I use the term "sexual freedom" in this book as shorthand for all of this. In this sense, the term "sexual" addresses far more than sex and the term "freedom" addresses far more than freedom in the bedroom.

hostility toward the broader freedoms that are important to each side. Hopefully, together, we can work to reframe these issues in a more productive way.

Of course, reframing these issues in a productive way cannot be done by burying our heads in the sand. Religious freedom and sexual freedom do conflict in several situations. For example, what should be done when a closely held for-profit entity denies benefits or services to employees based on religious objections? How can religious universities or adoption agencies representing faiths that oppose same-sex marriage continue to serve their missions in light of the issues raised by legal recognition of same-sex marriage? What should be done about government officials who refuse to grant marriage licenses to same-sex couples based on religious objections? And, of course, should Mandy Rodriguez in the hypothetical example have any legal recourse to avoid expulsion from her university?

These questions are important and serious. They will be addressed in detail in later chapters, but for now it is important to understand that many religious freedom claims are more like Jonathan Stein's situation. They have no impact on sexual freedom. Moreover, in many cases religious freedom claims have much in common with claims for LGBT and reproductive rights. After all, in all these situations people are seeking to keep government from interfering with or denying them their most fundamental, and often personal, aspects of being. Opposing or blocking all religious freedom laws to prevent discrimination could actually end up fostering discrimination against religious minorities, as well as mainstream Christians, in contexts where there is no discrimination against anyone else.

Mandy's situation is somewhat different from Jonathan's. Mandy's situation raises what is often called a "conscience claim." These claims sometimes, but not always, impact third parties. Conscience claims run the gamut from less controversial issues (at least less controversial in the twenty-first century), such as conscientious objection to military service to more controversial issues, such as the refusal of county clerks to issue marriage licenses to same-sex couples and the refusal of hospitals to allow abortions to be performed in their facilities. As will be seen, common ground may be found in some of these cases, but whether this can be done is a fact-sensitive question. The answer depends on the impact that accommodation of religion-based conscience claims will have on others.

II BALANCING RELIGIOUS FREEDOM, LGBT RIGHTS, AND REPRODUCTIVE FREEDOM

Stepping back from all the rhetoric, fear, and accusations launched by the most radical combatants in the culture wars, we can see some common elements within the struggles of the LGBT community for civil rights and civil liberties, religious people seeking to live their faith without being penalized by laws or policies that may have never considered them, and women seeking reproductive freedom without government interference. Each of these important struggles will be addressed in turn.

As Janet and Michelle's case demonstrates, LGBT rights, including the recently recognized right to same-sex marriage, are about fundamental things that most people never have to think about but have created untold pain and stress for members of the LGBT community. Think about the following questions: Can my bond to the person I love be legally recognized just like anyone else's? Can the person I love share my health and retirement benefits like anyone else in a similar relationship? Can I visit the person I love in the hospital in an emergency as spouses are able to do? Can I prevent my employer from discriminating against me because I chose to marry the person I love, and so on?[1]

Most couples take these things for granted, but until June 2015 same-sex couples could not in many parts of the United States, despite the fact they are consenting adults, some of whom have been together for decades. Moreover, no federal antidiscrimination law protects LGBT individuals from discrimination and many states lack such laws as well. One of the outcomes this book advocates for is the combination of antidiscrimination laws protecting the LGBT community and religious freedom laws protecting people of faith. Having both types of laws can help create a balance that can maximize protection and minimize harm for the LGBT community, as well as maximizing accommodation for people of faith. The balance between these sorts of laws when they appear to conflict is complicated, but I will explain these interactions and the best way to approach them in an easy to understand manner in Chapters 3, 4 and 5.

Thankfully, some states already have both sorts of laws. We can look to these states as examples. Utah recently passed a fascinating law aimed at balancing religious freedom and LGBT rights. This law, and others, will be explained throughout the rest of this book. They serve as evidence that when people sit down and talk with a willingness to compromise, both religious freedom and sexual freedom can be protected.

Despite the promise of what has become known as the "Utah Compromise," at a national level religious freedom has been increasingly, and unfairly, framed as the irrational enemy of LGBT rights. This misunderstands religious freedom claims and underestimates the role that religion plays in Americans' lives. Two sub-issues rise from framing religious freedom in this way: first, that it is the enemy of LGBT rights; and second, that it is irrational, especially where it conflicts with LGBT rights.

There are certainly cases in which religious freedom claims conflict with LGBT rights, but these do not represent the majority of religious freedom claims. Moreover, the fact that a religious freedom claim can be asserted does not mean that it will be victorious. Much of the rest of this book is devoted to navigating religious freedom claims that *do* conflict with sexual freedom and determining if and when they should be, or will likely be, victorious. Each side will win on some issues and lose on others, but I hope to demonstrate that the key to these determinations should be whether the religious freedom claim poses a direct and meaningful harm to third parties. The meaning of "direct and meaningful" is key to this analysis and will be explained and discussed beginning in the next chapter.

Debates and dialog over the rationality of religion have become more popular in recent years, with some militant secularists lambasting and lampooning everything religious. The question of whether religion is irrational could be the topic of a multivolume set, and a detailed discussion is far beyond the scope of this book; but it is necessary to address the topic at some level, because if religion were as irrational and immoderate as some in the current debate allege it to be, there would be strong arguments against protecting it. Of course, those who attack religion either turn it into a monolithic caricature or engage in the very sort of rhetoric and deductive thought that they accuse religious people of engaging in. Not all religions are the same, and even within a given religion there can be a wide range of views.

Moreover, in the United States religious freedom and freedom of conscience have been given special attention and protection, albeit inconsistently, since the founding of the nation. If anything, the problem has not been that religion has received too much protection over time but rather that sometimes dominant religions have been protected while less dominant religions have not. The solution to this problem is not to decrease protection for larger religions but rather to increase protection for religion generally.

At the same time, it is essential to protect the LGBT community from discrimination, and a balance must be found that will minimize harm for members of the LGBT community while allowing religious freedom claims that do not inflict direct and meaningful harm on others to be accommodated. As will be seen in the following chapters, this will not necessarily lead to conflicts with LGBT rights; when it does, it may be that religion must yield unless religious concerns can be accommodated without harming the rights of others. This suggestion will ring hollow to those who wish to undermine religious freedom generally, as well as to those who wish to expand religious freedom regardless of its impact on others. It could be a good thing if it upsets those firmly entrenched on each side of this polarized debate, because ruffling those feathers could indicate progress toward greater equality and protection of rights on both sides.

The sorts of religious freedom claims that have often arisen under the Constitution and religious freedom laws, however, do not generally create serious conflict with the rights of others. For example, can I receive a simple accommodation to miss school to observe a holiday central to my faith without being penalized? Can the courts empower my doctor to force me to get a blood transfusion when my religion forbids it? Can our tribe continue to follow its ancient traditions on land taken, and now owned, by the federal or state government? Can a local zoning board prevent our church from building a facility to feed the poor or from using our existing facilities to do so? Can I grow a short beard in prison because my faith requires it, even though the prison rules say no beards? Can the government punish me for following my faith's long-standing tradition of drinking hallucinogenic tea in a highly controlled ceremony? Can the government require an autopsy of my brother or sister after a car accident even though our faith strictly prohibits autopsies? All of these questions are adapted from real cases; if religious accommodations were given in every one of these cases, there would be no significant negative impact on the freedom of others.

Mandy's situation is also loosely adapted from a real case.[2] In that case, the plaintiff prevailed, in part, because no direct harm would have been inflicted on the clients who were referred, and because the policy at the university in question allowed for referrals in other situations. The result in that case was almost certainly correct, but perhaps more for the former reason than the latter. Other conscience claims may raise much harder questions, and the answers will vary depending on the specific facts involved.

In light of a world that has changed quickly, both individuals and faith traditions that oppose same-sex marriage on religious grounds may ask: "In a nation of freedom, why must I be forced to accept these cultural changes that conflict with my religion, so long as I do not harm anyone else? Why am I under attack for holding to my faith and conscience when I mean no ill will toward anyone else? Why is freedom of conscience suddenly under attack?" This does not mean that religion should give people a free pass to discriminate, but it does mean that writing these people and faiths off as a bunch of unrepentant bigots will likely lead to bigger problems within the culture wars than would taking the claims seriously. As a religious person who believes strongly in LGBT and reproductive freedom, I am always struck by how easily people on one side or the other simply write off claims made by those with opposing viewpoints, as though those claims are not even worth consideration.

Like LGBT rights, reproductive freedom goes to the core of self-determination and the freedom to control one's body without government interference. Similar concerns about personal autonomy motivate those seeking reproductive freedom. Here the question is whether government should be able to interfere with core issues of self-determination and personal freedom, such as one's ability to control one's own body, career, and education. All of these issues come into play when government or any other entity tries to limit a woman's right to reproductive freedom. Unlike the right to same-sex marriage, however, reproductive freedom has been recognized as a national right since *Roe v. Wade* was decided in 1973.[3]

Opposed to reproductive freedom are a variety of interests, many of which are religious. The positions of these religions vary from viewing contraception itself as a sin to rejecting products or procedures that abort a fetus,[4] whether from the time of conception or later in the fetus's development. The key here is that these people believe deeply that aborting a fetus after conception is murder and against God's will. Therefore, if they do anything that helps facilitate abortion, even indirectly, they are complicit in what they view as a fundamental violation of God's law. Thus, we sometimes hear of doctors, pharmacists, and hospitals from certain religious traditions that refuse to perform procedures or give out medication that they believe will take a life.

The conflict between this worldview and that of those advocating reproductive freedom is stark. Yet, compromises have been reached at both the state and federal levels that allow conscientious objections by doctors and hospitals but also protect the rights of doctors and hospitals that perform abortions and other procedures to which conscientious objections are raised, and most importantly do not deny women access to these procedures. Problems have arisen, however, when the scope of protections for conscientious objectors has combined with other laws that are designed to minimize women's access to these procedures.

Importantly, however, if we look carefully common themes emerge between reproductive freedom and religious freedom. Both seek to keep government from interfering with the most fundamental aspects of a person's autonomy, self-determination, and being. Of course, this commonality may be of little solace to people of faith who view many reproductive choices as sin. The subject of conscience claims by religious organizations, doctors, and pharmacists is complex and will be discussed in Chapters 3 and 6 of this book.

For now, it is useful to note that many religions do not oppose – and some even advocate for – reproductive freedom. This is often forgotten in the black-and-white, polarized world of the extreme culture warriors on each side. Of course, the fact that some faiths do not oppose reproductive freedom does not remove the conflict between religions that oppose it and the people and organizations that support it. This conflict leads to some of the most significant barriers against balancing religious freedom and sexual freedom, but as we will see, even these barriers are surmountable, at least legally.

When I look at these questions I see common themes, not inherent conflict. While culture warriors on both sides may view these as disparate or irreconcilable concerns, many people of faith and many within the U.S. LGBT community – which includes a large number of people of faith[5] – as well as many reproductive freedom advocates, can envision common ground. Unfortunately, moderate voices are often drowned out by those who yell the loudest.

III THE DIFFERENCE BETWEEN INTEREST ADVOCACY AND RELIGIOUS AND SEXUAL FREEDOM

Significantly, there is a fundamental difference between religious freedom, which seeks to accommodate people of faith so that government cannot interfere with or penalize them for practicing their religion without an adequate government interest, and religious interest advocacy, which seeks to influence broader government policies and actions. Certainly religious freedom is an important issue in religious interest advocacy, but it is just one of many issues. Religious freedom has often been understood in terms of results in specific cases and in terms of the legal tests used to decide those cases. Religious interest advocacy often focuses on influencing public opinion and on affecting entire legal regimes on issues such as reproductive freedom and LGBT rights.

Religious lobbying can conflict with (or support) LGBT and reproductive rights, but religious advocacy and religious freedom are not the same thing. Religious freedom does not, contrary to what you may have heard in the media, involve getting government to do your bidding.

In fact, until the U.S. Supreme Court decided *Burwell v. Hobby Lobby*,[6] a case in which for-profit entities were given religious exemptions that allowed them to deny certain contraceptives to female employees, religious freedom was never understood to allow direct imposition on the rights of others.

It is true that accommodation in the land-use context, which is governed by the Federal Religious Land Use and Institutionalized Persons Act (RLUIPA), could possibly impose some burden on those who do not want the increased construction or traffic related to a religious land use. This could be viewed as imposing a burden on others as a result of accommodating religious land use. Yet, not until *Hobby Lobby* did the Court support a direct imposition on third parties as a result of religious accommodation. The Court denied there would be any imposition on third parties in that case, but as will be explained in the next chapter, the tenor and implications of the *Hobby Lobby* decision leave open the distinct possibility religious accommodations may harm third parties in other situations.

The very claim in *Hobby Lobby* – to deny certain federally mandated reproductive benefits to female employees – involves imposition on the female employees of the company. As will be seen in the next chapter, the *Hobby Lobby* Court's protestations to the contrary – claiming that the burden placed on female employees was "precisely zero" – ring hollow over the long run in light of political reality. Therefore, *Hobby Lobby* may be fairly viewed as a case where religious freedom was recognized in a fashion that might directly harm third parties. Yet, *Hobby Lobby* is the exception not the rule in religious freedom cases.

Interest advocacy has led some states to consider religious freedom laws that cloud traditional notions of religious freedom by providing broad protection for for-profit entities. Such laws have been considered in Arizona, as well as in a number of other states, but they have mostly failed to pass state legislatures or have been vetoed by the governor as happened in Arizona. Yet those who attack such legislation often ignore the fact that these laws are usually attempts to accommodate people of faith in a quickly changing world. There is no doubt that religious freedom claims by for-profit entities can create conflict, but as will be seen those claims threaten religious freedom as much as sexual freedom, and they have weak legal purchase.

Most of what we hear about the conflict between religious freedom and sexual freedom from interest advocates on both sides turns rights into straw men and eschews rational, moderate thinking in favor of propaganda. For example, Jim Daly, president of Focus on the Family, wrote in response to the Supreme Court's ruling on same-sex marriage: "We are also concerned that this decision will fan the flames of government hostility against individuals, businesses and religious organizations whose convictions prevent them from officiating at, participating in, or celebrating [same-sex] unions."[7] On the other side, Elliot Mincberg from People for the American Way, wrote in *Salon*, "[Recent state religious freedom laws] are, in part, a component of the far right's efforts to reframe their decades-long war against every advance in societal acceptance and legal rights for lesbian, gay, bisexual, and transgender (LGBT) Americans into a noble effort to protect 'religious liberty.'"[8]

These are among the more moderate statements we have seen from partisans on each side. Yet, both are mostly wrong. Jim Daly talks about the threat to religious freedom of "individuals, businesses and religious organizations," but it is businesses that are most likely to have issues; prior to the *Hobby Lobby* decision, many courts did not think for-profit businesses could exercise religious freedom. Meanwhile, there is no serious threat to an individual's right to believe or practice his or her faith. No one is forced to attend same-sex weddings or take birth control pills. Moreover, no church or minister will be required to perform same-sex marriages despite what you may have heard. There may be issues with tax exemptions and government grants to religious organizations, but as will be explained in detail in later chapters the impact should be limited.

Other issues, such as county clerks who refuse to issue marriage licenses to same-sex couples and adoption agencies that refuse to place children with same-sex couples are fact sensitive and complex. The specific facts, such as the availability of other clerks or agencies in the same community willing and able to serve in the place of a clerk or an agency that receives a religious exemption, as well as the adequacy of these alternatives, would be central to answering these questions if religious accommodations were available. These nuanced issues can not be carefully addressed through partisan rhetoric.

At the same time, Mincberg's characterization of recent religious freedom restoration act laws as an attempt by the far right to harm LGBT rights mistakes the motives of some religious freedom advocates for the purpose of religious freedom laws more generally.[9] Many who support religious freedom, myself included, also support same-sex marriage and reproductive freedom. In fact, we view these rights as part of a continuum of freedom. Most of us are hardly part of the Christian Right. In many cases, religious freedom protects religious minorities, as well as those from more dominant religious groups who have suddenly found themselves out of public favor in a fast-changing world. Religious freedom applies to everyone regardless of the size or power of their religion. Yet a garden variety religious freedom case such as Jonathan Stein's is a far cry from condoning discrimination against LGBT individuals or couples.

Significantly, and I cannot stress this enough, advocates of conservative religious values and advocates of progressive secularist values have the right to freedom of speech, just as they have every right to engage in partisan rhetoric and to advocate for laws that protect their interests. As things stand now, it appears that both religious conservatives and militant secularists risk losing these battles in the long run if they continue to frame the issues as they do; but as will be explained in Chapter 5, the risk currently seems greater for religious freedom than sexual freedom. Religious conservatives are not likely to succeed over the long run in changing the outcome of *Obergefell v. Hodges* (the same-sex marriage decision) either before the Court or through legislation. The real risk is that their rhetoric and actions will enable militant secularists who want to stereotype religious freedom as an invitation to discriminate to succeed in imprinting that characterization on the court of public opinion. This will lead to the defeat of religious freedom bills that are not designed to harm third parties. Ironically, religious minorities, religious progressives, religious moderates, and politically uninvolved people of faith are all caught between religious conservatives who want to roll back advances for LGBT and reproductive freedom and secular progressives who view all religious freedom laws as dangerous.

This is not to say that the core values of religious conservatives and secular progressives are free from risk in the current state of affairs. The fast progress of LGBT rights has seemed like an assault on the values of some religious conservatives; without strong religious freedom protections, religious conservatives' core values could be trampled. The same is also true for secular progressives, who view religious objections to progress on LGBT and reproductive freedom as a fundamental risk or barrier to equality, as well as an assault on human rights. In Chapters 4 through 7, we explore attempts to balance these concerns in a productive way, such as recent laws in Utah and a few other states, and see that some of these laws can help protect religious freedom, LGBT rights, and reproductive freedom. As you will see, other legal proposals are not so productive and will likely lead to the long-term degradation of rights on one side or the other.

Of course, both the religious conservatives and secular progressives miss the vast expanse of common ground and common purpose between religious freedom and sexual freedom. The possibility of seeing this common ground has often been overshadowed by rhetoric on both sides of the culture wars, and a media all too willing to report on every ridiculous action or word. As an example, in 2015 a lot of attention was paid to statements by Roy Moore. Moore is the unabashedly religious conservative and brazenly anti-LGBT Alabama Supreme Court justice who advocated that Alabama need not follow a federal trial court decision ordering the state to recognize same-sex marriage, and who later claimed the U.S. Supreme Court decision on same-sex marriage was worse than *Plessy v. Ferguson*, a case decided by the Supreme Court in 1896 that upheld racial segregation.[10]

More recently, Moore grabbed national headlines when he issued an order under his authority as the "Administrative Head of the Unified Judicial System of Alabama," telling Alabama probate judges not to issue any marriage licenses to same-sex couples because doing so would violate Alabama law. Moore's order clearly conflicts with the Supreme Court's ruling upholding the constitutional right to same-sex marriage. Moore's legal arguments supporting his order are unsound and violate basic principles of constitutional law. Yet, his actions captured the national spotlight for several days and are likely to do so again as his showdown with the U.S. Constitution and common sense continues. He was recently suspended after charges were filed against him by the Alabama Judicial Inquiry Commission.[11]

Focusing on these sorts of statements and situations does tremendous harm to religious freedom because it makes religious freedom and those advocating for it seem incapable of compromise. Yet Moore is a caricature, albeit a real-life one. He does not speak for most people of faith, nor does he speak for the vast majority in the legal community.

Every public official who openly seeks to use religious freedom to discriminate actually puts religious freedom further at risk. While many in the media and some radical sexual freedom advocates focus their attention on these sideshows, the many religious freedom claims made by people like Jonathan Stein, Mandy Rodriguez, and others, whether Christian, Jewish, Muslim, Native American, Buddhist, Sikh, Hindu, or otherwise, are put at risk and minimized. It is like confusing the forest for the trees. Claims like those addressed in *Hobby Lobby* represent one tree in a vast forest of religious freedom concerns. Chopping down the entire forest because a few trees have become diseased does not make sense. We can try to heal those trees, and we can chop them down if necessary to save the forest, but the forest itself is not the danger.

We sit on freedom's edge, and if a balance is not struck between protecting both sexual freedom and religious freedom, we will fall off the edge in one extreme direction or the other and lose a piece of what it means to be an American in the process. This book shows how to keep from falling off the edge and how to maximize freedom on all sides. It will not be easy, but it must be done, lest we let the extremes define American freedom.

2 RELIGIOUS FREEDOM

The term "religious freedom" and the related legal term "free exercise of religion" are used a lot in public discourse and in decisions by courts, but what do these terms mean? The answer is both simple and immensely complex. A comprehensive understanding of religious freedom requires years of study, and even then one might find the answer to be elusive. However, to understand what most people mean when they use the term "religious freedom," and what most courts mean when they use the term "free exercise of religion," the answer is simpler. We focus on what "religious freedom" means to many of those in society who seek to protect it and what courts mean when they use the term "free exercise of religion."

Considering these perspectives, religious freedom is the freedom to follow one's religion without inordinate government interference. It is essential to understand that this is a shorthand definition for a complex set of ideas. Whether government interference is inordinate depends on a number of legal factors explained later. The legal factors do not always reflect the essential nature of religious freedom for people of faith, but they are all that we have under the law.

Before delving into the law, however, let's address several bits of mythology that seem to affect many of those opposed to religious freedom.[1] First and foremost is the idea that religion is just about faith, and in the minds of many opponents of religious freedom, blind faith. This is based on a stereotype of Christianity, and of religion more generally. Of course, for many people religion is about more than faith. It is about how they conduct their daily lives, who they are, and the most fundamental aspects of existence.[2] The same is true for sexual orientation and reproductive freedom, so rather than being alien to each other, religious freedom and sexual identity share a depth that goes to the core of being. Moreover, for many religions, religious practice is as, and often more, important than faith.

Religion is at the core of many people's identity. Government interference with religious freedom can scar a person at the deepest levels. This scarring might be legally acceptable if religion did not receive any special protection under the Constitution, history, and laws of the United States, but religion has received special protection. This special protection does not necessarily allow interference with the rights of others, such as the right to same-sex marriage or the right to reproductive freedom. The key is understanding the boundaries of religious freedom.

It is ironic that many of those who have attacked religion in recent years do so in a stereotypical Christocentric way – in the sense that they stereotype all religion based on a straw man view of Christianity that fails to even consider the diversity within Christianity, let alone among other religions. Those who attack religion as anti–civil rights ignore the fact that religion was at the core of the American civil rights movement and that many faiths and people of faith strongly support same-sex marriage and reproductive freedom. It is easy to create a straw man by assuming religion is monolithic, or by assuming religion is an inherently conservative idea. The reality is, however, that religion generally, including many Christian denominations, spans the range of ideas and positions on every issue imaginable.

Most importantly, the vast majority of religious freedom concerns have no impact whatsoever on LGBT or reproductive rights. In fact, many such cases have no impact on anyone's rights other than those of the religious person asserting the claim. A small list of examples includes requests for exemptions to school policies requiring students to take tests or attend class on holy days; claims for access to kosher or halal food in government-run facilities such as prisons; claims by Muslims, Jews, Sikhs, and others to be able to cover their heads in places where the law generally requires the removal of head coverings; claims by adults to refuse certain medical treatments that they believe threaten their eternal being; claims by Native Americans to be able to follow rituals regardless of contrary government regulation; and claims by churches to not be bound by laws that fundamentally impact their religious values and for which exemptions would harm no one else. These basic religious freedom claims have little or no impact on anyone but the claimants and their coreligionists.

Recently, much attention has been paid to bakery owners who do not want to make wedding cakes for same-sex marriages and to florists and caterers with similar objections, but these claims are the exception, not the rule in the religious freedom context. Moreover, for the reasons discussed later and in Chapter 5, these entities that serve the general public are likely to lose their claims under religious freedom laws, absent provisions specifically designed to protect them. Chapter 5 explains why entities that serve the general public, such as shops, should be treated less favorably than religious institutions such as churches and religious charities when they seek religious exemptions that would allow them to discriminate against others. This may be of little solace to the shop owners, but the law can and should draw a line between religious institutions that serve their own congregants and businesses such as florists and bakers who serve the general public and are creatures of state law.

I RELIGIOUS FREEDOM LAW 101: THE BASICS

This section provides the background necessary to understand the law related to religious freedom claims. You do not need to be a lawyer to understand this law. In fact, you can view it as a story with good cases and bad cases in the roles of heroes and villains. Of course, not everyone agrees on which cases are good and which are bad.

Whether we like it or not, the legal arena is a major battleground for these issues. Without an understanding of the law relating to religious freedom and the law relating to sexual freedom, it is hard to have a truly informed dialogue on these issues. Yet, as is true of most professions and professionals, we lawyers and law professors have a remarkable ability to speak among ourselves with legal jargon that often makes the discussions impenetrable for people without a legal background. I have been as guilty of this as anyone. One goal of this book is to demystify the law on each of these issues so we as a nation can have a more informed discussion on their particulars. Even if you do not agree with the conclusions in this book, if you come away more informed about the legal and social dynamics of these issues, the dialogue will hopefully become more informed.

Most religious freedom claims seek exceptions to laws or government practices that burden religion. Granting these exceptions in some cases does not mean they will be granted in all cases; so society will not be confronted with the parade of horribles, such as human sacrifice, which some have argued will result from successful religious freedom claims. In religious freedom cases, if the law provides a basis for bringing a religious freedom claim, that claim is usually weighed against the interests of government and society. Religious freedom claimants do not get an automatic pass to run roughshod over social values and government interests.

Religious freedom can be protected against government interference in three ways: first, claims under the U.S. Constitution or state constitutions; second, religious freedom laws; and third, government practices that allow accommodation of religious freedom even when accommodation is not required under the law.

Since 1990, the U.S. Constitution, despite having a clause protecting the free exercise of religion, has done little to protect religious freedom. That year, the U.S. Supreme Court decided a case called *Employment Division v. Smith*.[3] The case involved two members of the Native American Church in the state of Oregon who were fired and then denied unemployment benefits for using peyote as part of a ritual service. Peyote and similar substances have been used for thousands of years as part of rituals in some Native American religions, and members of the Native American Church were only allowed to chew peyote as part of a carefully supervised ritual. Moreover, unlike other controlled substances, there was no substantial market for peyote, and both the federal government and many states had exemptions to drug laws for ritual use of peyote by Native Americans.

The case made its way to the Supreme Court. A majority of the justices held against the members of the Native American Church. The Supreme Court held that government has no duty to give an exemption to a generally applicable law, even if not giving the exemption substantially burdens religion and punishes those who engage in a religious practice that predates the founding of the United States. The Court held, however, that the government *may* give exemptions if it chooses to do so. This part of the holding figures prominently in the discussions about balancing religious and sexual freedoms throughout this book.

The Supreme Court's ruling rejected precedent that had been in place for almost thirty years. That precedent, *Sherbert v. Verner*,[4] said that the government must provide exemptions to generally applicable laws (laws that apply the same to everyone) when those laws substantially burden religion. This was not an automatic win for religious claimants, however, because the government had no duty to give exemptions when the government interest against providing the exemption was compelling (an extremely important interest) and the means the government used were narrowly tailored (the only practical way) to meet the government's interest. This precedent was not applied consistently before *Smith*, but it remained in place from the early 1960s until *Smith* was decided in 1990. The *Smith* decision was especially troubling because the state of Oregon did not argue that the long-standing precedent should be overturned, but rather that the state's interest was compelling (extremely important).

There was a remarkable outcry against the *Smith* decision from politicians, religious groups, and civil liberties groups. An amazing element of this outcry was its bipartisan and diverse nature.[5] The result was a new law called the Religious Freedom Restoration Act (RFRA), which was designed to restore the legal standard that applied to free exercise claims prior to *Smith*.[6] The federal RFRA was passed by a 97-3 vote in the Senate and a unanimous vote in the House and was signed into law by President Clinton in 1993.[7]

Under RFRA, if a law or government action imposes a substantial burden on an individual's or religious organization's religion, the government must provide an exemption unless the government has a compelling (extremely important) interest and the law or government action is the only practical way to meet that interest. Given the vast bipartisan and public support for RFRA, it is obvious that exemptions to generally applicable laws (laws that apply to everyone) for people of faith were not extremely controversial when RFRA was passed in 1993.

When the Supreme Court held four years later that Congress had exceeded its authority by imposing RFRA on the states,[8] numerous states passed state RFRAs.[9] Other states continued to interpret their state constitutions in a manner consistent with pre-*Smith* law.[10] Congress also reacted by passing the Religious Land Use and Institutionalized Persons Act (RLUIPA), which applies the same test as RFRA to situations involving religious land use, as well as to religious exemption claims by prisoners. The Supreme Court has since upheld RLUIPA as applied both to the federal government and the states.[11]

The general public did not view these laws as controversial when they were passed; yet, in recent years RFRA has become a central issue in the culture wars in the United States, and state RFRAs are now subject to serious opposition. Part of the reason is that some proposed state RFRAs explicitly protect for-profit entities and/or government employees, something the federal RFRA was not understood to do when it was passed. This has led to significant backlash against some recent state RFRAs, most famously in Indiana, where the state faced serious boycotts after passing a RFRA in 2015. However, even state RFRAs that do not explicitly protect for-profit entities, and which were modeled on the federal RFRA, have been defeated by strong public outcry. The fight over state RFRAs is addressed later.

Two of the major reasons that RFRAs have faced such strong opposition are (1) fear that they will be used to require exemptions that will harm third parties and (2) fear that they will protect for-profit entities that can use RFRAs to impose the owners' religious values on employee rights and on customers. Prior to 2014, it seemed that neither of these scenarios was particularly likely (and as will be seen, even today it is less likely than most people think because of compelling government interests in many of these situations). In 2014, however, the Supreme Court decided *Burwell v. Hobby Lobby*. The Court for the first time held that for-profit entities are protected under RFRA, even when doing so could, as a practical matter, place a burden on third parties. It is important to note that the majority of the Supreme Court held that there was no actual burden on third parties in that case. As we will see, however, this conclusion was questionable and says little about the potential impact of the holding in other situations.

In fact, many of the religious freedom issues that are hardest to negotiate involve for-profit entities, especially those that serve the general public, and situations where accommodating someone's religious freedom has a direct negative impact on third parties, such as failure to provide benefits or denial of service. This is exactly the can of worms the *Hobby Lobby* decision threw wide open. To understand the tactics currently used against religious freedom, it is essential to understand *Hobby Lobby* and the fact that many of those attacking religious freedom do not distinguish between claims by for-profit entities that may harm third parties and claims by religious individuals and religious institutions that do not generally affect anyone other than the individual or those who are part of – or seek to join – the religion.[12]

So let's look at the U.S. Supreme Court's decision in *Hobby Lobby*, and see what it actually says. I am on record that I think it is a terrible decision both legally and for religious freedom in the long run, because the stronger the arguments that third parties can be harmed and for-profit entities protected under RFRA, the more ammunition those who want to destroy religious freedom have. However, even with *Hobby Lobby* on the books, it is possible to protect LGBT rights and reproductive freedom. The outcry against *Hobby Lobby* is, in part, based on the perception of the case rather than likely long-term harms to LGBT and reproductive rights. I have argued elsewhere that it is exactly those perceptions that endanger religious freedom, but here we must take *Hobby Lobby* as a given and try to work to moderate its negative impact on the way in which religious freedom is viewed and minimize any impact it could have on the rights of third parties. I will argue in Chapter 5 that one of the best ways to protect religious freedom over the long run is to amend the federal RFRA (and state RFRAs) to exclude for-profit entities from coverage, which would undo the *Hobby Lobby* decision and give less ammunition to those who seek to repeal or prevent passage of RFRAs.

Hobby Lobby actually involves two cases that were consolidated by the Court. Both cases involved for-profit corporations that sued the government over the HHS Mandate under the Affordable Care Act (ACA), which is known by most people as "Obamacare." The HHS Mandate is a set of rules created by the Department of Health and

Human Services – the HHS – requiring employers to provide contraceptive services as part of their health care coverage. An employer that refuses to provide this coverage under its insurance plan is subject to hefty fines.

The first case involved a Pennsylvania corporation, Conestoga Woods, which is owned by the Hahn family and employs 950 people. Conestoga Woods sued to challenge the HHS Mandate. The second case, and the namesake of the Court's decision, involved Hobby Lobby, a large for-profit hobby and crafts chain incorporated under Oklahoma law. Hobby Lobby is owned by the Green family and has more than 500 stores and more than 13,000 employees. The Greens also own a chain of Christian bookstores called Mardel, which employs 400 people. Both companies sued, arguing that the HHS Mandate violates RFRA. The companies did not object to providing contraceptive coverage generally, but rather to providing what they considered to be abortifacients, including Plan B, Ella, and certain IUDs.[13]

The fines for noncompliance with the HHS Mandate are large. Significantly, however, the mandate contains exemptions for traditional religious entities such as churches, integrated church auxiliaries such as in-house religious schools, and associations of churches.[*] Moreover, it contains an exception for other non-profit religiously affiliated entities such as charities and schools. This exemption, in effect, requires third-party coverage for contraceptive services to which the non-profit religious entity objects. There is also an exception for employers with fewer than fifty employees. Therefore, the claim in *Hobby Lobby* only applied to for-profit entities with more than fifty employees.

The *Hobby Lobby* case raises two key questions under RFRA. Both of these questions are front and center in the current culture wars. First, are for-profit corporations covered under RFRA? Second, if so, what happens when a for-profit corporation denies its employees a benefit required under federal law because it has a religious objection to providing that benefit?

---

[*] The term "church" in this context is legal shorthand. It applies to all houses of worship, including synagogues, mosques, temples, and so on.

The Supreme Court held that closely held for-profit corporations are protected by RFRA. The Court explained that RFRA applies to for-profit companies because RFRA protects "persons." In many areas of law, corporations are considered "persons." Sometimes that characterization makes sense, and it has been part of the law for a long time. This characterization had not, however, been applied to for-profit corporations in the religious freedom context prior to the ACA. The Supreme Court nevertheless found no basis to exclude for-profit companies from the definition of "persons" under RFRA. RFRA specifically states that persons are protected from substantial burdens on religion, unless the burden is supported by a compelling state interest (extremely important interest) and the law creating the burden is narrowly tailored (the only practical means) to meet that compelling interest.

The *Hobby Lobby* Court's analysis on this issue, however, seems strained. The Court suggests there is no practical difference between protecting a religious entity or nonprofit under RFRA and protecting a closely held for-profit corporation. This breezes past the obvious points that religious entities serve their congregations, while for-profit corporations have many constituencies, and that the HHS Mandate specifically exempts religious entities and religious nonprofits.[14] Moreover, there is ample support for the notion that prior to *Hobby Lobby*, for-profit entities were viewed differently from nonprofit entities under the Free Exercise Clause and thus also under RFRA. This is important because before *Hobby Lobby*, it was generally believed that RFRA restored the law that existed prior to the *Smith* decision. The Supreme Court avoids these concerns in two ways.

First, the Supreme Court argues that since a free exercise challenge was allowed to proceed in a case involving Sunday closing laws, which had a negative impact on an Orthodox Jewish business, for-profit businesses are in fact covered by RFRA. This argument is weak. The Sunday closing law case, which was called *Braunfeld v. Brown*,[15] involved a sole proprietorship (a one-person business), and the Supreme Court treated the burden on the entity and the individual as the same. More importantly, as Justice Ginsburg points out in her

Hobby Lobby dissent, the plaintiff – who suffered a significant burden in that case – lost his free exercise claim.

Prior to the *Smith* decision, the Supreme Court specifically addressed the for-profit nature of an employer seeking a religious exemption in *United States v. Lee*.[16] The case involved a small Amish employer who sought a religious exemption to paying Social Security taxes for its employees because the Amish community provided its own social safety net. The Supreme Court held that a for-profit business has to follow a general law even if it burdens the owner's religious beliefs. The *Hobby Lobby* Court attempts to distinguish *Lee* based on the fact that it is a Free Exercise Clause case and that it involved taxation, but the relevant portion of *Lee* demonstrates that the discussion of for-profit entities is not so limited.

Another argument against using the *Lee* case to support the argument that for-profit corporations were not protected under the Free Exercise Clause is that the Supreme Court heard the case in *Lee*, meaning that the Supreme Court allowed the corporate entity to have standing (a basis to sue) under the Free Exercise Clause. This argument is what we often call a "red herring" in the law. The Supreme Court recognized the right to sue but then held that for-profit corporations must follow the law even when it conflicts with the religious faith of the owner. It is quite possible, therefore, that in subsequent cases under the Free Exercise Clause, there would not be standing (a basis to sue) because there is no way for a court to redress the harm and there may be no legally recognizable injury. This argument about standing is an interesting legal argument, but in light of the outcome in the Sunday Closing case, it is more of a distraction than a strong legal argument.

Second, the Supreme Court asserts in *Hobby Lobby* that RFRA, which was passed to undo the *Smith* decision and return the law to where it was before that decision, is no longer limited to the pre-*Smith* law because of the legislative history of the RLUIPA, which was passed after the Supreme Court found that RFRA did not apply to the states. The legal arguments here are complex, but looking at the history of RFRA and RLUIPA, I think that the *Hobby Lobby* Court was wrong on this point.[17] Of course, a number of excellent legal scholars would disagree with me and with my critique of *Hobby Lobby* generally,[18] while others would strongly agree with my position,[19] but it is hard to deny the political and social reality that *Hobby Lobby* has been used to damage religious freedom more generally.

The next major issue that the Supreme Court addresses in *Hobby Lobby* is whether the HHS Mandate imposes a "substantial burden" on the plaintiffs' religion. This is one of the toughest questions in the case because it requires a determination of whose religion is substantially burdened if we give for-profit corporations free exercise rights under RFRA. Is it the corporation? The owners? Some other group? Moreover, it requires a determination of what constitutes a "substantial burden" on religion under RFRA.

The Supreme Court held that in a closely held corporation, the owners' religious freedom is what should be considered. It also held that while state law creates corporations, they could still have values and expression. This is consistent with an equally controversial earlier decision by the Supreme Court dealing with campaign finance reform called *Citizens United*.[20] In that case, the Supreme Court held that corporations are entitled to free speech rights and are able to express themselves through campaign contributions.[21] Based, in part, on this earlier case, the *Hobby Lobby* Court rejected the notion that the purpose of a corporation is just to make money.

The *Hobby Lobby* Court also rejected the argument that religious exercise is inherently different from other forms of corporate expression and held that a closely held corporation can exercise religion. That exercise must be viewed from the perspective of the owners of the closely held corporation. This holding, too, is controversial.

Even if a closely held corporation can exercise religion, the question remained whether the HHS Mandate serves a compelling governmental interest (extremely important interest) and is narrowly tailored (the only practical way) to serve that interest. The Supreme Court assumed that the HHS Mandate met a compelling government interest by requiring that health plans include contraceptive coverage. It found, however, that the HHS Mandate was not narrowly tailored to meet that interest.

The Supreme Court noted that there are already several exceptions to the HHS Mandate. Ironically, two of these were to protect the religious freedom of traditional religious entities such as churches and religious non-profits. The former are completely exempt from the HHS Mandate, and the latter are not responsible to pay anything toward contraceptive care to which they have religious objections; rather, the entities' insurance carrier or a designated insurance carrier (if the entity is self-insured) would pay for the coverage. The HHS Mandate also has an exemption for employers with fewer than fifty employees, as is common for many federal statutes. This provision would, of course, protect small closely held for-profit entities whose owners have religious objections, but based on their size not on those objections. Finally, the HHS Mandate has a grandfather provision that allows companies to elect to keep their preexisting plans under certain conditions. This grandfather exemption was designed to allow plans that provided good coverage prior to the ACA to continue and to give companies time to adapt to the general requirements of the ACA. If grandfathered plans change their coverage or the costs for which the insured, is responsible they can lose grandfathered status.

The Supreme Court relied on these exemptions to suggest that the government need not have uniformity of enforcement to satisfy its compelling interest. Rather, the government had already created a system that could be used to protect its interest in universal access to contraceptive care – namely, the government could do what it already does for religious non-profits by setting up a third-party payer system that goes into effect once the employer certifies that it objects to providing contraceptive coverage (which is what the government has indeed done since *Hobby Lobby*), or the government could pay for the care itself. The Supreme Court held, therefore, that the burden on female employees would be "precisely zero."

This, of course, ignores the fact that other employers may object to contraceptives generally, or to other medical treatments, and that the solution of the government payer, whether or not politically feasible, can always be raised to show a less restrictive alternative. Moreover, the idea of requiring religious employers to self-certify thus triggering contraceptive coverage has already sparked numerous legal challenges as is discussed in Chapter 7. The idea that government could pay the way when for-profit entities object to government mandates will likely have a negative impact on religious freedom claims in the future.[22] The government has agreed to provide the accommodation suggested by the Court, but that could change with future administrations and says nothing about what might happen in situations where a religious employer objects to broader forms of contraceptive–or other healthcare–coverage.

The Supreme Court's tacit acknowledgment that exercising religious freedom could interfere with the rights of others is unprecedented. The Supreme Court says the impact on female employees is "precisely zero," but that is not the case. Reading the opinion as a whole, it is clear that negative impact on third parties is possible under *Hobby Lobby*. Justice Kennedy filed a concurring opinion arguing that the decision does not allow negative impact on third parties,[23] but as Justice Ginsburg points out in dissent that may just be wishful thinking.[24]

When it comes to religious freedom, RFRA and RLUIPA are not the only games in town. Important legal concepts called the Ecclesiastical Abstention Doctrine and the doctrine of Church Autonomy also apply to some religious freedom claims. These are fancy terms for the idea that courts will not get involved in answering religious questions nor can government force religious entities to alter religious doctrines. The Ecclesiastical Exemption Doctrine is an important and core concept that reaches back to an 1872 Supreme Court decision called *Watson v. Jones*.[25] The Ecclesiastical Abstention Doctrine has mostly been applied in cases involving battles over church property and church schisms. The doctrine of Church Autonomy is a related concept. Recently it was applied to protect a church from a claim by an employee under the Americans with Disabilities Act because the church considered the employee to be a clergy member.[26] These doctrines are quite important in the context of sexual freedom because many people have heard the frenzied arguments that religious institutions will be forced to hold same-sex marriages or provide contraceptives. They won't. Any statement to the contrary ignores these long-established principles of law and common sense. Even state mandatory contraceptive coverage laws have exemptions for traditional religious entities.

II WHAT WE KNOW AND WHAT WE THINK WE KNOW

Certain things are clear based on the law, while others are less so. First, most religious freedom claims have nothing to do with sexual freedom and place little or no burden on third parties. Of course, those are not the claims that have raised so much attention in recent years, so we focus on situations with potential tension between religious freedom and sexual freedom. The rest of this chapter presents a basic statement of what is clear and what is unclear under the law regarding the conflict between these freedoms. Topics that are unclear receive detailed attention throughout the rest of this book.

It is clear that no individual, religious or not, will be forced to attend same-sex marriages or use birth control. This is so obvious it should not even need stating, but some radical anti-LGBT or anti-contraceptive forces have argued that people will be required to do so. This is one of the few things in the law that is absolutely clear. Government cannot make anyone attend a wedding he or she does not want to go to or use contraception he or she does not believe in: period, the end.

What about churches and other religious entities? The answer to this question is also clear. No clergy member will be required to preside over same-sex marriages, and no religious entity will be required to allow same-sex marriages. Of course, many religious entities and clergy will allow and perform same-sex weddings because their theology allows or supports them in doing so. This is not due to government compulsion, but rather quite the opposite: It is a result of religious doctrine. If a given religion were to decide to stop performing these ceremonies, the government could not interfere. Moreover, no church or religious house of worship will be required to provide contraception since houses of worship are exempt from the Affordable Care Act's contraception mandate – and even if they were not, they would most likely be protected under RFRA and several other laws as discussed in Chapter 6. Again, many religious entities will provide contraceptive care because doing so is consistent with or mandated by their faith, but no religion will be forced to do so.

These are of course the easy cases, but what about the hard ones? What happens when government employees seek a religious exemption to performing their duties? What happens when for-profit corporations seek a religious exemption in states not governed by a RFRA that covers for-profit companies? Finally, what happens to religious institutions such as universities, adoption agencies, and charities that do not want to recognize same-sex marriages or contraceptive care for benefits purposes? Chapters 4, 5, and 7 address each of these issues in greater depth, but it is helpful to briefly answer these questions now to provide context for later discussion.

Government officials swear an oath to serve the public, but that does not answer the question of whether they should be entitled to religious exemptions. Certainly, if multiple people in an office can perform the same duties and someone requests a religious exemption not to perform that duty, the appropriate authority can grant the exemption, but unless there is a law that mandates religious exemptions, no government employee or official is entitled to one. In Chapter 4, I argue that the government should grant these exemptions when other government employees or officials are available to perform the duties, even if the government is not required to do so.

Some states have passed or proposed laws that would exempt government officials who do not want to provide marriage licenses for or perform same-sex weddings. However, government officials are not entitled to nor should they be given an exemption when they are the only government official(s) who can perform the duty or when every government official who can perform the duty seeks an exemption. The laws passed so far are consistent with this.

As the discussion of *Hobby Lobby* demonstrates, for-profit entities are entitled to exemptions under the federal RFRA. This may also be true under some state RFRAs. Chapter 5 explains how this may end up harming religious freedom for traditional religious entities such as churches. Protection of for-profit corporations was a major impetus for the intense backlash against several state RFRAs. Still, as a practical matter, for-profit entities will lose these claims in many

cases because government will have a compelling interest for denying the exemption, and because the government action will be the
only practical way to meet that interest. If, for example, a for-profit
entity sought to deny all benefits to same-sex couples, broad forms of
contraception to any employee, or blood transfusions, government could
well deny the requested accommodation based on a compelling interest
and narrow tailoring. This is also addressed further in Chapter 5.

Finally, religious non-profit charities and universities are concerned
they may lose government grants or tax-exempt status if they refuse
to recognize same-sex spousal benefits. Remember, these entities are
exempt under the Affordable Care Act.[27] This topic is extremely
complex and is addressed in Chapter 7. What happens when
a religious non-profit entity refuses to provide benefits required by
law? Similar issues can arise under state anti-discrimination laws that
cover sexual orientation. Currently, no federal anti-discrimination law
does so.

It is possible that these entities could lose government contracts or
even tax-exempt status. The latter is highly unlikely, but there is precedent for it in the context of race discrimination by a non-profit
entity.[28] First, the Internal Revenue Service or a state taxing authority
would have to seek to remove the tax-exempt status of one of these
entities. Next, it would have to prove that the entity does not meet the
requirements for tax-exempt status because of its failure to grant
benefits or because of discriminatory practices. Finally, the taxing
authority would most likely have to prove this in court after being
sued. Each of these steps is addressed in more detail in Chapter 7.

Some non-profit entities that refuse to provide benefits to same-sex
spouses might lose government contracts. This would depend on how
the government decides to proceed in light of the recent recognition
of same-sex marriage. It is certainly possible that some government
entities may decide at some point to deny contracts to religious non-
profits that refuse to provide benefits to same-sex couples. These
entities might raise a claim under RFRA if this were to happen, but
how that would play out is unclear.

It is also possible that laws may be passed protecting religious non-
profits in these areas. Ironically, protection of for-profit entities under
RFRA may help foster backlash against such laws protecting non-profit

entities. Again, the likely legal impact of *Hobby Lobby* is much less than its social impact of undermining religious freedom more generally. Chapter 7 proposes a way to avoid the conflict. The resolution will make neither side completely happy but will allow both sides' interests to be protected.

3   SEXUAL FREEDOM

I INTRODUCTION

The term "sexual freedom" is not an ideal term. Clearly, LGBT and reproductive freedom is about far more than sex. Both LGBT and reproductive freedom concern one's ability to be oneself, to be free, and to control one's destiny. LGBT rights are about, among other things, being who you are without government interference or discrimination in the most fundamental aspects of life. Reproductive freedom is about, among other things, the ability to control your own body and to determine your own future. The term "sexual freedom," as I use it in this book is shorthand for all of this.

There is a certain irony here. Recall in the last chapter that many progressive secularists assume religious freedom is about just faith. As we learned in the previous chapters, it is about far more than that. It is about who people are, how they experience life, and what they perceive to be essential to a fulfilled existence. Yet, each of these things can also be said about LGBT rights and reproductive freedom. It is just as unfair for people of faith to assert that sexual freedom is only about personal choices – unattached to core aspects of being – as it is for secularists to assume that religious freedom is just about protecting blind faith.

I understand that none of this is as simple as throwing aside our core assumptions, which is not simple at all, of course. Even if people were able to do that – and an open goal of this book is to challenge people on both sides to reflect on their horizons and how they perceive each other – fundamental questions about what matters in society, about values, and about morals may keep people from finding common ground. Agreement with specific elements of freedom on one side or the other may be hard to achieve. Yet, if we are unable to even perceive, and more importantly get a palpable sense of, the importance of a given issue to one side or the other, compromise will be even harder.

This chapter explores both LGBT rights and reproductive freedom. Section II addresses LGBT rights, with a significant focus on the law from the 1980s through the present time. Therefore, I focus on the freedom of members of the LGBT community to engage in sexual relations without government interference, the freedom to marry, and the current state of antidiscrimination laws protecting members of the LGBT community.

Section III addresses reproductive freedom, also with a significant focus on the law. This includes the right to use contraception, abortion rights, attempts by states to limit abortion rights, and of course the questions posed in this context by *Hobby Lobby*. I also explore three federal laws: the Church Amendments, the Weldon Amendment, and Section 245 of the Public Health Service Act. These laws protect the rights of doctors and other healthcare practitioners to refuse to provide abortions based on conscience without suffering discrimination or reductions in funding, but the Church Amendments at least, may also protect the rights of doctors and others who provide abortions based on conscience to be free from discrimination and retaliation by government entities, employers, and so on. These laws, and conscience claims generally, are addressed in greater detail in Chapter 6.

II LGBT RIGHTS

In recent years, same-sex marriage has been a central issue in the fight for LGBT rights. In June 2015, the U.S. Supreme Court held that marriage is a fundamental right that can not be denied based on sexual orientation. That case, *Obergefell v. Hodges*,[1] has raised many of the fascinating religious freedom questions addressed in this book. Yet, even before the Supreme Court decided *Obergefell*, a number of states had already recognized same-sex marriage, through statutes, amendments to state constitutions, or state supreme court decisions upholding the right to same-sex marriage under state constitutions. Moreover, lower federal courts had regularly held that state laws denying the right to same-sex marriage violated the U.S. Constitution.

Same-sex marriage is not the only important issue in the context of LGBT rights. Other issues include the right to engage in same-sex intimate relations without legal interference, as well as the right to be free from discrimination based on sexual orientation or transgender status. This section addresses these issues in turn before addressing same-sex marriage.

A Sodomy Laws

Given the recent progress on LGBT rights, it may come as a surprise to many people that until 2003 it was unclear whether sodomy laws targeting same-sex intimate relations were unconstitutional. Sodomy laws prohibit certain sexual acts, including oral and anal sex, and originally applied to both straight and gay individuals who engaged in these acts. Over time, these laws became disfavored in most states and were generally not enforced. More recently, however, some states passed sodomy laws that applied only to same-sex couples or enforced their existing laws only against same-sex couples. In a 1986 decision called *Bowers v. Hardwick*,[2] the Supreme Court upheld application of a state sodomy law as applied to same-sex couples. The law itself applied to both heterosexual and homosexual acts of sodomy, but it was raised against two men who were having private, consensual sex in one of the men's home.

The U.S. Supreme Court had to answer the question of whether same-sex intimate relations could be criminalized by a state without violating the U.S. Constitution. The Supreme Court held that states could criminalize same-sex intimate relations because these relations were not protected by the Constitution. The decision was heavily criticized not only by those who supported sexual freedom generally but also by those who questioned the government's right to regulate private behavior between consenting adults that occurs within the home. In this sense, the decision not only upset progressives and those who supported LGBT rights but also many small government conservatives and libertarians who did not support government interference with highly personal behavior in the privacy of one's home.

The decision remained valid law until 2003, when the Supreme Court decided a case called *Lawrence v. Texas*,[3] which overturned *Bowers v. Hardwick*. *Lawrence v. Texas* involved a Texas law that criminalized only homosexual sodomy. By 2003, most of the states had repealed their sodomy laws. However, fourteen states still had sodomy laws on the books, although many of these states did not enforce those laws. Four of these states, including Texas, had sodomy laws that applied only to same-sex relations. The Court held that every adult, including members of the LGBT community, has a fundamental right to private sexual relations in his or her home without government interference so long as both parties consent. States could still enforce laws against prostitution, even when consensual, for a variety of reasons.

The key to the Supreme Court's decision in *Lawrence v. Texas* is that no state can enforce a law that criminalizes consensual adult sexual conduct without violating the Due Process Clause of the Fourteenth Amendment to the U.S. Constitution. The Supreme Court specifically held the following:

> The petitioners are entitled to respect for their private lives. The State cannot demean their existence or control their destiny by making their private sexual conduct a crime. Their right to liberty under the Due Process Clause gives them the full right to engage in their conduct without intervention of the government. "It is a promise of the Constitution that there is a realm of personal liberty which the government may not enter." [Citing *Planned Parenthood of Southeastern Pa. v. Casey*, 505 U. S. 833, 847 (1992)]. The Texas statute furthers no legitimate state interest which can justify its intrusion into the personal and private life of the individual.[4]

The legal balancing test used – whether the "statute furthers no legitimate state interest which can justify its intrusion into the personal and private life of the individual" – has been criticized as being too weak, too strong, or unprecedented, but it remains good law and is further reinforced by *Obergefell v. Hodges* (the same-sex marriage case).

Additionally, Justice Sandra Day O'Connor filed a concurring opinion arguing that the law violated the Equal Protection Clause of the Fourteenth Amendment to the Constitution as well because the law targeted only same-sex acts and not heterosexual acts, so that it denied LGBT individuals the equal protection of the law. Since the majority of the Supreme Court held the Texas law violated the Due Process Clause of the Constitution, the majority opinion did not address the equal protection claim directly as Justice O'Connor did. Regardless, Justice O'Connor is almost certainly correct that the laws violated the Equal Protection Clause as well.

It is important to note that the Supreme Court's opinion also protects private heterosexual sexual conduct. The *Bowers v. Hardwick* decision did not answer the question of whether heterosexual conduct could be outlawed, so the ten states that had laws on the books criminalizing various forms of private consensual sexual conduct (regardless of sexual orientation) could have enforced those laws against anyone. The Supreme Court's holding in *Lawrence v. Texas* protects sexual conduct between consenting adults in the home regardless of sexual orientation.

B Antidiscrimination Law

A major element of LGBT rights is the quest for antidiscrimination laws. The reality is that members of the gay and lesbian community are sometimes the victims of discrimination in employment, housing, and even public accommodations. Some states and localities have antidiscrimination laws to protect against this sort of discrimination; yet, no federal antidiscrimination law protects members of the LGBT community, and most states do not have these laws either. Of course, the LGBT community includes transgender individuals, who are sometimes not even protected in locations that have antidiscrimination laws protecting members of the gay and lesbian community, but a discussion of this issue is beyond the scope of this book. The focus here is on antidiscrimination laws that protect members of the gay and lesbian community.

The issue of antidiscrimination protection for gays and lesbians is far more connected to religious freedom than it might appear at first glance. One of the biggest concerns expressed by those who oppose religious freedom laws is that these laws would allow widespread discrimination against members of the LGBT community by for-profit entities. The reason I mention for-profit entities specifically is that most antidiscrimination laws, including national ones such as Title VII of the Civil Rights Act of 1964, have exceptions for traditional religious entities; so, for example, a Baptist church can discriminate based on religion when hiring its ministers or other religious personnel. It would be odd indeed if a Baptist church could not require that its ministers be Baptist. Moreover, as a result of something called the ministerial exception, Title VII does not apply to clergy, so the Catholic Church can require that its priests be male. Whether this is a wise decision is none of the government's business, and the ministerial exception, which is based in part on the doctrine of Church Autonomy discussed in Chapter 2, ensures this.

The same is true for most antidiscrimination laws that protect members of the LGBT community. Churches and their affiliates can do what they want in regard to having gay clergy, performing same-sex marriages, or welcoming congregants who are members of the LGBT community. So if antidiscrimination laws protecting the LGBT community are passed, an exception is likely for traditional religious entities such as churches.

But what about for-profit entities? Antidiscrimination laws have not generally allowed religious exceptions for them. This means that if we had national antidiscrimination laws that protected against discrimination based on sexual orientation, exemptions are unlikely for religious companies such as Hobby Lobby. So how would this work given that the *Hobby Lobby* case protects for-profit entities under the Religious Freedom Restoration Act (RFRA)? The likely outcome is that antidiscrimination laws would serve as a compelling interest (an extremely important interest). If government has such a compelling interest, it is far more likely that it could prevent for-profit companies from discriminating. Moreover, an antidiscrimination law that gives religious exemptions to traditional religious entities might be viewed as narrowly tailored (the best practical way) to meet the government's compelling interest in preventing discrimination. If so, traditional religious entities would be completely protected under RFRA and the religious exception in antidiscrimination laws. For-profit entities, however, could not discriminate.

Antidiscrimination laws protecting the LGBT community are not only essential to protect against discrimination based on sexual orientation, but they are also essential in helping support more state RFRAs because the arguments that RFRAs promote discrimination would ring more hollow if RFRA protections were balanced against antidiscrimination laws. As discussed in Chapter 5, concerns about discrimination have prompted the defeat of several state RFRAs.

If those states had solid antidiscrimination protection for members of the LGBT community, or if there were a national antidiscrimination law protecting members of the LGBT community, it would be much harder to seriously argue that state RFRAs would cause widespread discrimination. Unfortunately, we are still a long way from having national antidiscrimination protection. Hopefully, that will change sooner rather than later. Let's look at the current state of antidiscrimination laws protecting the LGBT community, and at the one Supreme Court decision that touches on this issue.

No current national law protects gays and lesbians from discrimination based on sexual orientation. In 2014, however, President Obama signed Executive Order 13672, which prohibits discrimination based on sexual orientation by companies and non-profits that contract with the federal government. The Equal Employment Opportunity Commission (EEOC) and some courts have also upheld employment discrimination claims under Title VII of the Civil Rights Act of 1964. That law does not protect against discrimination based on sexual orientation, but it does protect against discrimination based on gender. The EEOC and a few courts have upheld claims based on sexual orientation using the argument that discrimination based on "sex," which is prohibited under Title VII, can include discrimination based on sexual orientation under some circumstances. These are complex and interesting legal arguments, but it is unclear what the U.S. Supreme Court would say on these issues. A law directly protecting against discrimination based on sexual orientation would answer any such questions; moreover, it could help provide the balance needed to generate greater public support for religious freedom laws.

Significantly, as of the time of this writing, 22 states protect against discrimination based on sexual orientation in public and private employment. An additional nine states protect public employees against discrimination based on sexual orientation but do not provide such protection in the private sector. Twenty-one states protect against discrimination based on sexual orientation in public accommodations such as hotels and restaurants. Moreover, numerous cities and counties have ordinances that prohibit discrimination based on sexual orientation. Yet in many places, there is no protection under federal, state, or local law.

Some states have attempted to prohibit localities from passing antidiscrimination laws that protect against discrimination based on sexual orientation. This most recently occurred in North Carolina, when a law commonly known as HB2 was passed. The law has gotten a lot of attention because of its provisions regarding the use of public restrooms by transgender individuals. Yet, one of the most far-reaching provisions in the law denies local governments the ability to pass antidiscrimination laws. This provision seems targeted at the city of Charlotte, which had passed an ordinance protecting members of the LGBT community from discrimination. HB2 prevents Charlotte, or any other North Carolina local government, from providing such legal protection to members of the LGBT community. This provision of HB2 is almost certainly unconstitutional.

In 1996, the U.S. Supreme Court decided a case called *Romer v. Evans*.[5] In that case, the Supreme Court held unconstitutional a Colorado constitutional amendment banning local governments from protecting against discrimination based on sexual orientation. The Supreme Court held that the law was discriminatory because it prohibited only one group of people – gays and lesbians – from gaining protection under antidiscrimination law without first amending the state constitution. Thus, people could gain protection based on any trait, including hair or eye color, without amending the state constitution, but members of the gay and lesbian community would need to amend the state constitution before they could even get a local law to protect them. This violated the Equal Protection Clause of the Fourteenth Amendment to the Constitution. Thus, any state laws aimed at preventing localities from passing antidiscrimination ordinances prohibiting discrimination based on sexual orientation are suspect and unlikely to pass constitutional muster.

The recent North Carolina law prevents passage of any local anti-discrimination law regardless of whether it provides protection for members of the LGBT community. This will not likely save the law under the *Romer v. Evans* analysis. First, a lot of evidence indicates that the purpose of this provision of HB2 was designed precisely to prevent local governments from protecting members of the LGBT community from discrimination. Second, to gain protection from discrimination at the local level, members of the LGBT community would need to have the state law overturned.

North Carolina would likely argue that HB2 is different from the Colorado constitutional amendment struck down in *Romer v. Evans*, because the Colorado amendment applied only to members of the LGBT community, whereas HB2 prevents any local antidiscrimination law. Yet, the history of HB2 and its practical effect demonstrate that it was designed to serve the same purpose as the Colorado amendment struck down in *Romer*. Perhaps more importantly, the relevant constitutional precedent is no longer limited to *Romer*, and since that case was decided *Lawrence v. Texas, United States v. Windsor* (a case holding that the federal Defense of Marriage Act unconstitutionally discriminated against same-sex couples whose relationship was recognized in their home state), and *Obergefell v. Hodges* have lent more ammunition to those who seek to challenge HB2.

Significantly, for present purposes, laws such as North Carolina's HB2 – which is not based in religious freedom – do great damage to good-faith attempts to protect religious freedom. In an environment where laws such as HB2 regularly make headlines, and there is no national antidiscrimination protection for members of the LGBT community, it becomes easier for those who oppose religious freedom laws to argue that they are part of a broader attempt to promote discrimination.

C Same-Sex Marriage

If this section had been written before June 2015, it would have been an exceptionally long and detailed explanation of the patchwork of protections for same-sex marriage among the states. Some of these protections were passed by state legislatures, state supreme courts decided others, and still others were based on orders by federal courts to recognize same-sex marriage. In spite of all these decisions, before June 2015 not every state recognized same-sex marriage.

Moreover, the Supreme Court had not addressed the constitutional right to same-sex marriage directly. There was an understanding based on earlier cases that marriage is a protected constitutional right.[6] The Supreme Court had also held in a case called *United States v. Windsor*,[7] that DOMA (the Federal Defense of Marriage Act), which defined marriage for the purposes of federal law as being between a man and a woman and allowed states to deny recognition of same-sex marriages performed in other states for, was unconstitutional.

In June 2015, however, in *Obergefell v. Hodges* the Supreme Court held clearly that same-sex couples have a fundamental right to marry, and that denying that right violates both the Due Process Clause and the Equal Protection Clause of the Fourteenth Amendment. As a result, there is no longer a legal barrier to same-sex marriage. The right is constitutionally guaranteed.

Some state officials have raised claims that they should not be required to perform same-sex marriages or issue licenses. As seen in the next chapter, these officials' claims can only be accommodated if someone else can perform the functions without any delay, and so long as certain other factors are met; so even if religious objections are recognized, the right to same-sex marriage still cannot legally be denied.

III REPRODUCTIVE FREEDOM

Reproductive freedom, like LGBT rights, is not only about sex. It is also about health, the ability to control one's own body and mind free from government interference, and the right to control one's future. These are major elements of self-determination. If a patient and her doctor agree that an abortion is necessary to save her life or to protect her health or her future, why should government be able to interfere with her ability to gain information about or have the abortion before the fetus is viable and therefore the government has a legally recognized interest in protecting the Fetus? Why should a woman have her future dramatically altered because of someone else's religious beliefs? These are fundamental questions in current reproductive freedom debates.

Reproductive freedom is perhaps even more contentious than LGBT rights for some. Yet, some forms of reproductive freedom have been recognized at the national level since the Supreme Court decided *Griswold v. Connecticut* in 1965.[8] That case held that it is unconstitutional for a state to criminalize the use of contraceptives (the state ban precluded even the use of condoms). Today the right to use contraception is not especially controversial. Religious individuals and entities, however, have sought exemptions from prescribing, paying for, or supporting the use of contraceptives. The most recent example of this is the *Hobby Lobby* case discussed later and in Chapters 2 and 5. As you may recall from Chapter 2, Hobby Lobby and two other companies sought to deny coverage for particular intrauterine devices (IUDs) and emergency contraceptives, such as Plan B and Ella.

Of course, abortion is a far more controversial reproductive freedom issue; yet, the right to have an abortion, at least prior to the viability of the fetus, has been recognized since *Roe v. Wade* was decided in 1973.[9] Since that time, there have been numerous attempts to limit information about or access to abortions. Some of these will be discussed later. As with contraception more generally, religious individuals and entities have sought exemptions to protect their rights not to perform, pay for, or otherwise support abortions.

The discussion in this section focuses mostly on contraceptives and abortions performed during the time before fetal viability, which includes the vast majority of abortions. Late-term abortions certainly raise important issues, but the Centers for Disease Control (CDC) has demonstrated that 89 percent to 92 percent of abortions occur in the first trimester, and most of the remaining abortions occur in the second trimester.[10] The very few late-term abortions that occur are almost always performed to protect the life or health of the mother.

Most current attempts to limit abortion rights involve requiring permission from someone other than the woman seeking the abortion (such as parental consent), requiring dissemination of information that tries to dissuade against abortion (even when the doctor does not agree with that information), requiring waiting periods, or attempting to regulate what facilities can and cannot perform abortions, so as to limit access. As I will explain, these attempts, which have been "successful" in some states, are likely to backfire in the long run; in fact, I assert that they will ultimately backfire right into the conscience claims and religious exemptions to protect those conscience claims that currently exist. Thus, current attempts to limit reproductive freedom will not only harm reproductive freedom but will also harm religious freedom in the long run.

I have tried throughout this book to make the case for both religious freedom and sexual freedom, knowing full well that many people heavily entrenched on one side or the other may be unable to empathize with the "other side." I also realize that it is especially hard to build bridges between people who think that abortion – or even contraception – is murder and those who view contraception and abortion as core questions of self-determination, privacy, and the control of one's own medical care and body. As a religious person who supports reproductive freedom, I can empathize with both sides.

As will be seen in the next few sections, we currently have a reasonable balance between reproductive freedom and religious freedom in this context. Reproductive freedom is legally protected, as are conscience claims by medical professionals and religious hospitals that have religious objections to performing abortions or other procedures. Both reproductive rights and conscience claims are reasonably well protected, although some states are pushing the envelope to limit reproductive freedom in ways that are likely to backfire.

If religious entities continue to push for increasing restrictions on abortion rights at the state and federal levels, I fear that the current compromise will erode and it will actually be religious freedom that loses in the long run. Short-term victories in some states will build greater national resistance against religious freedom, as has already occurred since *Hobby Lobby* was decided; in the long run, protection for conscience may erode. It would be a classic case of winning the battle but losing the war.

Society is changing, and an inability to compromise – especially on the most morally and religiously charged issues – while damaging to both sides may be most damaging to religion. People who oppose abortion based on religion could easily characterize my position as a vast over-simplification. Indeed from certain religious perspectives, it may be, because I am prescribing exactly what it sounds like I am prescribing, namely, compromising on issues that make up the very fabric of theology and morality. I ask no less of the other side, however, by requesting that conscience claims be protected even when entire hospitals assert those claims. This will be addressed further in Chapter 6.

Compromise on issues that affect fundamental aspects of being is a horrific choice for some on either side, but losing all legal protection for even broader aspects of being is potentially worse, because if a side loses the culture wars or issues *in toto*, even the ability to persuade others will be significantly reduced. I understand that for some any compromise may not be possible because doing so would be to make oneself complicit in evil on the one side or complicit in discrimination on the other side; but given the stakes, winning the battle but losing the war on either side because of an inability to compromise would be to make oneself complicit in greater harm.

Ironically, I respect those on both sides who may think my position is naïve or simplistic. Perhaps these people give my position too much of a kind spin, because I understand full well the struggle it would take for people and entities with these concerns to compromise. It is a pragmatic approach, but in this context pragmatism could end up helping freedoms on both sides. After all, as a practical matter what is at stake in compromising is balancing legal protections on both sides in a practical way. There will still be winners, losers, and controversy, but within a more balanced system. What is at stake in the culture wars is far more: It is the legal protections *and* the social capital to persuade others and have your voice considered relevant. If you lose the culture wars, you lose not only the battle for legislation in the long run but also the ability and credibility to change behaviors through persuasion and example.

The following sections address some of the legal principles relevant to reproductive freedom. Addressed first are questions raised about reproductive freedom in the *Hobby Lobby* case. Next, three laws designed to protect conscience claims at the federal level – the

Church Amendments, the Weldon Amendment, and Section 245 of the Public Health Service Act – are addressed. Finally, state laws limiting access to abortions on bases other than conscience are discussed.

A Reproductive Freedom and the *Hobby Lobby* Case

Hobby Lobby has often been characterized as a case about religious freedom. I, too, have characterized it that way.[11] Yet, at its core, it is a case about reproductive freedom as well. In fact, the very issue in that case reflects the core theme of this book: namely, balancing religious freedom and sexual freedom. The problems with the *Hobby Lobby* resolution of that balance – which barely considered the sexual freedom side of the equation – were addressed in Chapter 2. Here, I specifically address the reproductive rights issues involved in the *Hobby Lobby* case.

Hobby Lobby, Conestoga Woods, and Mardel, three for-profit companies, challenged the federal government's requirement that they provide insurance coverage for certain IUDs and for emergency contraception under the Affordable Care Act. The companies argued that providing these contraceptives violated their religious freedom because it would require them to facilitate what they believed to be a sin. They argued, therefore, that requiring them to provide these benefits violated RFRA. In a highly controversial decision, the U.S. Supreme Court sided with the companies.

This case, like few others, exposes the tension between religious freedom claims and reproductive freedom, because providing the religious accommodation sought by the companies' owners denied federally protected benefits to female employees. The Supreme Court suggested that the government could provide the benefits or could find some other way to accommodate female employees' access to these forms of contraception, but the practical result is that one side's religious accommodation negatively impacted the other side's access to reproductive choices. It also required the female employees to expose their choices to their employers' scrutiny to defend the right to coverage. It is not an easy choice for female employees to risk the possible negative impact on their jobs and/or other forms of discrimination they might face after coming forward to assert their right to or need for contraceptive coverage.

Significantly, it is possible that in another case a company may want to deny all contraceptive coverage based on a religious objection (that is exactly what happened in Amy's situation in Chapter 1). This would certainly impose significant costs on female employees seeking to exercise reproductive freedom. It also could have serious medical impact going well beyond contraception issues since many women are prescribed birth control pills for reasons other than contraception, and many of these pills are not inexpensive over the course of the year.

The Supreme Court asserted in *Hobby Lobby* that no burden would be imposed in that case, but this assumes that the government would either pay to subsidize the companies' religious accommodation or amend the law and/or the regulations to provide for-profit entities with the same religious accommodations provided to religious non-profits: accommodations that are being challenged by those non-profits. Currently, HHS is providing such an accommodation as a result of *Hobby Lobby*, but a change in administration or a win by the non-profits currently challenging the accommodation could easily affect the current situation.[12] Chapter 5 addresses the many practical differences between religious entities and for-profit companies. These differences suggest a different result from the one reached in the *Hobby Lobby* case. Yet, for now at least, the *Hobby Lobby* case is the law, and Chapters 5 and 6 also address what this means for reproductive rights.

In Chapter 6, I argue that religious accommodations make sense when a traditional religious entity, such as a church or a religious non-profit, is involved. Someone working for the Catholic Church, for example, should not be surprised to learn that contraception is not covered under the church's insurance. Yet, Hobby Lobby was a company with thousands of employees and millions of customers, many of whom do not share the owners' religious values. In this context, religious accommodation is more problematic.

B Legal Protection of Conscience Claims and Reproductive Freedom

Unlike the LGBT rights area, where laws protecting conscience claims specifically (as opposed to religious freedom generally) are uncommon, a number of laws protect conscience claims surrounding reproductive freedom by religious doctors, hospitals, and pharmacists. At the federal level, three such laws are the Church Amendments, the Weldon Amendment, and Section 245 of the Public Health Service Act. Each of these three laws operates to protect conscience claims by medical professionals and/or facilities against government-imposed requirements. Interestingly, some provisions in the Church Amendments can be easily interpreted to protect conscience claims by both doctors who are opposed to performing and those who perform abortions. Chapter 6 is devoted to conscience claims, but this section lays out some specific legal provisions that operate in the context of reproductive freedom.

The Church Amendments, named for Senator Frank Church, can be found in Title 42 of the United States Code at section 300a-7. The Church Amendments mandate that no federal government official or agency can require any individual to violate his or her religious or moral convictions by performing or assisting in an abortion or sterilization procedure. The same prohibition applies to any entity, such as a hospital, which has a religious or moral conviction that does not allow it to make its facilities available to perform abortions or sterilization procedures. These protections apply even to individuals and entities that receive federal grants, contracts, or loans. The Church Amendments also include protections against discrimination based on an individual's or entity's religious or moral convictions about performing abortions or sterilization procedures. Interestingly, these antidiscrimination provisions might be interpreted to protect doctors who refuse to as well as those who do perform these procedures based on religious or moral commitments. Most states have passed similar laws over the years.

The Weldon Amendment states in pertinent part that

> None of the funds made available in this Act [the act referred to is a broad federal funding law that includes funding for the Department of Health and Human Services] may be made available to a Federal agency or program, or to a State or local government, if such agency, program, or government subjects any institutional or individual health care entity to discrimination on the basis that the health care entity does not provide, pay for, provide coverage of, or refer for abortions.[13]

To the extent that the Weldon Amendment prevents vast amounts of federal funding from going to federal agencies or states that "discriminate" against entities that do not provide abortions, it is reminiscent of the Church Amendments; although it applies to state and local entities and federal programs rather than just federal officials and agencies.

The bigger issue raised by the Weldon Amendment is that it denies funding to government entities that "discriminate" against healthcare entities that do not provide coverage for "or refer for abortions." The first element of this could conflict with a number of state laws that require contraceptive coverage. This is not likely to be a major issue, however, if the healthcare entity is affiliated with a religious entity because most of these state laws have exceptions for religious entities.

The second element is far more troubling and could have an especially vicious impact on reproductive freedom. Some states and localities require that healthcare providers provide informed consent – a legal term that essentially means clear notice – that they do not perform abortions, and others require that they provide adequate information to allow patients to find alternative providers. Finding alternative providers can be quite hard in some areas of the country. If a state or local government enforced these laws against a healthcare entity that refused to meet these requirements, the Weldon Amendment might be violated, and significant amounts of federal funding could be denied. This could lead to non-enforcement of these laws or to the defeat of proposed laws, thus leaving women without adequate information in areas dominated by hospitals affiliated with some religions, such as the Catholic Church, or areas where few healthcare providers are willing to provide these services even when a patient's health is at risk.

Section 245 of the Public Health Services Act requires that any government entity (federal, state, or local) that receives federal funding not discriminate against a healthcare entity that "refuses to undergo training in the performance of induced abortions, to require or provide such training, to perform such abortions, or to provide referrals for such training or such abortions." This is quite broad and raises many of the same problems as the Weldon Amendment, especially the referral provision. In fact, the main difference between the two laws is that Section 245 applies not only to the refusal to perform abortions but also to the provision of training about abortions. Moreover, it applies to all federal funding rather than just the – still significant – funding at issue under the Weldon Amendment. In addition to these three federal laws, a vast array of state laws protect conscience claims by doctors, hospitals, and other healthcare providers.

C Attempts by States to Limit Access to Reproductive Freedom

Since *Roe v. Wade*, many state laws limiting access to abortion have been proposed or passed. These laws differ from those designed to protect conscience claims because rather than focusing on protecting conscience, the vast majority of these laws focus on limiting access to abortions, and sometimes even certain kinds of contraception. Addressing the vast array of these laws would require an entire book, or perhaps even a multivolume set; however, while taking a basic look at these laws, some common themes emerge, which can be addressed more succinctly than can the many laws that try to encompass them.

First, there are laws that require information to be provided to patients about abortions. Most of the time, this information includes alternatives to abortion, including adoption. The information required under these laws ranges from just listing and providing basic alternatives to abortion to requiring graphic material on what happens to the fetus during an abortion procedure. The former have been upheld as constitutional,[14] while the latter have been found unconstitutional.[15]

Second are "permission" laws. These laws often require that minors seeking abortions have permission from a parent, or when gaining such permission is not possible or could pose a risk to the young woman, from a judge. These laws put young women, especially those from religious and/or conservative households, in an exceptionally difficult position because their parent may not grant permission, and in some situations the young woman may be the victim of abuse at home or fear abuse if she seeks permission. The alternative of going before a judge is terrifying for a teenage girl who is already scared and possibly embarrassed. Yet, these laws have been upheld so long as they do not require the consent of both parents, which could pose a number of problems.[16] Even more controversial are partner permission laws, which require that women get the consent of the fetus's father before having an abortion. These laws have been found unconstitutional.[17]

Third are waiting period laws. These laws require that women have a waiting period between their initial visit to an abortion provider and the actual procedure. These have been upheld when the waiting period is not unreasonable.[18] All three of these types of laws have been combined in some states.

Fourth, and perhaps impinging on reproductive freedom more than the other three, are attempts by states to regulate facilities that provide abortions. These regulations are often cast as an attempt to protect women's health by carefully monitoring the facilities, but as a practical matter these laws result in closing numerous facilities and requiring women to go to hospitals, many of which will not allow an abortion to be performed. This means that women have to travel great distances to receive an abortion, even when not having one could put the woman's health at risk. This may make getting an abortion impossible for poorer women. Of course, this is exactly what these laws are designed to do. The Supreme Court has agreed to hear a case from Texas challenging one of these laws, and a decision should be forthcoming in 2016.[19]

Finally, there are laws aimed at preventing late-term abortions. These abortions are rare and usually performed to protect the health of the mother. The CDC has estimated that no more than 1.4 percent of abortions are late term (occurring after twenty-one weeks or more of gestation), and that the vast majority of these are performed to protect the health of the mother.[20] The Supreme Court has upheld a ban on one of these procedures, and states have more recently begun to pass laws often referred to as "fetal pain bans," which prohibit abortions after the time at which the state – often in contradiction to medical evidence – determines that a fetus can feel pain.[21]

Given the core importance of reproductive freedom to women's health and self-determination, any limitation on this freedom should be necessary to protect some other fundamental value. The Supreme

Court has held that in the abortion context, the state takes on such an interest in the fetus after viability. Prior to viability, the state's interest would not allow it to prevent an abortion.[22]

In contrast, at this point religious conscience claims are more about protecting religious conscience than limiting access to reproductive freedom more generally. Those asserting a conscience claim are asking the government not to interfere with their core religious conscience. Yet, when religious entities go beyond this and seek to use government to interfere with reproductive freedom, even though these attempts are also based in religious conscience, they exceed the zone of conscience claims protected by religious freedom and enter the distinct but also protected realm of interest advocacy.

Under these circumstances, the rights of women to determine their own medical care, control their own bodies, and determine their own futures are directly under attack. Of course, certain kinds of conscience claims, when aggregated, can have practical effects not too different from laws directly attacking reproductive freedom. As I argue in Chapter 6, this would pose a special problem, and the answer could lead to the denial of specific sorts of conscience claims: for example, in the context of "zombie hospitals," where the conscience claim is not made by a religious entity directly, but rather a secular entity that has bought a formerly religious hospital.

4 COUNTY CLERKS AND OTHER GOVERNMENT EMPLOYEES

I INTRODUCTION

The story of Rowan County, Kentucky, clerk Kim Davis made headlines across the country in 2015. Almost everyone is familiar with Davis's refusal to provide marriage licenses after the U.S. Supreme Court held that same-sex marriage is a fundamental right that cannot be denied to same-sex couples.[1] Ironically, however, her case may have done more to obfuscate the issue of religious accommodations for government officials than to enlighten people about the issue.

This is in part because of the grandstanding that occurred in her case. Davis and her attorneys turned her into a cause célèbre, in the process making claims that turned out to be false,[2] some of which did not relate directly to her legal arguments.[3] Meanwhile, around the country other government employees in other locations have sought accommodation without becoming causes célèbres. These cases raise many questions that this chapter addresses.

Must religious freedom claims by government officials be accommodated when the requested accommodation involves not performing duties for which the official was elected or hired? If such accommodations are not mandatory, should they be given, and if so, under what circumstances? Does the availability of other officials who can perform the duties make a difference? What about the argument that when a government official requests that someone else perform her duties, the dignity of those requesting government services may be harmed (this is often referred to as "dignitary harm")? Does media attention figure into the question of dignitary harm?

As will be seen, the biggest problem with Kim Davis's claim was not her personal refusal to issue marriage licenses, but rather her initial refusal to allow anyone in her office to do so. There is a fundamental difference between a government official seeking accommodation and an official seeking to keep others, even those whom she supervises, from following the law. Additionally, the media firestorm her situation generated, and which she helped foster, raises additional questions that may not be present when a county clerk simply asks that others in her office issue same-sex marriage licenses.

II ISSUES WITH ACCOMMODATING GOVERNMENT OFFICIALS

Should we accommodate government officials and employees who seek religious exemptions in cases involving sexual freedom? The answer is a qualified "yes." Of course, the details matter. A balance can be reached that will maximize protection for sexual freedom while allowing religious accommodation of government employees in some situations. In states that have Religious Freedom Restoration Acts (RFRAs) or other laws that protect the religious freedom of government officials, the boundaries drawn would determine when accommodation is mandatory. In all other states, the boundaries drawn would determine when permissive accommodations are allowed if the relevant government entity seeks to accommodate.[4]

I argue that accommodations should be given except when doing so will impose a direct and meaningful harm on others. Of course, the question of what accommodations will result in direct and meaningful harm when those seeking accommodation are government officials raises a number of unique problems. From a legal perspective, there is no duty to accommodate unless a RFRA or other law requires doing so. Thus, my argument is not that government entities must accommodate in the absence of a legal requirement to do so, but rather that they should accommodate regardless of whether or not there is a legal mandate to do so, but only when doing so will not result in direct and meaningful harm to others. On the flip side, even in states with RFRAs or other relevant laws that apply to government officials or employees, accommodation may not be required unless certain parameters are met. These parameters are discussed in detail in Section IV. First, however, some of the specific issues raised in the context of accommodating government officials and employees must be addressed.

A number of factors make situations involving government officials especially complex. Government officials are elected or hired to serve the public generally so when they seek an exemption to refuse service to a specific group within the public, especially in relation to a right recognized by the Supreme Court, alarm bells should sound. For example, if a government official refused to grant marriage licenses to interracial couples based on a religious argument, no court would allow such an injustice to stand. Why should the situation be any different when a government official asserts a religious objection to issuing marriage licenses to same-sex couples?

First, an analogy can be made on the subject of basic rights. The Supreme Court in *Obergefell* did rely – and I would assert correctly so – in part on *Loving v. Virginia*[5] (the 1967 case holding that laws prohibiting interracial marriage are unconstitutional) to support its holding that denying the right to same-sex marriage violates the Due Process and Equal Protection Clauses of the Fourteenth Amendment. Yet, this does not address the question of religious accommodations. The nature and history of religious objections to interracial marriages and the nature and history of religious objections to same-sex marriages are quite different.[6] Second, religious objections to interracial marriage were directly connected to a broader system of racism, whereas religious objections to same-sex marriage are often limited to the issue of marriage itself.[7] In fact, this is reflected directly in the opinions finding a constitutional right to interracial marriage and to same-sex marriage. In *Loving v. Virginia*, when the Supreme Court held that anti-miscegenation laws (laws that prohibited interracial marriage) are unconstitutional, the Court wrote:

> The fact that Virginia prohibits only interracial marriages involving white persons demonstrates that the racial classifications must stand on their own justification, as measures designed to maintain white supremacy.[8]

Yet in *Obergefell v. Hodges*,[9] the case in which the Supreme Court held there is a constitutional right to same-sex marriage, it specifically noted the following:

> Finally, it must be emphasized that religions, and those who adhere to religious doctrines, may continue to advocate with utmost, sincere conviction that, by divine precepts, same-sex marriage should not be condoned. The First Amendment ensures that religious organizations and persons are given proper protection as they seek to teach the principles that are so fulfilling and so central to their lives and faiths, and to their deep aspirations to continue the family structure they have long revered.[10]

Some people certainly object to same-sex marriage based on bigotry, and not truly on religious principle. If any of these people were government officials and asserted a religious objection to issuing same-sex marriage licenses based on the argument that members of the LGBT community are inferior or should not interact with the hetero-sexual community on an equal basis, the exemption should be denied.[11] The level of harm caused by granting an exemption in these circumstances would far outweigh the government official's religious freedom interest. It is not because the request for an exemption is religiously based.

This is not the only concern with granting exemptions to government officials and employees. Two other factors are highly relevant. The first concern is the very fact that the person seeking the exemption is a government official. Government officials are elected or hired to serve the public generally. Allowing them to pick and choose whom they will serve could set a dangerous precedent. Should a devout Christian government official's refusal to serve Jewish, Muslim, Buddhist, and atheist citizens be accommodated if she believes that she can only interact with Christians? What about an extremely devout Wahhabi Muslim man who objects to interacting with female citizens?

The answer is "no," because the accommodation would prevent the official from doing his or her job for a large percentage of the public: So although the government could give a permissive accommodation, there are good reasons why it should not. How can we determine the line of demarcation between these situations and that of a clerk who seeks an accommodation to not issue same-sex marriage licenses? The key is in the parameters discussed in Section IV of this chapter. Unless the person's main duty is issuing marriage licenses, he or she can fulfill other duties; so long as someone else can issue the licenses without any inconvenience to any citizen. The former situation is more akin to someone who refuses to serve any LGBT citizens for any purpose. The government has the strongest interest in not accommodating such a person.

Next, accommodating government officials for religious reasons might raise Establishment Clause concerns that are not raised in other accommodation contexts.[12] For example, wouldn't accommodating a government official who refuses to issue marriage licenses to same-sex couples or who refuses to perform a same-sex civil ceremony be a violation of the Establishment Clause? The short answer is "no," but with one major exception discussed later. In *Employment Division v. Smith*,[13] the Supreme Court specifically held that permissive accommodations are allowed. In *Cutter v. Wilkinson*,[14] the Supreme Court specifically addressed this issue and held that application of the Religious Land Use and Institutionalized Persons Act (RLUIPA), a statute that applies the same (or perhaps an even more stringent level of protection) than RFRA, does not violate the Establishment Clause.

The major exception is when government endorses or advances religion through the accommodation given to an official. This can happen when states pass laws that are designed to promote religion, rather than simply accommodate it. For example, if a state designed a law to favor specific religious values or passed a law that favors those values in a manner that could harm the rights of others, there is a significant likelihood of an Establishment Clause violation. This could happen if a law were passed that mandated accommodation for government employees but did nothing to protect the rights of same-sex couples in areas where no government employee is available to issue a marriage license or perform a civil ceremony. This could also happen if a state ended all civil ceremonies and made no allowance for other nonreligious means to validate a marriage, therefore only allowing marriages to be validated through a religious entity.[15]

Two states have already provided legal models for accommodating religious government employees without harming the rights of same-sex couples. Both Utah and North Carolina have passed laws that require someone be available to grant marriage licenses and perform civil ceremonies for same-sex couples, while also allowing for religious accommodations for government employees.[16] These laws are not perfect, but they do protect the right of same-sex couples to get marriage licenses and civil ceremonies without delay or a reduction in available services while also protecting religious freedom claims by employees who object to issuing marriage licenses to same-sex couples or performing same-sex ceremonies. Neither law addresses parameter five set forth in Section IV, but they do balance rights in a manner that should not violate the Establishment Clause.

III DIRECT AND MEANINGFUL HARM

I raised the concept of direct and meaningful harm on third parties in Chapter 1, but I did not define the term there. This section addresses that term, since it is central to the framing of the parameters discussed later and to the ideas discussed in each of the remaining chapters in this book. What constitutes a direct and meaningful harm in a given situation can be quite fact sensitive, but this section provides you with a working definition and understanding that will help you apply the concept to various situations.

For a harm to be direct, it must impose a burden on others that arises as a direct result of the accommodation, such as interference with rights, imposition of a financial burden, denial of a benefit available under the law, or similar sorts of situations. For a harm to be meaningful, it must be more than minor emotional discomfort, such as offense taken when someone is aware that a given individual or individuals disapprove of his or her relationship. This does not mean that more direct dignitary harms, such as when someone expresses a discriminatory motive, are not meaningful. We do, however, live in a diverse society where many views are protected, and we must be willing to deal with ideologies with which we disagree. Whether such a situation is meaningful is fact sensitive and depends on how the negative perceptions of a given classification are expressed.

This chapter provides one of the best examples of the difference between a direct and an indirect harm. When a government official, such as a county clerk, refuses to issue a marriage license and no one else in the office is able to do so, the harm resulting from accommodating the official would be direct. The result would be that the person applying for the license would not be able to receive it or would incur delay in receiving it. If, however, someone else in the office could issue the license, there would be no direct harm from accommodating the request for a religious exemption because the person applying for the license would receive it at the same time as he or she would have, had the accommodation not been granted. In this situation, if the person applying for the license had to wait an extra minute or two for the official who can issue the license to finish a phone call or serve another person, the "harm" would not be meaningful as discussed below. If, however, the wait for the other official was significant, the delay could be both direct and meaningful. How much time is reasonable? That would be a question of fact, but the key difference would be whether the delay was the sort that might happen in any government office while waiting for an official versus a longer delay.

Hobby Lobby provides another great example of a direct harm. The accommodation in that case denied female employees coverage that they were otherwise entitled to under the Affordable Care Act. This is a direct harm. The Supreme Court claimed that there was no harm at all as a result of the accommodation in that case, because alternatives would prevent any harm. Even if that were true one could easily envision a situation like Amy's in Chapter 1, where there is unquestionable harm. Amy's harm is direct because it results from accommodating her employer's religious objection to providing contraceptive coverage otherwise required by law. Without the accommodation, the coverage would be available.

The term "meaningful" is important because of concerns about dignitary harms. Some have asserted that dignitary harm results any-time a religious accommodation is given in the context of same-sex marriage or some other sexual freedom contexts. At one level, this is almost certainly correct. If, for example, a government official is accommodated so as not to have to issue same-sex marriage licenses because someone else in the office can do so, some people applying for those licenses will no doubt be offended. Others might simply view it as part of living in a diverse society and not feel offended.

The term "meaningful" requires more than this sort of dignitary harm. It involves a pragmatic balance. On the one side, we have accommodation of religious freedom in a diverse and ever-changing society. On the other side, we have a potential sense of offense when learning that another person has been accommodated because of a religious objection, but unless there are extenuating circumstances such as a direct confrontation by the government official, the balance falls on the side of religious freedom for all the reasons discussed in Chapters 1 and 2.

Of course, in some cases there is more. For example, Kim Davis did not just suggest that the couples who came to her office wait while she got someone else to issue the license. She informed the couples of her belief that it was a sin to issue the licenses, while denying them a license altogether.[17] This is meaningful and is the basis for parameter five. Such direct confrontation goes beyond someone just being aware that another person is being accommodated and feeling offended. It is meaningful for purposes of this analysis because it goes beyond being aware of someone's need for a religious accommodation in a diverse society.

The distinction between dignitary harms that result from living in a society with religious accommodations and dignitary harms that result from being denied access to a right or benefit one is entitled to and knowing why is quite different. Another example demonstrates this. Assume a same-sex couple goes into a shop to buy a cake for their anniversary. The person behind the counter seems to disapprove of them but says nothing and asks someone else to help them. The other person helps them and they get the cake. This would certainly be offensive if they sensed the first worker's reason for not helping them, which could happen if he asked for the other person to help after learning that they wanted an anniversary cake. It would be a dignitary harm arising directly from his religious objection. Yet, for purposes of the direct and meaningful approach, it would not be the sort of meaningful harm that would prevent the worker from being accommodated (this assumes that there is a right to accommodation when dealing with for-profit shops, which as Chapter 5 demonstrates, there may not be).

Now envision the same situation, but rather than saying nothing and getting someone else, the first worker says, "we do not make wedding or anniversary cakes for gays," and the couple cannot get the cake from that shop. This is more than just awareness that someone has a religious objection to same-sex marriage. This is an explicit denial of service based on the fact that the couple exercised their right to get married. This also causes dignitary harm, but in this case that harm is meaningful. It goes beyond the couple just being aware that someone disapproves of their marriage. Even without the statement by the worker, this situation would present a direct and meaningful harm. It is essential to note that the direct and meaningful analysis I urge in this book would not apply to religious entities that primarily serve their own flocks, such as churches, synagogues, mosques, and so on. Rather, this analysis applies to individuals and entities that serve the public more generally, yet still seek religious accommodations. The reasons for this distinction are explained throughout the book, but arise heavily from the Ecclesiastical Abstention and Church Autonomy doctrines discussed in Chapter 2, as well as other religious freedom concerns.

You are, of course, free to disagree with the direct and meaningful harm approach I use. The discussion throughout this book focuses on trying to balance freedoms when they conflict and to point out where they do not conflict. I find the direct and meaningful harm concept helpful, but even if you do not, the rest of the discussion in this book should be relevant to determining what the stakes are on both sides and how one might be able to resolve or prevent conflict between freedoms on each side.

Finally, for those of you with a constitutional law background, it is worth noting that I am not a fan of using any sort of direct/indirect analysis in constitutional law. It was highly problematic in the Commerce Clause context and also when used under the Free Exercise Clause in *Braunfeld v. Brown* (the Sunday closing case). My use of the idea here is not intended to be formalistic in any way. What counts as a direct harm under the approach I suggest is based on the facts on the ground and not a formalistic distinction. Moreover, it is connected to meaningful harm that is hardly a formalistic concept.

IV THE PARAMETERS NECESSARY FOR ACCOMMODATING GOVERNMENT OFFICIALS WITHOUT DIRECTLY AND MATERIALLY HARMING THE RIGHTS OF OTHERS

In this section, I set forth, and then explain, the basic parameters necessary to accommodate government officials and employees without imposing direct and meaningful harm on others. The parameters are designed to minimize harm to same-sex couples while protecting religious freedom. They are designed to work both in the RFRA and permissive accommodation contexts.

Here are the five parameters:

First, government officials and employees should be accommodated in cases where a government official seeks a religious accommodation and others are able to fulfill the duties of that official without causing any delay or reduction in service to individuals or couples, unless the fifth parameter is violated.

Second, there should be no accommodation where the only government official able to carry out a function or all officials able to carry out the function seek an accommodation to avoid doing so. Moreover, under these circumstances, there should be no accommodation even under a RFRA.

Third, accommodation should be given where a government official seeks an accommodation beyond excusal from performing a specific duty, such as having his or her name removed from marriage license forms, so long as the accommodation would not invalidate or call into question the right or benefit conferred on any individual or couple, and so long as the fifth parameter is not violated.

Fourth, there should be no accommodation where the accommodation sought is an exemption from performing, on an equal basis, the primary duty that the official was elected or hired to perform.

Fifth, accommodation should be denied or revoked when a government official acting in his or her official capacity calls attention to the refusal to perform a duty, either through contacting the media or through direct confrontation with the individual or couple he or she refuses to serve.

The first parameter makes sense as a balance between religious freedom and same-sex marriage rights. So long as there is no denial, delay, or reduction in service, the fact that a specific official or employee does not issue a license or perform a civil marriage ceremony would not violate or infringe on the rights of any citizen. The key is that there be someone else who is ready, willing, and legally able to issue the license or solemnize the marriage. This is precisely what the Utah and North Carolina laws require. These laws are reasonably clear that no denial or reduction in service is allowed, but the Utah law could be improved by spelling out more clearly that no *delay* in services should be allowed either. Also, Utah law provides very strong religious freedom protection generally, and that may have helped facilitate the compromise which also protected sexual freedom. Yet, even in states that provide less religious freedom overall compromise is a good idea because it allows both sides to be protected.

This parameter is the one that most clearly works against Kim Davis. Having others perform the duty in question is an obvious accommodation, yet one she did not seek. From the start, she had at least one clerk willing to issue licenses, and subsequently all but one, yet she initially refused to allow it. Her reason for refusing this obvious accommodation was concern about facilitating sin by having her name on the licenses, but while facilitating something that violates one's deepest religious convictions is serious, parameter three clearly addresses this concern. Having her name removed from the forms could accommodate her, but that too was not adequate for her.[18] If accommodation is available, but the person seeking accommodation refuses to accept available accommodations and insists on accommodations that would directly and materially have a negative impact on third parties, that individual cannot be accommodated.

The second parameter is a natural corollary to the first. If no one else can issue a marriage license or perform a civil ceremony without delay, there should be no accommodation. This could occur because only one person is authorized to issue the license or perform the ceremony, as in the case of a small county office, or it could occur because everyone authorized to do so seeks an exemption. The North Carolina and Utah laws require that someone be available to issue the license or perform the ceremony so that this problem is avoided. The Utah law expands the range of officials who can perform these duties to help facilitate this,[19] and the North Carolina law sets up a system that could provide immediate backup in situations where exemptions are given.[20]

One accommodation that should never be available is outright denial or limited access to marriage licenses (and by analogy civil ceremonies). This is a logical corollary to the Supreme Court's decision in *Obergefell v. Hodges* upholding same-sex marriage, and a point specifically spelled out in Judge Bunning's opinion in the Kim Davis case. Allowing such an accommodation would violate the fundamental rights of couples denied the licenses. The fact that the couples might go to other counties does not solve this problem. Since there is a fundamental right to marriage, and that right cannot be denied to same-sex couples, it follows that limiting the times and places that right can be effectuated to preclude same-sex couples from receiving marriage licenses in a given location violates this fundamental right, in addition to denying the couple equal protection of the law.

Marriage laws are generally applicable (they apply the same to everyone), so there is no right to a religious exemption under the Free Exercise Clause of the First Amendment to the U.S. Constitution.[21] Therefore, any countervailing free exercise right would arise under a statute such as RFRA, under a state constitution, or as a matter of permissible accommodation. The Supremacy Clause of the Constitution answers any doubts as to which law prevails when a federal constitutional right, such as the right to marry, is violated by federal statute, state constitution, or state law. The right under the U.S. Constitution prevails.[22]

The third parameter is quite interesting. It raises the question of "facilitating evil," which is a major focus of conscience claims and is discussed in more detail in Chapter 6. What happens when a county clerk or other government official does not want his or her name on marriage licenses issued to same sex-couples? The Kim Davis case raised this issue; however, two things kept the issue from being the primary focus.

First, the then state attorney general and the then governor announced that licenses altered by Davis to remove her name are valid under state law.[23] This seems consistent with the state law governing marriage licenses at that time,[24] but one could read the state law as requiring licenses to have the clerk's name on them.[25] The governor's and the attorney general's reading seems to be both the better legal interpretation and the best practical approach.

Second, Davis initially refused to allow other clerks in her office to issue the licenses, which made whether her name appeared on the licenses secondary to the question of issuing the licenses. These questions were certainly intertwined. The fact that Davis's name would be on the licenses was one of the reasons why she refused to allow others in her office to issue the licenses in the first place. She also initially believed that if her name were removed from the licenses, they would be invalid, although she later changed this position. Davis was initially wrong on the latter point, but the reason for parameter three is to ensure that when a clerk is willing to allow others in her office to follow the law, concerns about having her name on a document that violates her fundamental religious tenets can be accommodated.

The best way to approach this would be to include just the name of the county or a state office on marriage licenses. This is, of course, a question of state law. It may be impossible to accommodate a clerk who wants her name removed if a state requires the name of the clerk to be on the license for it to be valid. If a state does not require the clerk's name on marriage licenses, even when the practice is to include the name, an objecting clerk should be accommodated in taking his or her name off marriage licenses, so long as it is done on all licenses and not just those for same-sex couples.

The reason for allowing this accommodation, where doing so does not directly and materially harm others, is to protect the religious freedom of someone who cannot do something that violates a core tenet of his or her religion. It is important to accommodate these sorts of concerns so long as they can be accommodated without materially harming others, lest we impose our values on people with different beliefs and traditions. Of course, the removal of the name must be applied equally to all marriage licenses and could only be done if licenses issued without the name would remain valid.

The fourth parameter is a matter of common sense. If the main duty of an official is to issue marriage licenses or perform civil ceremonies, and the official cannot do so equally based on religious objections, there could be no accommodation because the official can not evenhandedly fulfill his or her primary job function. One option in this context, at least where the official is not an elected one, would be to relocate the employee. This would be at the discretion of the agency and would need to be done without negatively impacting others: for example, where someone else in the office wants to perform the objecting employee's job and the objecting employee can be transferred without harming other employees. In the case of officials elected to perform that specific duty, however, performing the duty equally for all citizens or stepping down are the only options allowed short of violating the Constitution. As a practical matter, this may rarely come up because county clerks and civil magistrates often perform many functions, only one of which is issuing marriage licenses or performing civil marriage ceremonies. In these cases, parameters one and two would govern.

The fifth parameter is both important and problematic. It is important because of the severity of the dignitary harm that can be fostered in situations where a government official seeks out media attention for the denial of service to citizens, or where the official directly confronts the citizens in a disrespectful manner. The mere existence of potential dignitary harm is not enough to deny exemptions. Yet, in some situations the dignitary harm is severe and exacerbated by the behavior of the government official(s) who seek religious exemptions. In these cases, as opposed to where a government official simply has someone else perform the duty or tells the citizens that he or she cannot perform the duty but will immediately get someone who can, the dignitary harm caused to the citizens would be direct and material.

This parameter is problematic because we are dealing with issues that could impact freedom of speech. Here, however, the fact that we are dealing with government officials and employees helps answer the question. The Supreme Court has long drawn a distinction between government officials and employees speaking as private citizens on matters of public importance, as opposed to those speaking in their capacity as government officials or employees. When speaking in their capacity as government officials or employees, these individuals' speech can be limited. When government officials or employees speak as private citizens on matters of public concern, however, their freedom of speech is more carefully protected.

Here the very issue arises from performance of government duties, so any speech involved would be in the actors' capacity as government officials or employees. Therefore, if the government official or employee contacts the media to announce that he or she will not serve same-sex couples or confronts the same-sex couples in a disrespectful way, the individual is speaking in his or her capacity as a government official or employee. Therefore, such speech can be limited. In this case, the limitation would result in the denial of an accommodation because of the harm inflicted on those seeking a marriage license or civil ceremony. Simply saying "I cannot help you with that but I will get someone who can" is not the sort of speech that would raise these concerns.

What about the Kim Davis situation? Kim Davis did not make the initial contact with the media, so as an immediate matter the problem was that she violated parameters one and two. As the situation progressed, however, she and her lawyers called additional attention to the matter. This creates a sort of chicken and the egg problem. Had the media not already been paying attention to her case, perhaps it would violate parameter five; but since the media was already focused on the case, it is a tougher call. Davis's direct contact with the couples she refused to serve, however, would violate parameter five. She did more than say something like, "sorry, I can't serve you; I will get someone who can." She refused to allow anyone to serve these couples, and she made sure that the couples knew why in no uncertain terms.[26]

This is significant because when Davis refused to issue marriage licenses on the basis of her religious objection to same-sex marriage, she made clear that it was because she thought same-sex marriage was a sin, and she said so in her capacity as a government official. The fact that she denied licenses to all couples, whether same sex or not, does not change the analysis because her reasons for doing so were openly and directly based on her objection to same-sex marriage. Moreover, she confronted same-sex couples; even though she did not act viciously or in an openly mean-spirited manner toward same-sex couples, she denied them the license because she viewed their exercise of their constitutional rights as a sin and openly said so. Therefore, she violated parameter five. The sort of dignitary harm caused by such a direct refusal and denunciation by a government official is different from a situation where a government official simply asks someone else in the office to perform a duty.

It may be that in the latter situation, the couple knows, or can easily figure out the reason for the change in service. As a result, they may feel some sense of dignitary harm, or they may simply respect the rights of the clerk and view the situation as part of living in a pluralistic society. Such an indirect dignitary harm should not be a basis to deny a religious accommodation in a diverse society. When the government official directly confronts citizens in the manner Kim Davis did, the situation reaches a different level and would violate parameter five. In addition, it may also violate the Establishment Clause.

Religious freedom and same-sex marriage need not conflict, even in contested contexts such as requests for accommodation by government officials. Religious accommodations can and should be given in instances where doing so would not delay service or lower the level of service provided to same-sex couples. In some contexts, such as where only one official can perform a specific function, this may mean that the official cannot be accommodated, because the accommodation would infringe on the fundamental rights of same-sex couples.

The Kim Davis case is a bad example because she made herself almost impossible to accommodate without violating the rights of others. Yet, for every Kim Davis there are numerous government officials who would welcome accommodations such as allowing others in the office to perform the duties to which they object or having their name removed from forms so long as the forms remain valid under state law. Davis rejected both of these accommodations at one point or another. The recent laws in Utah and North Carolina protecting the rights of same-sex couples while accommodating religious exemptions requested by government employees demonstrate that it is possible to accommodate religious freedom claims without delaying or lowering the level of service provided to same-sex couples. These laws are not perfect, but they provide excellent and workable proof of concept. They show we can protect religious freedom and sexual freedom even when those freedoms appear to conflict.

5 FOR-PROFIT COMPANIES, SHOPS, AND COMMERCIAL LANDLORDS

A central source of conflict between religious freedom and sexual freedom arises in the context of for-profit entities such as shops, closely held corporations, commercial landlords, and many other venues. Prior to the U.S. Supreme Court's decision in *Hobby Lobby*, it was unclear whether these entities would be protected under the federal Religious Freedom Restoration Act (RFRA). As set forth in Chapter 2, prior to *Hobby Lobby* there were strong legal arguments that for-profit entities are not protected, or even if theoretically protected, they are not able to experience a substantial burden on religion in the same ways as an individual or a religious entity because of the many constituencies involved in operating and patronizing a for-profit entity.

We no longer live in that world. The Supreme Court's decision in *Hobby Lobby* makes it clear that today closely held for-profit businesses are protected, at least under the federal RFRA. This is not the end of the discussion, however, because some of the biggest issues that arise in the context of for-profit entities involve religious accommodations that conflict with civil rights and antidiscrimination laws. As I have noted repeatedly, even when a RFRA exists to provide protection for religious freedom, there is no guarantee that all religious freedom claims will be successful. Government may still burden religion when it has a compelling (extremely important) interest and the law that burdens the freedom of religion is narrowly tailored to meet that interest. This issue has been analyzed in several cases; in most of these cases, religious exemptions were denied because the exemption would conflict with antidiscrimination laws. In fact, this is the likely result in most cases involving for-profit entities claiming a right to discriminate under a religious freedom law.

Moreover, many states do not yet have religious freedom laws. In these states, it is possible that any future law could exclude for-profit entities – or at least public accommodations such as hotels, restaurants, and catering halls – from the definition of "person" under the law, which would prevent these entities from being protected. This is the approach I advocate because it supports the passage of state RFRAs, which are often essential to protect religious freedom, while protecting against discrimination in employment, public accommodations, and other services available to the general public.

I have also advocated throughout this book that government should give permissive accommodations for religious freedom claims when doing so will not interfere with the rights of others. Certainly when discrimination by for-profit entities is involved, the rights of third parties could be interfered with. Therefore, a government entity should not give a permissive accommodation that conflicts with an antidiscrimination law, despite the arguments in favor of giving permissive accommodations in other contexts.

Ironically, as you will see in this chapter, protection of for-profit entities under *Hobby Lobby* and some state RFRAs has led to an extreme public backlash against religious freedom, which actually endangers that freedom for even traditional religious entities. This is an excellent practical reason to amend RFRA to deny protection to for-profit entities. However, I should be clear that in advocating for the denial of religious accommodations for for-profit entities, I depart from the positions of many of my colleagues who support protecting for-profit entities because of the serious burden that denial of religious freedom claims may place on the owners of these businesses. It is not that my colleagues are wrong. In fact, they are correct that denying religious exemptions may place a significant burden on the owners of these companies. Rather, it is the impact that these exemptions may have on employees and customers, as well as the practical threats they pose to religious freedom more generally – as recent situations in Arizona, Michigan, Indiana, Georgia, and other states demonstrate – that tips the balance strongly in favor of amending RFRA to deny exemptions to for-profit entities.

This chapter begins by addressing cases where small businesses that serve the general public, such as bakeries and photographers' studios, are alleged to have violated antidiscrimination laws. As you will see, while there are a number of pending cases, in the two major cases decided recently, the small business owners lost.

Next, the chapter focuses on *Hobby Lobby* and addresses what should happen when an exemption is available to for-profit businesses under a religious freedom law, but the exemption sought violates anti-discrimination laws or otherwise violates the rights of third parties. This issue was not clearly addressed by the Court in *Hobby Lobby*. The cases involving small businesses that serve the general public are helpful in analyzing this issue as well. As part of this discussion, we explore the exceptional backlash against religious freedom generally that has been caused by protection of for-profit entities. This includes an analysis of several state RFRAs that failed as a result of this backlash, as well as state RFRAs that were enacted but caused significant backlash and fostered damaging economic consequences for the states involved. Following this, the chapter addresses questions involving commercial landlords who may be protected by the Federal Religious Land Use and Institutionalized Persons Act (RLUIPA) but are also governed by numerous state antidiscrimination laws and the federal Fair Housing Act.

I SMALL BUSINESSES THAT SERVE THE GENERAL PUBLIC

A number of cases involve bakers, florists, and caterers who refuse to provide services for same-sex couples because the owners have a profound religious objection to same-sex marriage. Even before these more recent cases, situations arose involving smaller local or regional health clubs whose owners had religious objections to alleged conduct by specific LGBT patrons. The behavior of the small businesses in these earlier cases is quite different in tone from the more recent ones because many of the small businesses in the more recent cases have no other objection to serving LGBT customers than providing wedding-related services.

Perhaps the most directly on-point case thus far is *Elane Photography, LLC v. Willock,*[1] because it involved a claim by a lesbian couple under the New Mexico Human Rights Act against a photographer who refused to photograph a same–sex commitment ceremony. The parties agreed that the ceremony was essentially a wedding, but the case occurred before the Supreme Court upheld the right to same-sex marriage nationally and the couple used the term "commitment ceremony." The New Mexico Human Rights Act protects against discrimination based on sexual orientation. New Mexico also has a RFRA, and the decision in the case by the New Mexico Supreme Court addressed the potential conflict between the two laws, albeit in a manner that may not answer some of the questions that could be raised in states that interpret their RFRAs differently. Still, as will be seen, the result in this case is in keeping with similar cases in other states, as well as with the approach suggested in this book.

The New Mexico Human Rights Act protects against discrimination in public accommodations such as hotels, restaurants, catering halls, photography studios, and shops open to the general public. Unlike a number of states, New Mexico's law protects against discrimination not only based on race, religion, sex, ethnicity, disability, and so on but also based on sexual orientation. Ironically, as I argue throughout this book, having such antidiscrimination protection based on sexual orientation is not only good for the LGBT community but also for religious freedom. It helps set a boundary on harms to third parties that may make religious freedom laws and claims more palatable to the general public and therefore less likely to be, or perceived to be, a basis for discrimination. Moreover, as the New Mexico Supreme Court (and other courts) hold, applying these laws to businesses does not violate the Free Speech Clause of the First Amendment to the U.S. Constitution, which applies to the states through the Fourteenth Amendment.

New Mexico is also an ideal of sorts because it has strong antidiscrimination protection based on sexual orientation, as well as a RFRA. This allows for general protection for religious freedom in cases like Mandy Rodriguez's and Jonathan Stein's in Chapter 1, but it prohibits such claims from being a basis for discrimination. This might make Mandy's case harder than Jonathan's, but as will be seen, Mandy would win in this context, while Elane Photography correctly lost.

Vanessa Willock contacted Elane Photography seeking a photographer for the ceremony for her and her partner, Misti Collinsworth. The owner of Elane Photography, Elane Huguenin, told the couple that she only photographed "traditional weddings." When asked for clarification, she explained that she does not "photograph same-sex weddings." Vanessa Willock then filed a discrimination claim against Elane Photography under the New Mexico Human Rights Act with the New Mexico Human Rights Commission. The commission found that Elane Photography was a public accommodation, and that the business discriminated against Willock and Collinsworth based on sexual orientation. Elane Photography appealed, and the case eventually wound its way to the New Mexico Supreme Court.

The key to the case was that Elane Photography is a public accommodation because it offers services to the general public for a fee. New Mexico, like most states, has an antidiscrimination law that prohibits public accommodations from discriminating based on race, sex, and a number of other factors. New Mexico's law also explicitly prohibits discrimination based on sexual orientation. Discrimination by public accommodations and private educational institutions was a big issue during (and after) segregation, when many businesses discriminated against African American customers and refused to serve them outright or declined to serve them on the same terms as white customers. Occasionally, a public accommodation or private educational institution tried to justify the discrimination based on religious objections. Significantly, they lost virtually all of those cases (and today would certainly lose all of them).[2]

The Elane Photography situation is a bit different, however. Elane Photography did not refuse to serve gay or lesbian customers. Rather, Elane Photography refused to photograph same-sex couples in any romantic context, including same-sex weddings. This does not save Elane Photography from losing, however, because the New Mexico Supreme Court held – and correctly so – that Elane Photography cannot discriminate in the services it provides to clients based on sexual orientation, because the New Mexico Human Rights Act prohibits discrimination in broad terms by forbidding "any person in any public accommodation to make a distinction, *directly or indirectly*, in offering or refusing to offer services" (emphasis added).[3] The court noted that Elane Photography is primarily a wedding photographer, and it provides services "to heterosexual couples but it refuses to work with homosexual couples under equivalent circumstances."[4]

The only way Elane Photography could legally prevail given this seemingly obvious violation of the New Mexico Human Rights Act would be if it could prove that its discrimination was not based on sexual orientation or that it had a right under the federal or state constitution or the state RFRA. Elane Photography argued that it did not discriminate when it refused to photograph the same-sex ceremony because it would photograph gays and lesbians in non-romantic contexts. Elane Photography also argued that applying the New Mexico Human Rights Act's antidiscrimination principles to its refusal to photograph same-sex ceremonies violated its right to freedom of speech and the free exercise of religion under the First Amendment to the U.S. Constitution, which is applicable to the states through the Fourteenth Amendment, and that doing so violated the New Mexico RFRA.

The first argument was the easiest for the New Mexico Supreme Court to address. Refusal to provide services to gays and lesbians on the same terms as heterosexuals goes to the very core of discrimination in public accommodations. The court addressed this directly:

> We are not persuaded by Elane Photography's argument that it does not violate the NMHRA [New Mexico Human Rights Act] because it will photograph a gay person (for example, in single person portraits) so long as the photographs do not reflect the client's sexual preferences. The NMHRA prohibits public accommodations from making any distinctions in the services they offer to customers on the basis of protected classifications ... For example, if a restaurant offers a full menu to male customers, it may not refuse to serve entrees to women, even if it will serve them appetizers.[5]

This is consistent with the *Masterpiece Cakeshop* case discussed later. Moreover, it makes complete sense.

Another element of the argument made by Elane Photography calls up an old concept that discrimination based on conduct – in this case, getting married – is not the same as discrimination based on status – in this case, being lesbian. The idea is that it is okay to discriminate based on conduct so long as the discrimination is not based on the status of the individual: for example, the individual's race, gender, religion, sexual orientation, and so on. This argument was rejected by the New Mexico Supreme Court and has been rejected repeatedly in other contexts by the United States Supreme Court in recent years. The New Mexico Supreme Court held as follows:

> We agree that when a law prohibits discrimination on the basis of sexual orientation, that law similarly protects conduct that is inextricably tied to sexual orientation. Otherwise, we would interpret the NMHRA [New Mexico Human Rights Act] as protecting same-gender couples against discriminatory treatment, but only to the extent that they do not openly display their same gender sexual orientation.[6]

One irony to the argument made by Elane Photography here is that the same argument could be used by public accommodations or employers to discriminate based on religious practice, so long as doing so was not based on an individual's religion. Therefore, a Christian could be fired for going or not going to church on Sunday, so long as the person was not fired just because he or she is Christian. This would most likely seem patently ridiculous to Elane Photography, but it is based on the same sort of reasoning that the business argued for in this case. Thankfully, this reasoning was rejected by the New Mexico Supreme Court and has been widely rejected by other courts as well.

Perhaps the best analogy to demonstrate the problems with both the limited service and status-conduct arguments in this case is the following. Imagine if a wedding photographer told an African American couple or a couple where one spouse is African American and the other white that it would not photograph the wedding because of the race of the couples. Would it make any difference if the photographer were willing to photograph a birthday party for one of the individuals? Of course not, and Elane Photography went beyond this because it would not photograph same-sex couples in any romantic context, even holding hands. Therefore, for Elane Photography to win, it would have to succeed on the basis of the constitutional right to freedom of speech, the free exercise of religion, or the New Mexico RFRA.

Elane Photography argued that photography is an expressive activity; therefore, the New Mexico Human Rights Act could not compel it to photograph a ceremony. This argument is based on a legal doctrine under the Free Speech Clause to the U.S. Constitution called the compelled speech doctrine: Government is not only prohibited from preventing free speech but also from compelling individuals to speak. This can be done in two ways. The government may not require someone to speak a message that the government wants the person to speak and the government may not require someone to "host or accommodate" someone else's message.[7]

The court held that requiring Elane Photography to follow the requirements of the New Mexico Human Rights Act and photograph the ceremony without regard to the sexual orientation of those involved violates neither element of the compelled speech doctrine. The court rejected the argument that Elane Photography was being forced to speak the government's message because all that is required under the New Mexico Human Rights Act is that if Elane Photography operates a business as a public accommodation, it cannot discriminate in violation of the act. It does not require that Elane Photography take wedding pictures, nor does it require that Elane Photography speak the government's message.

The court noted two famous compelled speech cases. In the first, the Supreme Court held that a Jehovah's Witness cannot be compelled to recite the Pledge of Allegiance because of that faith's belief that an oath can only be made to God (and importantly, not because of any lack of patriotism).[8] In the second case, the Supreme Court held that the state of New Hampshire could not require citizens to have the state motto of "Live Free or Die" on their license plates if the individuals found the motto "repugnant to their moral, religious, and political beliefs."[9] The court pointed out that in addition to the fact that the New Mexico Human Rights Act does not require Elane Photography to photograph weddings or do so for a fee, the government also does not necessarily send a message promoting specific government values other than equal provision of services in the market without regard to protected classifications such as race, gender, religion, and national origin and the prevention of humiliation and dignitary harm.

The court wrote as follows:

> The NMHRA does not require any affirmation of belief by regulated public accommodations; instead, it requires businesses that offer services to the public at large to provide those services without regard for race, sex, sexual orientation, or other protected classifications. The fact that these services may involve speech or other expressive services does not render the NMHRA unconstitutional ... Elane Photography is compelled to take photographs of same-sex weddings only to the extent that it would provide the same services to a heterosexual couple.[10]

The court also rejected the argument that the New Mexico Human Rights Act required Elane Photography to host or accommodate someone else's message:

> The United States Supreme Court has never found a compelled-speech violation arising from the application of antidiscrimination laws to a for-profit public accommodation. In fact, it has suggested that public accommodation laws are generally constitutional ... The United States Supreme Court has found constitutional problems with some applications of state public accommodation laws, but those problems have arisen when states have applied their public accommodation laws to free-speech events such as privately organized parades, and private membership organizations. Elane Photography, however, is an ordinary public accommodation, a "clearly commercial entit[y]," that sells goods and services to the public."
>
> The NMHRA does not, nor could it, regulate the content of the photographs that Elane Photography produces. It does not, for example, mandate that Elane Photography take posed photographs rather than candid shots, nor does it require every wedding album to contain a picture of the bride's bouquet. Indeed, the NMHRA does not mandate that Elane Photography choose to take wedding pictures; that is the exclusive choice of Elane Photography. Like all public accommodation laws, the NMHRA regulates "the act of

discriminating against individuals in the provision of publicly available goods, privileges, and services on the proscribed grounds." (citation omitted). Elane Photography argues that because the service it provides is photography, and because photography is expressive, "some of [the] images will inevitably express the messages inherent in [the] event." In essence, then, Elane Photography argues that by limiting its ability to choose its clients, the NMHRA forces it to produce photographs expressing its clients' messages even when the messages are contrary to Elane Photography's beliefs.

Elane Photography has misunderstood this issue. It believes that because it is a photography business, it cannot be subject to public accommodation laws. The reality is that because it is a public accommodation, its provision of services can be regulated, even though those services include artistic and creative work. If Elane Photography took photographs on its own time and sold them at a gallery, or if it was hired by certain clients but did not offer its services to the general public, the law would not apply to Elane Photography's choice of whom to photograph or not. The difference in the present case is that the photographs that are allegedly compelled by the NMHRA are photographs that Elane Photography produces for hire in the ordinary course of its business as a public accommodation. This determination has no relation to the artistic merit of photographs produced by Elane Photography. If Annie Leibovitz or Peter Lindbergh worked as public accommodations in New Mexico, they would be subject to the provisions of the NMHRA. Unlike the defendants [in cases in which] . . . the United States Supreme Court has found compelled-speech violations, Elane Photography sells its expressive services to the public. It may be that Elane Photography expresses its clients' messages in its photographs, but only because it is hired to do so. The NMHRA requires that Elane Photography perform the same services for a same-sex couple as it would for an opposite-sex couple; the fact that these services require photography stems from the nature of Elane Photography's chosen line of business.

The cases in which the United States Supreme Court found that the government unconstitutionally required a speaker to host or accommodate another speaker's message are distinctly different because they involve direct government interference with the speaker's own message, as opposed to a message-for-hire.[11]

Other cases have agreed with this analysis in similar circumstances,[12] but this addresses only the free speech claim. What about the free exercise of religion under the First Amendment to the Constitution? You read the answer to that question in Chapter 2. Recall the case involving the denial of unemployment benefits to members of the Native American Church who used peyote in a ritual ceremony (*Employment Division v. Smith*). The Supreme Court held that when a law is generally applicable, it applies to everyone regardless of religion, and the government does not have to provide a religious exemption to the law. The government may choose to do so, however. As you might recall, it was this case that gave rise to the need for the federal RFRA. To this day, I believe that *Smith* was wrongly decided, but it is the law and therefore Elane Photography's freedom of religion claims under the First Amendment to the Constitution easily fail because antidiscrimination laws are generally applicable (they apply to all for-profit employers and public accommodations in the same manner).

It is important to note that even if *Smith* were not the law, Elane Photography was likely to lose under the prior rule that required government to have a compelling interest (extremely important interest) – in this case preventing discrimination against groups that have often been the victims of discrimination – supporting any substantial burden on the free exercise of religion. This rule also required that the government's means of achieving that interest – antidiscrimination law – is narrowly tailored to meet the government interest. Preventing discrimination is clearly a compelling government interest, and antidiscrimination laws are narrowly tailored to meet that interest. Ironically, Elane Photography could argue that most antidiscrimination laws already have exemptions for some religious entities, but that is exactly the point. Under these exemptions, religious entities are non-profit entities that primarily serve their flocks, while the Supreme Court held under the pre-*Smith* compelling interest test that for-profit entities must follow generally applicable laws.[13] *Hobby Lobby* does not change this because it is interpreting the federal RFRA, which is a statute passed by Congress, not part of the Constitution.

The existence of a compelling interest in preventing discrimination would likely have doomed any claim made by Elane Photography under the New Mexico RFRA even if that law applied, but the New Mexico Supreme Court avoided the issue by holding that the state RFRA does not apply in this context. How could that be? The court held that the state RFRA does not apply because the lawsuit under the New Mexico Human Rights Act was brought by one private party against another, while the New Mexico RFRA only applies when "a 'government agency' restricts a person's free exercise of religion."[14]

I think it unlikely that other state RFRAs will be interpreted the same way. The passage of a RFRA by the legislature and application of a RFRA by a state civil rights commission and/or court is likely to be enough to enable a private party to raise a cognizable RFRA claim or defense. But as explained earlier, the RFRA claim or defense would not likely succeed when a private party whose conduct violated antidiscrimination laws raised it.

Yet what about the sincere religious beliefs of Elane Huguenin, the owner of Elane Photography? Think about the position she is now in. She built a business before the same-sex marriage issue or even civil commitment ceremonies were a major focus. She believed that her religion commanded her to refrain from supporting same-sex relationships, and this is exactly what she did. There is no serious argument that she hates gay or lesbian individuals because they are gay or lesbian, but rather she was unable to support same-sex relationships.

Justice Bosson captured the balance between these rights beautifully in his concurring opinion:

> The Huguenins are free to think, to say, to believe, as they wish; they may pray to the God of their choice and follow those commandments in their personal lives wherever they lead. The Constitution protects the Huguenins in that respect and much more. But there is a price, one that we all have to pay somewhere in our civic life.
>
> In the smaller, more focused world of the marketplace, of commerce, of public accommodation, the Huguenins have to channel their conduct, not their beliefs, so as to leave space for other Americans who believe something different. That compromise is part of the glue that holds us together as a nation, the tolerance that lubricates the varied moving parts of us as a people. That sense of respect we owe others, whether or not we believe as

they do, illuminates this country, setting it apart from the discord that afflicts much of the rest of the world. In short, I would say to the Huguenins, with the utmost respect: it is the price of citizenship.[15]

I agree wholeheartedly both with the respect shown for Elane Huguenin given the position she was placed in, and with the central importance of the freedom from discrimination that requires Huguenin to pay the price of citizenship. But what if there were a way to provide some accommodation for businesses like Elane Photography without allowing discrimination? I explain below how this is possible.

Keep in mind that after the case, Hugeunin must either violate a fundamental tenet of her faith or abandon a core aspect of her livelihood. She is a wedding photographer. Perhaps she could make a living doing other sorts of photography, but there is certainly no guarantee that she could support her business doing this, as anyone familiar with the photography industry could attest (a significant number of portrait studios, some from large chains, generally do not photograph events such as weddings, Bar and Bat Mitzvahs, etc.). Is there any way to accommodate her in a manner that does not violate the antidiscrimination tenets addressed in the court's opinion and throughout this book?

Quite honestly, many people – myself included – would relish watching her business fail if her act of discrimination were based on raw bigotry or a sense that gays and lesbians are not as capable as heterosexuals. Yet, her objection is based on a sincere religious concern over being complicit in same-sex relationships, not a belief that gays and lesbians are less capable or that they should be the subjects of discrimination in general. She was not accused of the sort of broader bigotry involved in denying services to any gay or lesbian individual regardless of context.

Admittedly she goes much further than those who refuse to perform services only for a same-sex wedding but are willing to otherwise perform services for gay and lesbian couples, because she will not do any photography showing a romantic relationship between same-sex individuals. This could be a basis for arguing that her situation is quite different from that of a baker or photographer who only objects to performing services for a same-sex wedding. Thus, one could argue that Huguenin does engage in the broader form of discrimination because she refuses to photograph the very conduct that defines one's status as gay or lesbian, as opposed to just a wedding ceremony. I have some sympathy for this argument, but it simply removes the question to the next level. Is there any way to accommodate the baker or photographer who will perform services in every context except a same-sex wedding? This is exactly the situation that arose in the *Masterpiece Cakeshop* case discussed later.

The main basis for Huguenin's actions (or inactions) is related to the theological concept of not facilitating (or being complicit in) what she views as a sin. This concept plays an important role in several Christian traditions, including Huguenin's Christian faith. That does not mean she does not love those she may view as sinners. We do not have to like or agree with Huguenin's religious perspective, but discomfort with her religious perspective does not deny her the right to hold her faith. It also does not justify subjecting her to the attacks and hatred directed at her after her case came to light. This was a legal battle over the boundaries between freedoms, and Elane Photography rightfully lost that legal battle. There was going to be pain on one side or the other for whoever lost, and it is callous to write off the tough position Elane Huguenin has been put in even if we agree that she should have lost the case.

Losers in the culture wars do not just go away. They often retrench and try to move forward. Writing them off because we disagree with them is a dangerous and small-minded approach. Some of the public commentary on this case, and on the following cases, reflects a remarkable inability to see the commonalities between religious freedom and sexual freedom and demonstrates the hypocrisy in some of the more radical commentary from both sides. Thankfully, however, there have been numerous balanced stories and some thoughtful public commentary on these issues.

There is a certain irony when people seeking to promote freedom and non-discrimination attack someone who is simply following her religion, not behaving in a manner that suggests she thinks gays and lesbians are somehow less human. What she did was devastating to Vanessa Willock and Misti Collinsworth, and they did the right thing by taking Elane Photography to court. They won, and balancing all the factors, that was the correct legal decision. If they had lost, it would have been devastating to them personally and to many other same-sex couples in New Mexico. Moreover, it would have been devastating for religious freedom because of the likely public backlash.

As I explained in the first few chapters of this book, there will be winners and losers when freedoms conflict, but if we approach each other with a sense of the pain these experiences may cause, we can better navigate the treacherous pass between these freedoms in a manner that allows us to maximize freedom where possible. Elane Photography lost because it is a public accommodation and what it did was discrimination. That is the correct legal result and it should be. Public accommodations serve the general public; when antidiscrimination laws are in place, they must serve everyone equally. My fear is that the result in this and similar cases may lead some states not to include sexual orientation in their antidiscrimination laws, and that would be a mistake. Having both antidiscrimination laws protecting people based on sexual orientation and religious freedom laws is one of the best ways to maximize freedom on both sides.

So what can be done for Elane Huguenin without allowing her to discriminate? This is a hard question. Even after thinking long and hard about this, no solution seems possible that would allow robust accommodation despite the impact on religious freedom. What are the options? First, states could refrain from passing or repeal antidiscrimination protection for members of the LGBT community. This is the worst possible option. Antidiscrimination laws protecting members of the LGBT community are not only good for members of that community but also good for religious freedom. Large segments of the public are concerned that religious freedom protection leads to discrimination against members of the LGBT community. The backlash against proposed or passed state RFRAs around the country has been heavily based on this. With antidiscrimination protection in place, religious freedom is less threatening.

A second option would be to exclude sole proprietorships or small family-owned businesses from antidiscrimination laws that govern public accommodations. This option is also problematic. While there are exceptions for small companies under some employment discrimination laws, these exceptions make little sense in the public accommodation context. Here the analogy to racial discrimination is apropos. Should a small family-owned restaurant be able to exclude African Americans? Or more analogous to Elane Photography, African Americans who choose to hold hands? Of course not. Is there a difference between this and a photographer who does not want to take pictures of an interracial couple for religious reasons in any context that demonstrates the romance between them? Of course not.

A common argument suggests that we should just allow the small business owner to do what he or she wants. This argument has often been made in the same-sex marriage context and was made after *Loving v. Virginia* struck down anti-miscegenation laws. The argument would sound something like this: The photographer is a racist (if the context is race) or homophobic (if the context is same-sex marriage) and should be boycotted. Since the couple can go elsewhere to be photographed, the photographer should not be forced to photograph something he or she does not want to photograph. Of course, that may be true in New York City, but what about a smaller town in the Deep South in 1965 in the race context? Or in many less urban areas today in the same-sex marriage context?

That is the situation presented by this argument. In large swaths of the country, it may be hard to find a photographer, bakery, or catering hall that would not discriminate against a same-sex couple getting married. In some places, there may only be one or two shops to begin with. To have to hold your wedding or seek services far away may be financially prohibitive and, of course, can create significant emotional harm. Thus, this option too is highly problematic.

What if, however, we follow an option modeled on the concepts suggested for county clerks in Chapter 4? It would be far from perfect for either side, but it would provide some accommodation for people like Elane Huguenin while not allowing any denial of service or delay for same-sex couples.

How would something like this work, especially in a sole proprietorship? It would not be simple, but here is a model for how it could work. A sole proprietorship or small family-owned business may not deny a service to a same-sex couple related to a same-sex wedding. However, it can be exempted from performing the service personally so long as someone else in the business or someone with whom the business has created a working relationship – even if only for referral purposes – is (1) equally qualified to perform the service and (2) is able to perform the service without delay or added cost.

There is no doubt that neither side will be completely happy with this option. For those who support religious accommodation, this solution still makes the service provider complicit in what he or she is forbidden to support, but the alternative is no accommodation at all; at least this accommodation allows the person(s) who directly object to providing the service to be accommodated. Some might respond by arguing that denying antidiscrimination protection for gays and lesbians will solve this problem, but that is naïve. In the long run, denying antidiscrimination protection will simply lead to less and less religious freedom for the reasons explained throughout this book.

For those who find even this accommodation repugnant because it still allows discrimination – even if that discrimination is less direct and may not even be known by those whom it affects – you have a point. This accommodation, however, would prevent the denial of service and decrease or erase any potential dignitary harm because the system would be in place to allow a smooth provision of service. Moreover, why would anyone want a person who is opposed to same-sex marriage to be the one performing the service? Even if that person is uniquely good at what he or she does, who is to say that skill will be reflected in the outcome when he or she is being forced to provide the service? Finally, and perhaps most importantly, why should those who have finally been given the long overdue freedom to marry and express the core of their being want to deny to someone else the freedom to express the core of his or her being (in cases where doing so will not lead to a denial of or delay in equal service)?

I must admit that I share the Elane Photography court's view that public accommodations that charge a fee for services should not be able to discriminate against a class that is protected under antidiscrimination law. Yet, the religious harm caused to people such as Elane Huguenin through being made complicit in something forbidden by her religion is significant enough to attempt even a problematic solution. After all, finding common ground is essential for us to move forward as a nation. A pure legal victory on either side feels good for a while but may prove to be pyrrhic as society responds.

The situation referenced earlier, where a public accommodation refuses only to provide a service for a same-sex wedding rather than any other context came up in an even more recent case. Unlike in the Elane Photography case, where the owner refused to photograph any scene depicting same-sex couples in a romantic context, no evidence indicated that the owner of the small shop in the following case objected to providing services for the same-sex couple for anything other than the same-sex wedding. In fact, he expressly stated that he would make them baked items for any other event and never made any statement that the other events could not reflect a romantic relationship.

Craig v. Masterpiece Cakeshop, Inc.[16] involved a claim filed under the Colorado Anti-Discrimination Act against a cake shop and its owner for refusing to sell a same-sex couple a wedding cake. The Colorado Court of Appeals decided the case well after *Hobby Lobby* was decided, but Colorado does not have a RFRA, so the case does not involve a direct conflict between a state antidiscrimination law and a RFRA. It does, however, involve conflict between free speech and religious freedom claims by the bakery and its owner and a clear antidiscrimination law prohibiting discrimination based on sexual orientation by public accommodations.

The reasoning of the Colorado Court of Appeals could prove relevant even in states with a RFRA, but as you have already learned, a RFRA would require the state to show that enforcing the antidiscrimination provision serves a compelling interest and is narrowly tailored to meet that interest. The *Masterpiece Cakeshop* court did not engage in this analysis for the reasons explained later. It did, however, rely heavily on the *Elane Photography* case, which held that application of an antidiscrimination law to a public accommodation meets the compelling interest requirement.

After discussing the *Masterpiece Cakeshop* case, I explain why applying antidiscrimination laws to public accommodations should always meet the compelling interest and narrow tailoring requirements. I also explain why applying these laws to traditional religious entities would generally fail the compelling interest requirement and sometimes violate the Ecclesiastical Abstention Doctrine discussed in Chapter 2. Many important distinctions exist between a for-profit entity that serves the general public and a religious entity or non-profit.

The *Masterpiece Cakeshop* case follows the analysis from *Elane Photography* closely, but the facts are somewhat different. Charlie Craig and David Mullins went to Masterpiece Cakeshop to buy a wedding cake. Masterpiece Cakeshop's owner Jack Phillips was there and explained that he could not bake a cake for a same-sex wedding based on his religious beliefs. Phillips told Craig and Mullins that he would be happy to make them any other baked item and, of course, to sell them any baked items already in the shop. There was no evidence that Phillips had any objection to a romantic relationship between same-sex partners, which differentiates the case a bit from *Elane Photography*. Phillips's only objection was to baking a wedding cake for a same-sex wedding.

Craig and Mullins did not dispute the sincerity of Phillips's religious beliefs, and the evidence showed that Phillips has been a devout Christian for more than thirty-five years. Phillips also did not dispute that his bakery was a public accommodation. Therefore, the primary issues in the case, other than some specific issues relating to administrative law in Colorado that are beyond the scope of this discussion, were (1) whether Masterpiece Cakeshop violated the Colorado Anti-Discrimination Act, which prohibits discrimination based on sexual orientation by public accommodations, and (2) whether the Free Speech Clause or the Free Exercise Clause of the U.S. Constitution and a similar provision of the Colorado state constitution provide a valid defense to a claim of discrimination under the Colorado Anti-Discrimination Act.

On the first issue, Masterpiece Cakeshop made a similar argument to the one made by Elane Photography. Masterpiece argued that it did not discriminate based on sexual orientation because it was willing to bake any item and serve all customers, including gay and lesbian customers, except that it would not bake a wedding cake for a same-sex wedding. Thus, Masterpiece argued that it did not refuse to create the wedding cake "because of" Craig's and Mullins's sexual orientation, which would be a basis for discrimination under the law. Rather, Masterpiece asserted that it refused to create the cake because of Phillips's religious objection to same-sex marriage. If anything, the argument was stronger in this case than in the case of Elane Photography, where the owner refused to provide any services that reflected a romantic relationship between a same-sex couple. Yet the court rejected this argument, with good reason under the Colorado Anti-Discrimination Act, and for reasons similar to those set forth in the *Elane Photography* opinion.

Masterpiece Cakeshop's argument attempts to draw a distinction between a protected status, sexual orientation, and conduct connected to that status, same-sex marriage. The *Masterpiece Cakeshop* court relied on two Supreme Court decisions, including *Obergefell v. Hodges*, to explain that this sort of distinction has been rejected:

> In these decisions, the Supreme Court recognized that, in some cases, conduct cannot be divorced from status. This is so when the conduct is so closely correlated with the status that it is engaged in exclusively or predominantly by persons who have that particular status. We conclude that the act of same-sex marriage constitutes such conduct because it is "engaged in exclusively or predominantly" by gays, lesbians, and bisexuals. Masterpiece's distinction, therefore, is one without a difference. But for their sexual orientation, Craig and Mullins would not have sought to enter into a same-sex marriage, and but for their intent to do so, Masterpiece would not have denied them its services.[17]

Masterpiece Cakeshop also argued that since it was willing to create and sell other products to gay and lesbian customers, it did not violate the Colorado Anti-Discrimination Act. This argument loses its force once the court found that refusal to create the cake for the same-sex wedding was discrimination in violation of the act, and the court thusly rejects this second argument:

> We reject Masterpiece's related argument that its willingness to sell birthday cakes, cookies, and other non-wedding cake products to gay and lesbian customers establishes that it did not violate CADA. Masterpiece's potential compliance with CADA in this respect does not permit it to refuse services to Craig and Mullins that it otherwise offers to the general public.[18]

The court then addresses Masterpiece Cakeshop's argument that even if it violated the antidiscrimination law, it was justified in doing so

based on the Free Speech and Free Exercise Clauses of the First
Amendment to the U.S. Constitution and Article II, Section 4, of the
Colorado constitution, which covers the free exercise of religion.
The court's reasoning on the free speech issue closely mirrors the
reasoning on that same issue in *Elane Photography*. Like photography,
creating a cake can be an activity expressing the perspective of
the baker in some contexts but as in *Elane Photography*, that does not
save Masterpiece Cakeshop since Phillips voluntarily chose to make
money selling to the public and cannot discriminate in doing so.
The compelled speech argument failed for some of the same reasons
as in *Elane Photography*. If Phillips created cakes for his own purposes
or for charity, the expressive activity would be more protected.
However, an additional issue worked against one of Masterpiece
Cakeshop's compelled speech arguments, namely the fact that
Phillips never discussed the design of the cake and simply rejected
making it outright. Therefore, he had no idea whether it would convey
a particular message such as having two grooms, a rainbow symbol,
and so on. It seems that regardless of this factor, the court would have
held against Masterpiece Cakeshop, but this factor might provide other
courts with a basis to distinguish the case.

Regarding the free speech arguments more generally, the court
explained:

> Masterpiece contends that wedding cakes inherently communicate
> a celebratory message about marriage and that, by forcing it to
> make cakes for same-sex weddings, the Commission's cease and
> desist order unconstitutionally compels it to express a celebratory
> message about same-sex marriage that it does not support.
> We disagree.
>
> ... Masterpiece's argument mistakenly presumes that the legal
> doctrines involving compelled speech and expressive conduct
> are mutually exclusive. As noted, because the First Amendment
> only protects conduct that conveys a message, the threshold
> question in cases involving expressive conduct – or as here,
> compelled expressive conduct – is whether the conduct in
> question is sufficiently expressive so as to trigger First
> Amendment protections.

We begin by identifying the compelled conduct in question. As noted, the Commission's order requires that Masterpiece "cease and desist from discriminating against [Craig and Mullins] and other same-sex couples by refusing to sell them wedding cakes or any product [it] would sell to heterosexual couples." Therefore, the compelled conduct is the Colorado government's mandate that Masterpiece comport with CADA by not basing its decision to serve a potential client, at least in part, on the client's sexual orientation. This includes a requirement that Masterpiece sell wedding cakes to same-sex couples, but only if it wishes to serve heterosexual couples in the same manner.

Next, we ask whether, by comporting with CADA and ceasing to discriminate against potential customers on the basis of their sexual orientation, Masterpiece conveys a particularized message celebrating same-sex marriage, and whether the likelihood is great that a reasonable observer would both understand the message and attribute that message to Masterpiece.

We conclude that the act of designing and selling a wedding cake to all customers free of discrimination does not convey a celebratory message about same-sex weddings likely to be understood by those who view it. We further conclude that, to the extent that the public infers from a Masterpiece wedding cake a message celebrating same-sex marriage, that message is more likely to be attributed to the customer than to Masterpiece.

First, Masterpiece does not convey a message supporting same-sex marriages merely by abiding by the law and serving its customers equally ...

[W]e conclude that, because CADA prohibits all places of public accommodation from discriminating against customers because of their sexual orientation, it is unlikely that the public would view Masterpiece's creation of a cake for a same-sex wedding celebration as an endorsement of that conduct. Rather, we conclude that a reasonable observer would understand that Masterpiece's compliance with the law is not a reflection of its own beliefs.

We do not suggest that Masterpiece's status as a for-profit bakery strips it of its First Amendment speech protections. However, we must consider the allegedly expressive conduct within "the context in which it occurred." The public recognizes that, as a for-profit bakery, Masterpiece charges its customers for its goods and services. The fact that an entity charges for its goods and services reduces the likelihood that a reasonable observer will believe that it supports the message expressed in its finished product . . .

By selling a wedding cake to a same-sex couple, Masterpiece does not necessarily lead an observer to conclude that the bakery supports its customer's conduct. The public has no way of knowing the reasons supporting Masterpiece's decision to serve or decline to serve a same-sex couple. Someone observing that a commercial bakery created a wedding cake for a straight couple or that it did not create one for a gay couple would have no way of deciphering whether the bakery's conduct took place because of its views on same-sex marriage or for some other reason.

We recognize that a wedding cake, in some circumstances, may convey a particularized message celebrating same-sex marriage and, in such cases, First Amendment speech protections may be implicated. However, we need not reach this issue. We note, again, that Phillips denied Craig's and Mullins' request without any discussion regarding the wedding cake's design or any possible written inscriptions.

Finally, CADA does not preclude Masterpiece from expressing its views on same-sex marriage – including its religious opposition to it – and the bakery remains free to disassociate itself from its customers' viewpoints . . . CADA does not prevent Masterpiece from posting a disclaimer in the store or on the Internet indicating that the provision of its services does not constitute an endorsement or approval of conduct protected by CADA. Masterpiece could also post or otherwise disseminate a message indicating that CADA requires it not to discriminate on the basis of sexual orientation and other protected characteristics. Such a message would likely have the effect of disassociating Masterpiece from its customers' conduct. (citations omitted).[19]

Masterpiece Cakeshop's arguments under the Free Exercise Clause were predetermined by the outcome in *Employment Division v. Smith*, the peyote case discussed in Chapter 2. A state has no duty to provide an exemption to a law that applies to everyone regardless of religion. The Colorado Anti-Discrimination Act applies to everyone regardless of religion, so the only way for Masterpiece to succeed would be to prove that its free exercise claim could combine with another constitutional claim, such as its free speech claim, to create what the *Smith* Court called a "hybrid right." The hybrid rights concept makes no legal sense and appears to have simply been a way for Justice Antonin Scalia, writing for the majority of the Supreme Court, to get around inconvenient precedent. The Colorado Court of Appeals notes this as well but adds that since it found no free speech violation, no hybrid rights claim was possible even if that concept made any sense:

> We note that Colorado's appellate courts have not applied the "hybrid-rights" exception, and several decisions have cast doubt on its validity. *See, e.g., Grace United Methodist Church v. City of Cheyenne*, 451 F.3d 643, 656 (10th Cir.2006) ("The hybrid rights doctrine is controversial. It has been characterized as mere *dicta* not binding on lower courts, criticized as illogical, and dismissed as untenable." (citations omitted)). Regardless, having concluded above that the Commission's order does not implicate Masterpiece's freedom of expression, even if we assume the "hybrid-rights" exception exists, it would not apply here.[20]

This left only Article II, Section 4, of the Colorado constitution as a defense. Colorado does not have a RFRA, so unless the court were willing to interpret the Colorado constitution to apply the legal standards that the Supreme Court applied prior to the peyote case, as some states have done, Masterpiece could not win. The court refused to apply these standards under the Colorado constitution; so since the antidiscrimination law applies to everyone, Masterpiece lost the case. The accommodation I suggested earlier might help here if Phillips were willing to bring someone else with a high skill level in to make the cake or if he entered into a contractual relationship with another shop for making cakes without additional cost.

Would a RFRA have made a difference in the *Masterpiece Cakeshop* case? I do not think it would have, and not just for the reason given by the *Elane Photography* court, which held that since the state was not involved, there was no valid RFRA claim. What I will assert here is controversial to some, but I think it is almost certainly correct: The state will always have a compelling interest under RFRA in enforcing antidiscrimination laws. Moreover, enforcement of those laws against public accommodations and other for-profit entities will always be narrowly tailored, unless for some reason the state enforces the antidiscrimination laws only against those with religious objections (which has never happened and is unlikely to happen).

I proudly count myself among those who support both religious freedom and sexual freedom, but I go a step further than many religious freedom advocates are willing to go because I argue that protecting for-profit entities under RFRAs at all is a huge mistake, but we leave that argument for the next section. For now, let's address situations where these entities are protected under a RFRA in a state that also has antidiscrimination protection for members of the LGBT community. Let's further assume that a conflict arises between these statutes such as occurred in *Masterpiece Cakeshop*. Finally, we assume that our state rejects the argument made in *Elane Photography* that since a transaction between private parties is involved, no government action implicates RFRA, which only applies when government interferes with religious freedom. This final point is important because many states are likely to find government action does exist for RFRA purposes in these situations: While the business transaction is between private parties, the violation of antidiscrimination law is enforced by a state agency and/or a court, which are part of government and, of course, the law itself is made by the government and reflects government norms and values.

The U.S. Supreme Court and numerous state courts have held that the government has a compelling interest in enforcing antidiscrimination laws.[21] RFRAs require that government have a compelling interest for interfering with religious freedom. Protecting groups that have traditionally been subject to discrimination from that discrimination is a core value that government may enforce through antidiscrimination law.[22] Thus, there is little doubt that these laws would serve as a compelling interest under RFRAs. That, of course, leaves the question of narrow tailoring: that is, whether there is no other way to serve the compelling interest than enforcement of antidiscrimination laws. Even if government has a compelling interest for placing a burden on religion, it must do so in a narrowly tailored way to win under RFRA.

Narrow tailoring is not an easy standard to meet. After all, the government needs to show that there is no other plausible way to meet its compelling interest. In fact, in numerous cases from various areas of constitutional law (where this legal test is most commonly used), the government has lost because the courts have found the government's approach was not narrowly tailored. We refer to this as a "means-ends test" in legal circles. Are the means – whatever government action is being challenged – narrowly tailored to the ends – the government's compelling interest? You can see how narrow tailoring is often the government's undoing. Even if the government's ends are compelling, it loses in court if it could have used some other plausible means to meet that interest.

Yet, courts have held that enforcing antidiscrimination laws, which generally impose civil penalties rather than criminal penalties, is narrowly tailored to meet the government's interest in preventing discrimination.[23] In the present context, the government is applying the law to all public accommodations that charge a fee and are open to the general public. Making exceptions for entities that serve the general public for a fee may be permissible, but the government need not do so – and in most cases will not do so – because doing so would undermine enforcement of the antidiscrimination principle the government seeks to enforce.

In fact, most of these antidiscrimination laws have exemptions for religious entities, which, if anything, makes them even more narrowly tailored. The government's interest is to prohibit discrimination in employment or public accommodations, and it has tailored the law to apply to those entities that serve the general public for profit. Religious entities often serve their own flocks, and even those open to the public are generally non-profit. This does not mean that religious non-profits do not raise issues, but those issues, which are addressed in Chapter 7, are separate from the current discussion.

Of course, this assumes the state has an antidiscrimination law that protects based on sexual orientation. As advocated throughout this book, these laws are desirable for both sides of the religious freedom/ sexual freedom debate. On the sexual freedom side, the reasons are obvious. With or without same-sex marriage, members of the LGBT community have been subject to significant discrimination.

Antidiscrimination law is one of the most important ways to combat this discrimination. On the religious freedom side, the very existence of robust religious freedom may rely on the existence of antidiscrimination protection for members of the LGBT community. Religious freedom has increasingly been framed as a basis to discriminate, and the core values and reasons for religious freedom have become muddied by the backlash caused by *Hobby Lobby* and other situations where public accommodations or private employers discriminate against members of the LGBT community and offer justification based on religious freedom. Antidiscrimination protection for members of the LGBT community is essential to allow religious freedom to be seen for what it usually is (and ought to be): a way to protect people like Mandy Rodriguez and Jonathan Stein (see Chapter 1), as well as religious entities such as churches, synagogues, and mosques and religious non-profits.

You have now had a chance to learn about two actual cases involving small businesses that made it to court. The stakes are high on both sides, and ironically the core freedoms on each side share a number of elements. Public accommodation cases involving small businesses that engage in expressive activities are the hardest cases involving for-profit entities that serve the general public; as we have seen, the balance generally favors not allowing these entities to violate antidiscrimination laws where those laws exist. It is ironic then that the Supreme Court has interpreted the federal RFRA in a manner that protects much larger closely held corporations that serve the general public when they violate a different sort of law based on religious objections. This, of course, refers to *Hobby Lobby*. Would the result in that case be different if Hobby Lobby refused to sell items to customers for use in a same-sex wedding ceremony and there were a federal antidiscrimination law prohibiting discrimination based on sexual orientation? I think even after the *Hobby Lobby* decision, the answer would be "yes." The next section addresses this and other concerns relating to the *Hobby Lobby* case.

II HOBBY LOBBY

The *Hobby Lobby* case was addressed in Chapter 2 and that discussion need not be repeated here. The purpose of this section is to argue that granting for-profit entities religious freedom rights under a RFRA is not just a legal error but also a strategic error of epic proportions for religious freedom advocates. Simply put, *Hobby Lobby* is bad for religious freedom. Even if I did not think it was a terrible legal decision, the fact remains that it is a strategic catastrophe for religious freedom generally. Ironically, one of the best ways to protect religious freedom for individuals and traditional religious entities against the immense backlash religious freedom has been facing would be to amend the federal RFRA and state RFRAs to deny protection to for-profit entities. This is the opposite of what many state legislatures have been attempting to do.

In making this argument, I am not disparaging the Green or Hahn families, who no doubt had sincere religious beliefs that forced their hand. Nor am I disparaging the excellent lawyers who advocated on their behalf (in my opinion, it was a great job of lawyering since they were able to sell Justice Samuel Alito and the majority of the Supreme Court, except for perhaps Justice Anthony Kennedy, the legal equivalent of the Brooklyn Bridge). I am pointing out the simple reality that *Hobby Lobby* will prove to be worse for religious freedom than *Employment Division v. Smith* (the peyote case). I realize this is a radical statement, so I will back it up later in this chapter. Unfortunately, backing it up becomes easier almost every week as the country experiences more cultural backlash and fallout from the *Hobby Lobby* Court's protection of for-profit entities' religious freedom in a manner that could potentially harm third parties' rights.

Both the protection of for-profit entities' religious freedom and the implication that religious freedom claims could negatively affect third parties were unprecedented. But even assuming that these were the correct legal decisions, the fallout from these arguments both before and since *Hobby Lobby* has been stunning. Again, I am not attempting to belittle the impact that owners of closely held companies such as the Greens and the Hahns face. In fact, you could add Elane Huguenin and Jack Phillips to that list. These people are faced with a Hobson's Choice: violate the tenets of your faith and become complicit in something you believe to be sin, thus damaging the very core of your being and depending on your belief perhaps your eternal life, or give up the profit-making element of your business.

Of course, there is a profound difference between a religious entity and a for-profit corporation. This is the problem. Once we begin protecting for-profit entities, the likelihood of claims of discrimination will increase dramatically. We witnessed public outrage over the argument that a for-profit business can discriminate based on religious freedom even before *Hobby Lobby* was decided, but that outrage has reached a fever pitch since and will only increase.

A Why Protecting For-Profit Entities Is a Strategic Mistake That Could Doom the Long-Term Future of Religious Freedom in the United States

Protecting for-profit entities under RFRAs is a bad idea. Let's assume for the sake of this argument that there are good legal reasons for protecting these entities under a RFRA,[24] and even better spiritual reasons. Doing so is a mistake.

Three factors are abundantly clear in this context. First, the owners of closely held for-profit entities do suffer serious harm when they are forced to become complicit in actions that violate the tenets of their faith. The struggle over whether to close down their businesses or facilitate what they view as a sin affects them at the deepest levels. The emotional, spiritual, and psychological fallout from these situations can be staggering. People may be forced to choose between a business they have spent decades building and which employs many people who need work and becoming complicit in something that violates the very fabric of their being by violating God's law, and perhaps condemning their eternal souls – in which they believe as deeply as some secularists believe souls do not exist.

Imagine for a moment that you are a dog lover (for many this does not require imagination). You love your dog and view it as a part of your family. In fact, you identify deeply with its emotions and see its personality. So do your partner and your children. Others, who do not share your love of dogs, think you are a bit overzealous or are just imagining things. You have had your dog for ten years and it is a core part of your life, and you have always had dogs in your life since you were a child. One day the government decides that keeping dogs in the home is unsanitary, and that in fact animal rights protections generally were a big mistake. You are told you must give up your dog or your house will be taken away from you. Others feel bad for you but tell you to get over it. After all, "it's just a dog," they say. Others who share your love for their own dogs identify with you, but dog lovers have become less powerful in public debate. Do you give up your dog or your home?

Please don't assume I am equating one's religious faith directly with loving one's dog. In fact, for many people of faith their religious convictions go so deep that no analogy may be possible. Yet this hypothetical scenario captures the struggle that the owners of for-profit entities may be placed in when they must choose between the businesses they have built and becoming complicit in what they view as the unthinkable. What could the Greens and the Hahns have done if, as I suggest, they lost their cases?

I am painfully aware of the costs involved in compromising the religious freedom rights of the owners of for-profit businesses, but the second and third factors discussed later demonstrate why this must be done. Perhaps it is easier for me to make this argument since I do not think that the religious freedoms of for-profit entities were ever protected under the First Amendment, and that the *Hobby Lobby* Court misinterpreted RFRA when it protected for-profit entities under that statute. And perhaps it is easier for me to make this argument because I also deeply believe in protecting sexual freedom and can envision the equally painful situations that employees of for-profit entities who are denied benefits or discriminated against will suffer, but that changes nothing. Even if I did not hold these views, the pragmatic reality remains that protecting the religious freedom of for-profit entities will doom religious freedom generally in the long run.

Second, there is a fundamental difference between for-profit entities and religious entities. Religious entities generally serve their own flocks, and to the extent that they reach out through charity to serve others, they do so as part of their religious mission and not for any profit motive. The purpose of these endeavors is religious. When a church opens a "restaurant" and only serves food for free to the poor, we call it a soup kitchen, not a restaurant. If a church opened a department store for the general public and did so as a profit-making venture, the store could lose its status as a protected religious entity.

In fact, a Supreme Court case called *Hosanna-Tabor Evangelical Lutheran Church v. EEOC*[25] drives this point home. The case did not involve a RFRA, but rather a conflict between the Americans with Disabilities Act and the Ecclesiastical Abstention Doctrine, which prevents courts from interfering with religious matters. A sub-concept of that doctrine called the "Ministerial Exception," which prevents government from interfering in employment decisions involving clergy, was the main focus of the case. A teacher in the church school filed a complaint against the church under the Americans with Disabilities Act, and the church fired her because it goes against the tenets of the faith to file a civil suit against the church rather than relying solely on the church's internal dispute resolution mechanisms.

The key issue in the case was whether the teacher was considered a minister for purposes of the Ministerial Exception. If so, a court could not hear a challenge to her termination because that was entirely within the province of the church's doctrines; therefore, it would violate both the Free Exercise Clause and Establishment Clause of the First Amendment, which together support the principle of noninterference in religious matters on which the Ministerial Exception is based. If not, she would not be clergy and the Ministerial Exception would not apply. The church argued strongly that because she was "called" to be a teacher and teaches religious subjects along with her secular subjects, the teacher is a minister under church doctrine. A unanimous – as contrasted with the close 5–4 vote in *Hobby Lobby* – Supreme Court agreed. If the employer had been a closely held for-profit company, the result in the case would have been impossible. The Court would have simply said that the company is bound by the Americans with Disabilities Act unless an exception applies, and it enjoys no protection under the Ministerial Exception because *it is not a religious entity.*

Moreover, as Justice Ruth Bader Ginsburg explained in her *Hobby Lobby* dissent, state law creates for-profit corporations as profit-making entities. They are not non-profits, and they receive numerous benefits, such as tax breaks, in many states and localities. This does not mean that they are incapable of some forms of non-profit-orientated expression, but it does mean that as a legal entity they have no religion to substantially burden in violation of RFRA. These entities have many constituencies including the owners, employees, customers, and in some cases non-owner board members. The *Hobby Lobby* Court assumed that the owners are the corporation, but this is overly simplistic when the employees are just as much a part of the corporate entity as the owners.

Finally, and perhaps most importantly, since for-profit entities serve the general public and often have a diverse array of employees, assertions of religious freedom by these entities have a greater potential to harm third parties who are not coreligionists as happened in *Hobby Lobby*, *Elane Photography*, and *Masterpiece Cakeshop*. It is these conflicts that most threaten religious freedom generally – the conflicts that *Hobby Lobby* enabled by *both* protecting for-profit entities and implying, over the objection of the dissenting opinions and Justice Kennedy's concurring opinion, that religious accommodations could harm third parties. Religious freedom must give way when the rights of non-coreligionists are endangered or harmed lest religious freedom as an enterprise risk its own demise as demonstrated in the next section. Harm to third parties who are not coreligionists is more likely to happen in the for-profit context because employees and customers of larger companies are rarely, if ever, going to all be coreligionists. As you will see, this opens a can of worms that threatens to infest religious freedom generally.

Additionally, as noted, the evidence that protecting for-profit entities is harming religious freedom even for traditional religious entities is mounting. Moreover, it is casting religious freedom in a negative public light that tends to replicate itself and has become a trope regularly repeated by characterizing religious freedom as a basis for allowing companies to discriminate. This third factor and the vast evidence to support it are addressed in the next section.

The argument that the religious freedom of for-profit entities should not be protected will be uncomfortable for many religious freedom advocates. In fact, the highly pragmatic nature of the argument may be viewed by some as a lack of commitment to principle or a copout. If one is truly committed to religious freedom, the argument would go, there is no room for pragmatic compromise that would force people of faith to become complicit in what they view as sin. I respect this position, but I respectfully disagree.

If one is committed to religious freedom and the entire enterprise is at risk because a group of people – owners of for-profit businesses – who were never protected in the business context under the rubric of religious freedom as a historical matter have become protected, I say compromise before even traditional religious entities find their religious freedom at risk. Does this demonstrate a lack of true commitment to religious freedom or a half-hearted, naïve view of religious freedom? Well ... no. It demonstrates a pragmatic recognition of reality on the street and a commitment to save religious freedom from those who cannot compromise because they view the stakes in any compromise as too high. Again, I respect these people's commitment just as I respect the commitment of sexual freedom advocates who want no compromise that would allow even traditional religious entities to discriminate. They, too, are wrong despite the courage of their convictions.

In the real world of the culture wars, those who cannot compromise at all will eventually be at the mercy of any contrary social trend that goes against their position. In the twenty-first century, most social trends point against favoring religious freedom over sexual freedom and the overwhelmingly negative public and business response to state RFRAs in recent years, which is heavily based on concerns over protection of for-profit entities demonstrates this. These situations are addressed next.

B The Proof

Many advocates of religious freedom hailed the *Hobby Lobby* decision as an important and welcomed victory. If it is a victory, it is a pyrrhic one, because it threatens to undermine religious freedom more generally. I promised I would offer proof of this point. Offering that proof is the purpose of this section.

Religious freedom has recently come under blistering attacks in public discourse. Both the courts and the public have been slow to understand "lived religion," the idea that for many people of faith, religion is inseparable from other aspects of life and is lived daily, not just at services on Saturday or Sunday. Ironically, while the *Hobby Lobby* decision recognizes this, it does so in a context where lived religion is asserted by a for-profit entity to the detriment of employees who do not necessarily share the owners' faith commitments, thus giving further ammunition to those attacking religious freedom.

As this section explains, protecting for-profit entities, whether large closely held corporations such as Hobby Lobby or smaller public accommodations such as Elane Photography and Masterpiece Cakeshop, will undermine religious freedom in the long run. There are two reasons for this.

First, as rights have been applied to broader classes of people and situations, the courts have often interpreted those rights more narrowly for everyone.[26] Second, we are already witnessing significant backlash against the *Hobby Lobby* decision in battles over state RFRAs and other state and federal legislation. Moreover, arguments that for-profit corporations should be protected by RFRA and the decision in *Hobby Lobby* confirming this have helped push religious freedom directly into the culture wars in a way that it was not before these claims arose. Both in public discourse and in legislative battles, *Hobby Lobby* has left a wake of destruction for religious freedom and discourse about religious freedom, and this trend is only beginning.

RFRA was once seen as being about protecting religious minorities and other religious people from state intrusion on their religious freedom, but RFRA is increasingly being characterized as a license for religious entities to discriminate and harm third parties. This undermines arguments for passing more state RFRAs and may undermine existing RFRAs.

1 Broadening Rights Often Narrows Their Depth

The legal historian Philip Hamburger has explained that by expanding the substance of free exercise rights, advocates of religious freedom have actually narrowed the depth of those rights:

> "In this way, the conditions imposed [on free exercise] during the last half of the twentieth century suggest how well-intentioned efforts to enlarge a right can inflate it so far as to weaken it. It is

a strange legal trope, through which overstatement can have a cost. More really can be less."[27]

While I disagree with some of Hamburger's specific applications of the concept, his overall argument that courts often narrow rights after those rights have been enlarged is well supported in a variety of contexts. Other scholars have made the same point regarding freedom of speech and freedom of intimate association.[28]

Of course, the assertion made in this book is slightly different because RFRA is a statute, not a constitutional provision, and the expansion in this case is not of the right itself, but rather whom the right protects. Yet these two factors strengthen, rather than weaken, the concern that *Hobby Lobby* will move religious freedom for individuals and traditional religious entities backward. Courts deciding RFRA or state RFRA cases involving for-profit entities may be more wary in applying those statutes and in turn can set precedent for all claims under these statutes. Significantly, the phenomenon of "more being less" that Hamburger mentions in the free exercise context has been even more pronounced in the context of civil rights statutes.

The most obvious examples are the treatment by courts of sexual harassment, disparate treatment discrimination, disparate impact discrimination, and religious exemption claims under Title VII of the Civil Rights Act of 1964;[29] claims for accommodation and disparate treatment under the Americans with Disabilities Act;[30] and the application of 42 U.S.C. §1983 – a statute that allows people to sue when government violates certain civil rights generally.[31] Each of these laws was initially broadly interpreted by courts and the laws themselves were intended to be interpreted broadly, yet each was ultimately interpreted more narrowly – in some cases shockingly so – by the Supreme Court or lower courts. There are many other examples, but the civil rights examples are most similar to the RFRA context.

Moreover, both under civil rights statutes and the Constitution, expansion of the individuals/entities protected has led to a narrowing of rights. This can be seen clearly under the Americans with Disabilities Act and the Free Speech Clause. It is useful to explore some of these examples in further depth. The following three examples do so. The first explores the growth and retrenchment of hostile work environment law under Title VII of the Civil Rights Act of 1964. The second explores a remarkable limitation imposed by the U.S. Supreme Court under the Americans with Disabilities Act that was ultimately undone by Congress. The third example comes from constitutional law: the Free Exercise Clause itself.

a Example 1: Hostile Work Environment Sexual Harassment

The Supreme Court recognized a hostile work environment as a form of workplace sexual harassment at the federal level in 1986. That case, *Meritor Savings Bank v. Vinson*,[32] recognized a relatively broad right. The Court held that Title VII of the Civil Rights Act of 1964 is "not limited to 'economic' or 'tangible' discrimination"[33] and is aimed at "the entire spectrum of disparate treatment of men and women in employment."[34] In doing so, the Court held that a claim for hostile work environment could be established if unwelcome conduct in the workplace based on gender was "severe or pervasive" enough to create a "hostile or abusive work environment."[35] This right was quickly and appropriately expanded to apply to other areas protected under Title VII, including race, religion, and national origin.

Yet, two important questions remained regarding how one determines what constitutes a hostile work environment. First, what aspects of the workplace are to be considered in determining whether discrimination is severe or pervasive enough to create a hostile work environment? Second, from whose perspective must the environment be hostile? The victim's? The harassers? Some third option? The first question was far easier to answer than the second.

The answer to the first question is that courts should look to all of the circumstances to determine what constitutes a hostile work environment. The second question is more important, however, because it determines from whose perspective the conduct should be viewed. Should it be a reasonable person? A reasonable woman? Or some other perspective? Ultimately, the Court adopted a reasonable person standard.[36] In failing to adapt a reasonable woman standard (or reasonable member of the same protected class standard), the Court ignored both hints in earlier decisions that the standard is a reasonable woman standard and significant scholarly criticism of the reasonable person standard.

This was an important setback to the breadth of the hostile work environment cause of action, but the retrenchment was far from over. Lower courts seemed uncomfortable with the breadth of the right, even before the Supreme Court applied the reasonable person standard.[37] After that, however, courts had an easy tool to find no hostile work environment existed, even in cases where reasonable minds might disagree.[38] This trend has been significant, as the originally broad protection against hostile work environments has become weaker with fewer plaintiffs winning.[39] The right was born, expanded, and then after its expansion severely restricted. This is just one of many such examples under Title VII of the Civil Rights Act of 1964, including religious accommodation.

b Example 2: Reasonable Accommodation under the Americans with Disabilities Act   Numerous examples show the Supreme Court or lower courts limiting protection under the Americans with Disabilities Act, despite the fact that the law specifically states it is to be construed broadly.[40] Most of these cases involve claims by disabled individuals for reasonable accommodation. The judicial rollback of the Americans with Disabilities Act seems to be heavily motivated by the fact that the Act was designed to cover a broad range of people.[41]

One of the most notorious examples of this phenomenon can be seen in the Supreme Court's decisions in *Sutton v. United Air Lines, Inc.*[42] and *Murphy v. United Parcel Service, Inc.*[43] Congress ultimately overturned these decisions in an amendment to the Americans with Disabilities Act, but the holdings in these cases are a prime example of how courts often narrowly interpret a law because of the breadth of the law. The cases addressed whether the definition of an "individual with a disability" should be determined based on the individual's unmitigated condition (i.e., the condition without regard to medication or prosthetics) or the individual's mitigated condition (i.e., the condition as treated by medication or prosthetics). This question is exceptionally important because if the determination of who is disabled is made based on the mitigated condition, many individuals with disabilities will not be covered by the Americans with Disabilities Act. Therefore, these individuals would be unable to request accommodation for their disabilities even where failure to accommodate would exacerbate a disability to the point that it is no longer mitigated by medication.

Prior to the Court's decisions in *Sutton* and *Murphy*, the answer seemed clear. Mitigating measures such as medications and prosthetics were not to be considered in determining whether someone is disabled for ADA purposes. In fact, all three agencies charged with implementing the Americans with Disabilities Act, and all but one of the courts that had addressed the issue, considered this threshold question a straightforward one.[44] This view was supported by substantial legislative history.[45]

The Supreme Court disregarded all of this and held over strong dissents in both cases that the plain meaning of the law required mitigating measures to be considered in disability determinations.[46] This was a huge rollback of Americans with Disabilities Act protection, but it is only one of many examples. The Court's decisions in these cases effectively precluded many individuals with disabilities from getting accommodations under the act if their disabilities were controlled by medications – unless they could show that they were "regarded as disabled" under the act, which was an argument that the Court also substantially limited.[47] Ironically, as a result of these individuals not being considered disabled, employers could plausibly discriminate against them based on their impairments without running afoul of the Americans with Disabilities Act.[48]

These decisions were odd because the Americans with Disabilities Act has specific language stating it is to be interpreted broadly to prevent employment discrimination based on unfounded stereotypes of disabilities and disabled individuals.[49] By removing individuals from the act's coverage by answering the threshold question of whether they are disabled, the Court denied them protection entirely. And, because the Court also made it less likely that such individuals would meet the "regarded as" having a disability standard, even an employer's use of broad-based stereotypes may not be of help to these individuals.[50] This effectively removed many employees with disabilities from coverage under the act and may actually have protected employers who discriminate based on unfounded stereotypes, misconceptions, or outright animus. Congress corrected this by amending the law to make it clear – though it already was clear prior to the Court's decisions – that whether someone is disabled according to the Americans with Disabilities Act must be determined based on that person's unmitigated condition.

Simply put, courts know how to limit statutory protections – even against the weight of the rules of statutory interpretation – when they view the statute as too broad. While the Americans with Disabilities Act was initially interpreted to cover more individuals, both the substance of that protection and the protection itself – even for those obviously intended to be protected under the act – was significantly limited. And unlike religious freedom, the Americans with Disabilities Act was not smack in the middle of the culture wars at the time the issues arose.

c Example 3: The Free Exercise Clause   As you learned in Chapter 2, the history of claims for exemptions to generally applicable laws under the Free Exercise Clause is full of twists and turns, but in the end it demonstrates that as rights became more broadly recognized, a retrenchment occurred turning the promise of more religious freedom into a tale of less religious freedom. The U.S. Supreme Court's initial struggles with the issue led to the development of a dichotomy between belief and practice. *Reynolds v. U.S.*[51] is generally considered a major early precedent for this dichotomy. Essentially, the dichotomy suggests that belief must be protected to have religious freedom, but behavior/practice may be regulated (under generally applicable laws in the modern version) for the good of society. This dichotomy was formally altered in the landmark case of *Sherbert v. Verner*,[52] and in turn this was undermined by the Court's decision in *Employment Division v. Smith*,[53] which is discussed at length in Chapter 2.

I have argued elsewhere that this account of the evolution of free exercise rights and their subsequent destruction in *Smith* is flawed.[54] Sadly, the free exercise rights set forth in *Sherbert* were on the decline within fifteen years after that decision as the Court began to chip away at the broad protection recognized in that case. Also of note is the fact that religious minorities (especially non-Christian religious minorities) did not reap great benefits from *Sherbert*.[55]

In *Sherbert*, the Court abandoned the belief/practice dichotomy and held clearly that a state must have a compelling governmental interest for denying a religious exemption when a generally applicable law substantially burdens someone's religion.[56] In that case, the plaintiff was denied unemployment benefits after being fired for refusing to work on her Sabbath. The Court held that the state did not have a compelling interest for denying the benefits and, in fact, noted that the state unemployment laws contained a number of exemptions including one for Sunday Sabbatarians. *Sherbert* offered a broad recognition of rights under the Free Exercise Clause. Earlier cases had been a mixed bag, although as Philip Hamburger explains, the application of any test, including the compelling interest test, may narrow free exercise more than originally intended by the framers of the Free Exercise Clause.[57]

After *Sherbert*, it remained to be seen how the Court in subsequent cases would greet this broad reading of the Free Exercise Clause. In *Wisconsin v. Yoder*,[58] the Court held that Amish families with high school age children were entitled to exemptions from the state's compulsory education laws in the absence of a compelling state interest and narrow tailoring. The Court looked at the Amish community's track record of good citizenship, hard work, and the success of its young people within the community to demonstrate that the state had no compelling interest for denying the exemption.

Following *Yoder*, however, the Court decided a string of free exercise exemption cases in which the plaintiffs almost always lost, and in which non-Christian plaintiffs always lost.[59] With the exception of a few unemployment cases,[60] the compelling interest test was turned into a paper tiger. In some cases, the nature of the government institution – for example, the military or prisons – served as a basis for not applying the compelling interest test. In others, the relief requested was decisive in not applying the compelling interest test: for example, cases where the government entity involved would have had to change its policies to grant an exemption. Finally, in some cases the court ostensibly applied the compelling interest test, but in a manner that rendered it anything but strict scrutiny. It should be noted, however, that *Sherbert* and *Yoder* did influence the outcomes of some lower court cases.[61]

In *Employment Division v. Smith*, Native American employees of a drug rehabilitation center were fired and subsequently denied unemployment benefits because they used peyote at a ritual service. No evidence indicated that these employees used peyote at any time other than the ritual services; in fact, their religion forbade use outside of ritual ceremonies. They sued under the Free Exercise Clause of the First Amendment to the Constitution to receive unemployment benefits. In an opinion written by Justice Antonin Scalia, the Supreme Court explicitly restored the belief/practice dichotomy and held that the state need not create exemptions to laws of general applicability to accommodate religious practices. The Court noted that states remained free to create exemptions to laws that have an adverse impact on religious practices. Such exemptions are often referred to as "permissive accommodations." Such accommodations are a basis for providing some of the accommodations I argue for even when government is not required to do so by a state or federal law: for example, the accommodation of some county clerks suggested in Chapter 4 and the limited accommodation for public accommodations that I suggested earlier in this chapter.

Since the *Smith* Court held there is no duty to provide exemptions to generally applicable laws, the compelling interest test set forth in *Sherbert* was limited to the unemployment context, where a variety of exemptions are generally built into the unemployment laws. Furthermore, the Court held that the claim in *Smith* was different from earlier free exercise cases granting exemptions to unemployment laws because the claimants in *Smith* sought an exemption based on illegal conduct, while the claimants in the earlier cases sought an exemption based on religious conduct that was otherwise legal.

Yoder was harder to distinguish, but the Court created the concept of "hybrid rights" – and I stress the word "created" because the concept makes no legal sense. As you may recall, in "hybrid rights" cases the Free Exercise Clause right is connected to some other important right (in the case of *Yoder*, parental rights). This concept was used to distinguish several earlier cases that involved freedom of expression and free exercise concerns, as well as to distinguish *Yoder*. Yet, to characterize *Yoder* as a hybrid rights case is patently disingenuous.

Moreover, the concept of "hybrid rights" makes no sense whatsoever. Is the Court saying that two inadequate constitutional rights combined can make an adequate one? If so, it would not be hard to hybridize almost anything into a viable constitutional right. Or are hybrid rights the combination of two adequate constitutional rights? This possibility is precluded by the *Smith* Court's reasoning that clearly the Free Exercise Clause right would be inadequate by itself in an exemption case. This leaves two possibilities. First, the other constitutional right in the hybrid rights context would be adequate on its own and the Free Exercise Clause right is not; in which case, why mention the Free Exercise Clause in exemption cases when it essentially serves no function other than being an antidiscrimination principle? Second, and apparently accurately, hybrid rights are just a judicial creation to get around inconvenient precedent.[62] The last possibility seems to be the obvious answer.[63]

Divorcing *Smith* from all the important baggage regarding *stare decises* (the general idea that the Supreme Court should follow its own precedent) and so on, we are left with the basic notion that the Free Exercise Clause does not require exemptions to generally applicable laws. The argument seems to be that because these laws are religion neutral, the Free Exercise Clause has no impact on them except through the political process. This of course begs the question of whether such laws can ever be neutral given the vast array of religions and huge amount of government activity in the United States. The history of Free Exercise Clause jurisprudence, especially in the latter part of the twentieth century, is a staggering example of the "more is less" phenomenon.[64]

The "more is less" phenomenon is the first way in which religious freedom protection for for-profit entities might lead to less religious freedom for everyone else, including traditional religious entities. Sadly, the "more is less" phenomenon is not the biggest concern that protecting for-profit entities raises in this context. The biggest concern, addressed in the next section, is the public backlash against religious freedom and the effect of that backlash on limiting legislation that might otherwise have been passed to protect individuals and traditional religious entities.

2 *The Legal and Public Response to* Hobby Lobby
At the time of this writing, the *Hobby Lobby* decision has only been on the books for a short while. Yet it has already led, in part, to the failure

of state RFRAs in Michigan[65] and Georgia;[66] to serious challenges to a proposed RFRA in Maine,[67] and an earlier proposed RFRA in Georgia;[68] to the possible repeal of the Indiana RFRA, which was met with huge public backlash when it passed, was then amended to remove protection for most for-profit entities that discriminate, but has still faced at least one attempted repeal;[69] to legislation that could dramatically limit religious freedom even for traditional legal entities in California;[70] and to the potential weakening of state RFRAs in other states that require contraceptive coverage under state law.[71] Moreover, public outrage over the *Hobby Lobby* decision has blurred the line between traditional religious entities and for-profit entities and has changed the perception of RFRA from being a civil rights/civil liberties statute to one that threatens civil rights and civil liberties. And this is just the beginning.

For those who view *Hobby Lobby* as an important victory for religious freedom, the recent experience with the state RFRA proposed in Michigan should be quite sobering. Even those who deeply agree with *Hobby Lobby* cannot ignore the role it played in preventing passage of Michigan's RFRA. As will be shown, RFRA was often portrayed as a license for companies to discriminate and not meet their duties under state and federal law based on religious objections.[72] As will also be shown, the for-profit Health and Human Services (HHS) mandate litigation led, in part, to the failure of state RFRAs in Ohio and Kentucky (although a new bill has been moving through the Kentucky legislature).[73]

The Michigan Religious Freedom Restoration Act, HB 5958, was introduced on November 13, 2014, by state representative Jase Bolger. Another bill was introduced that would amend Michigan's Elliott Larsen Act (a civil rights law) to include statewide protection against discrimination in housing and employment for gays and lesbians. Notably, that bill did not include transgender individuals, which led to an alternative bill proposed by representative Sam Singh. Had either of these amendments passed the state House of Representatives, it would have provided a statewide compelling interest for government to protect gays and lesbians from discrimination based on religious assertions. Representative Bolger supported both bills. The latter bill seemed especially aimed at for-profit entities since the Elliott Larsen

Act has an exemption for traditional religious entities. The fact that its defeat was a key element that worked against the state RFRA becoming law is a great example of how passing antidiscrimination legislation protecting members of the LGBT community may be essential to robust religious freedom in some places and vice versa in others.

From the time HB 5958 was introduced, however, the Michigan RFRA was portrayed as a license for companies to avoid legal obligations and to discriminate. On December 4, 2014, the state house voted 59–50 to pass the Michigan RFRA, and it was then referred to the state senate. Media coverage regularly portrayed the law as a license for companies to discriminate and avoid legal obligations. Television ads were run doing the same. Opponents of RFRA must have been quietly grateful for the weapon that *Hobby Lobby* gave them.

Public support for the state RFRA weakened further when the state house voted down the proposed extension of the Elliott Larsen Act to protect gays and lesbians from discrimination on December 3, just one day before the state house approved the RFRA. Concerns were raised repeatedly about businesses using RFRA to support discrimination and avoid legal requirements. If traditional religious entities were the only ones that would have been protected by RFRA, the debate would have been quite different. Some might have still objected to allowing even churches to discriminate based on sexual orientation, but for many that was not the concern.

The concern was stated plainly in numerous news reports, articles, and op-ed pieces around the state. The worry was that companies, public accommodations, and landlords would be able to discriminate against LGBT individuals based on religious convictions, pharmacists would be able to refuse to fill prescriptions for contraceptives (an issue addressed in Chapter 6), and employers would be able to fire non-coreligionists, among similar concerns.

Others, including Representative Bolger, insisted that the bill was designed to protect religious freedom so that, for example, Jewish parents could object to autopsies being performed on a child as per Jewish law – in other words, the traditional bread-and-butter cases under RFRA. The problem was, however, that HB 5958 did not define "person" for purposes of the state religious freedom protection, and therefore the state supreme court might have interpreted the state

RFRA to include for-profit entities just as the U.S. Supreme Court interpreted the federal RFRA in *Hobby Lobby*.

The Michigan Supreme Court already protects religious freedom under the state constitution by applying the pre-*Smith* compelling interest test, but that could change in one decision, so the impetus for a state RFRA still existed. The state RFRA, however, was patterned on the federal RFRA; since it did not define the term "person" to exclude for-profit entities, there was a valid concern that the Michigan Supreme Court might follow *Hobby Lobby* if the state RFRA were enacted, even though it did not follow *Smith*.

Public pressure against the state RFRA was strong, and the bill languished for weeks in the state senate. Additionally, there was no guarantee that the governor would have signed the bill had it made it to his desk. The state RFRA had become a political hot potato even for the Republican-controlled senate, so the governor was wary. As the legislative session came to a close, the Senate had an opportunity to vote on the bill, but it never came to a vote and thus the quest for a state RFRA ended in the state senate. There is little doubt that if the bill enjoyed broader public support and was not seen as a license for businesses to discriminate, it would have passed. Thus, it is not an overstatement to say that without *Hobby Lobby*, the result might have been different.

If this were an isolated incident, perhaps it could be dismissed. It is, however, just one example in an evolving trend. As opposed to the wide-ranging support for the federal RFRA in 1993, today religious freedom claims are regularly characterized in the media and by some legislators as licenses to discriminate. In Arizona, Governor Brewer vetoed a "religious liberty bill" that would have included protection for for-profit businesses only a few months before *Hobby Lobby* was decided. The bill ignited a firestorm of condemnation and was opposed by women's rights groups, LGBT groups, business groups, a number of religious groups, the Chamber of Commerce, and others. The idea of protecting for-profit businesses from general laws based on religious objections was seen by many in Arizona and in the national media as backward and dangerous.

More troubling, however, was the bleed between exempting for-profit businesses and other religious organizations in some of the media coverage of the situation in Arizona. Much of the coverage, and certainly Governor Brewer's veto, were based on the protection the religious liberty bill would have afforded for-profit entities, but some of the rhetoric in Arizona opposed religious exemptions generally. This was also true in Ohio, Kentucky, and Georgia, where more traditional RFRA bills failed, in part, because of concerns that they would have allowed for-profit entities to discriminate. After *Hobby Lobby*, this bleed between the arguments against religious exemptions for for-profit entities and religious exemptions generally has increased, as was seen in Michigan. Michigan is not alone, however.

Recent RFRA legislation in Maine,[74] Indiana,[75] and a new bill in Georgia[76] faced strong opposition that would have been unthinkable a few years ago. In fact, the Indiana law was ultimately passed, resulted in significant public backlash because it included protection for for-profit entities, was amended to remove that protection where for-profit entities seek to use religious claims as a basis to discriminate, and yet may soon be repealed because of concerns by citizens, politicians, and local businesses. Even in Georgia, where one would think RFRA legislation might receive a warmer welcome, there has been serious backlash, and the governor recently vetoed a religious freedom bill passed by the legislature after the state was threatened with boycotts and other negative economic consequences.[77]

After *Hobby Lobby* this backlash is especially understandable. Business groups, LGBT groups, patients rights groups, and women's rights groups have all spoken out against these state RFRAs as licenses to discriminate, bad for business in the state, and bad for the freedom of third parties that might be affected by these exemptions. In Maine, similar opposition has formed and the bill has been portrayed by many in the media and by legislators who oppose it as a step backwards for the state of Maine.

Yet as noted earlier, most of the exemptions under these laws would go to religious individuals and entities that were not considered in the legislative process. It is the failure to define "persons" in a manner that excludes for-profit entities – or worse, defining "persons" explicitly to include for-profit entities that gives the opposition to these acts enough fuel to ignite a fire. Most troubling is that the lines between religious exemptions for individuals and religious entities and those for for-profit entities, government officials, and other individuals and groups that deal with the public generally are being blurred. The movement against RFRA is more and more against religious exemptions generally rather than just exemptions for for-profit entities.

Ironically, those promoting the RFRA legislation in state legislatures are either blind to or politically incapable of defining "person" to protect only religious individuals and traditional religious entities. This too is part of the culture wars. Many of those supporting this legislation *do* want to protect for-profit entities and others that serve the public generally from antidiscrimination laws based on sexual orientation or from providing services to which religious individuals object. This may seem to be laudable idealism, but it is in fact a shortsighted strategy. In trying to protect these individuals from modern views on social issues, protections for religious individuals who do not serve the general public and for traditional religious entities may be sacrificed.

This phenomenon has only become worse since the Supreme Court decision recognizing a constitutional right to same-sex marriage in *Obergefell v. Hodges.* In some states, legislators have openly proposed using RFRAs or religious freedom protections to discriminate against the rights of same-sex couples.[78] While this might play in their home districts, they might as well take a gun and point it at religious freedom in America and pull the trigger, because their pandering and/or shortsightedness is leading to the slow death of religious freedom more broadly. Thankfully situations such as the Utah compromise give us hope that there is a cure to this affliction.

Significantly, the laws that may be most helpful to religious freedom if they pass are those that seek to redefine "person" in federal or state RFRAs to exclude for-profit entities. These would protect the core of RFRAs in garden-variety cases, and perhaps remind the public that most RFRA claims are not about discrimination by for-profit companies but rather about protecting religious freedom for individuals and traditional religious entities in contexts that do not interfere with others' civil or political rights.

Legislation has also been proposed since *Hobby Lobby* that could be destructive of religious freedom generally; most notably, a California proposal would deny religious exemptions even to traditional religious entities.[79] These proposed laws are countered by legislation in still other states attempting to broaden RFRA protection for a wider array of religious entities, but these latter bills have received much negative media attention and are only likely to be successful in states where social conservatives have strong control, and those where the state legislature suffers from the same shortsightedness mentioned earlier. Yet, the trend nationally, fueled by *Hobby Lobby*, to characterize religious exemptions in a negative way seems the more charged movement at this point.

One final trend in a number of states involves a potential conflict that has arisen since *Hobby Lobby* between state mandatory contraceptive coverage laws and state RFRAs (or state constitutional interpretations that follow pre-*Smith* legal approaches). Most of these state mandatory contraception coverage laws have exemptions for traditional religious entities. Since *Hobby Lobby*, there has been concern that for-profit entities may be exempted in some states. Connecticut is a good example of this phenomenon. The movement seems to be toward making it clear that for-profit entities are not exempt from these contraceptive coverage laws, but some in the public have begun to question exemptions for any entity that employs people who are not coreligionists.

As the situation in Michigan and the other states demonstrates, public perception of religious freedom is changing. When the federal RFRA was passed more than twenty years ago, a wide range of civil liberties, civil rights, and religious groups supported it.[80] Today many of these same groups have shifted their positions and oppose RFRA legislation.[81] The raison d'être for this shift is the impact that religious freedom claims can have on innocent third parties. This concern is most obvious when for-profit businesses are protected by RFRA but also in other circumstances, such as when religious hospitals allegedly refuse to give proper medical treatment to pregnant women based on religious concerns. This latter issue raises a number of factors on both sides of the debate and is addressed in Chapter 6.

RFRA was once widely seen as landmark legislation protecting the religious freedom of those who are not considered in the legislative process. Now it is seen as a threat to women, LGBT individuals, and others who may be harmed if certain religious beliefs are accommodated. When a homeowner rented out a room and discriminated against LGBT individuals it made headlines,[82] but we still spoke in terms of that individual's religious freedom balanced against the state's interest in prohibiting discrimination. The homeowner might have won or lost in court depending on how the court viewed the weighing of those interests. Today, however, larger corporate landlords may try to discriminate citing *Hobby Lobby*. Whether they win or lose their cases, however, each such case will further alienate the public from the concept of religious freedom.

In a debate about *Hobby Lobby* several months before the case was decided, I argued that if Hobby Lobby won, within five years there would be significant backlash against religious freedom, and religious freedom would be eroded through the "more is less" phenomenon, legislative activity, public perception, and a failure to distinguish between traditional religious entities and for-profit entities. It seems I was naïve in thinking it would take five years for the decline in the perception of religious freedom to gain significant support from the *Hobby Lobby* decision. At the time of this writing, it has been less than three years since *Hobby Lobby* was decided, and *Hobby Lobby* has given significant PR support to those opposed to religious freedom.

As Douglas Laycock, a leading advocate for religious freedom who also supports civil rights for members of the LGBT community, has explained, both sides in the culture wars have dug in their heels, and coexistence of religious freedom and personal freedom is less the goal of either side:[83]

> There is no apparent prospect of either side agreeing to live and let live. Each side respects the liberties of the other only when it lacks the votes to impose its own views. Each side is intolerant of the other; each side wants a total win. The mutual insistence on total wins is very bad for religious liberty. The religious side persists in trying to regulate other people's sex lives and relationships so long as it thinks it has a chance of success. That motivates much of the other side's hostility to religious liberty. And those on the other side persist in demanding not only the right to live their own lives by their own values, but also the right to force religious objectors to assist them in doing so. And to that end, they are making arguments calculated to destroy religious liberty.[84]

In the long run, *Hobby Lobby* will add much weight to the political arguments on one side of the debate, and that side is not the one concerned about religious freedom. Failure to compromise in the public sphere when society is quickly changing in ways that go against what you believe, which may be important for some faiths or some people of faith, may be a victory of faith over modernity, but it is a sure way to lose in court and the court of public opinion over time.

3 A Brief Note on "Traditional Religious Entities"

I have used the term "traditional religious entities" throughout this book, and it is useful to elaborate on the meaning of this term. I engage in an in-depth discussion of the term in Chapter 7. The term, as used in this book, refers to those religious entities and adherents that have long been understood to be covered under the Free Exercise Clause of the First Amendment to the U.S. Constitution. These are also the individuals/entities that RFRA was designed to protect.

First, no one questions that individuals are protected under the Free Exercise Clause and RFRA. If government seeks to impose on an individual's free exercise of religion, it must meet the test set forth in RFRA (or state RFRAs, where applicable). A straightforward example of this is where a judge insists that a Muslim woman remove her hijab or a Jewish man remove his yarmulke in the courtroom. RFRA clearly prohibits the judge from enforcing this rule.

A number of religious entities have also been traditionally protected under the Free Exercise Clause and RFRA. The most obvious of these are churches, synagogues, mosques, temples, and so on. The Supreme Court long ago acknowledged that while the Free Exercise Clause (and therefore RFRA) was clearly designed to protect individuals, it could also protect the entities through which individuals of shared faith come together to express their religion.[85] While some have argued that these entities do not enjoy free exercise rights, the general consensus among judges, legislators, and scholars is that they do.

Next are affiliates or auxiliaries of religious entities: for example, a school or a soup kitchen run by a church. These entities too have been generally protected under the Free Exercise Clause and RFRA.[86] In a similar vein, non-profit religious entities such as Catholic

Charities or Jewish Family Services, to cite two examples, have been protected.[87] These entities are generally bound by the requirements of §501(C)(3) of the Internal Revenue Code. For-profit entities are, of course, not bound by §501(C)(3).

Finally, and perhaps most controversially, are hospitals, adoption agencies, and universities that are run by religious entities. These entities are the focus of Chapters 6 and 7, and an in-depth discussion of what should happen when the religious concerns of these entities conflict with the interests of third parties will be left to those chapters. For now, it is enough to note that powerful arguments have been made on both sides. Some have argued for excluding these entities from Free Exercise Clause and RFRA protections because they generally serve the broader community. Others have argued that these entities serve the core religious mission of the religious entity and that hospitals and healthcare providers already have religious exemptions to performing religiously objectionable procedures under state law in many states. These exemptions themselves have been controversial in their own right.

For purposes of defining "traditional religious entities," I include all of these entities – not because they will necessarily win when their actions conflict with the rights of others, but because they are generally non-profit parts of a religious sect's mission, and in most cases where exemptions are requested, they are openly serving the religious mission of the sect. This makes them different from for-profit entities and general public accommodations, even if that difference does not automatically determine the outcome in cases involving these entities. It is not surprising then that these entities too have generally been protected by the Free Exercise Clause and RFRA. Significantly, however, the government has a greater number of compelling interests and fewer means to meet those interests when a hospital or university serves the general public.

III CLAIMS FOR RELIGIOUS EXEMPTIONS BY LANDLORDS

A number of recent cases have been filed concerning discrimination by landlords against same-sex couples, but in a number of the ones that have received a good amount of media attention, religious freedom was not asserted as a basis for the alleged discrimination. For example a number of cases have been filed against landlords in New York City, mostly in rent-controlled or rent-stabilized buildings. In most of these cases, the landlord refused to add the same-sex spouse to the lease even after New York recognized same-sex marriage; but in almost all of these cases, the reasons appear to be financial because adding someone to a lease could prolong the period under which the lease could be renewed at the lower rates required under rent control and rent stabilization. These are cases of housing discrimination against same-sex couples, but they are not based on religion.

In a case filed in Colorado in January 2016, a psychic is alleged to have engaged in housing discrimination when she denied a lease to a same-sex couple. Apparently, her psychic abilities did not reach likely lawsuits. All joking aside, in this case too there seems to be no religious motivation. It is too early to tell what the psychic's defense will be; based on media coverage so far, she has not raised any religious basis and has asserted she was worried about noise from the couple's children. However, correspondence between her and the couple apparently refutes this as the basis for the lease denial. Regardless, unless a defense based in religion is raised during the litigation, this case too does not have religious elements. I only mention this and the New York cases because lawsuits have been filed in those cases, and they demonstrate that not every case of discrimination against same-sex couples by landlords will involve a religious freedom claim.

Yet incidents of housing discrimination have occurred based on marital status where the landlord has asserted a religious defense for the discrimination. These cases have not generally involved same-sex couples, but because they pit a violation of antidiscrimination laws governing housing against a religious defense, they are instructive. And, of course, now that same-sex marriage is a nationally recognized constitutional right, there will likely be additional cases of housing discrimination against same-sex couples.

What will make these cases especially sensitive when religion is raised as a defense is that RLUIPA, which has been found to be constitutional and binding on the states,[88] protects religious freedom claims in the housing context. Yet the federal – and many state and

Fair Housing Act has been increasingly interpreted to protect against discrimination aimed at same-sex couples, as have many state and local laws.[89] Moreover, *Obergefell v. Hodges* raises strong constitutional rights that also come into play. Making matters even more complicated, it appears that *Hobby Lobby* would protect large but closely held commercial landlords under RFRA and by implication RLUIPA, because the *Hobby Lobby* Court based its interpretation of RFRA heavily on RLUIPA.

I am a fan of the television sitcom *The Big Bang Theory*; at first glance, this seems to be one big game of rock, paper, scissors, lizard, Spock. I mean this to suggest that the rules for who wins against whom might be hard to determine without some sort of answer key. Fortunately, we have a shortcut to determine the likely winner of the game because we already have cases that have addressed the housing discrimination issue when a religious defense is asserted.

Two important cases address violations of antidiscrimination laws based on marital status by landlords who raised a freedom of religion defense: *Swanner v. Anchorage Equal Rights Commission*,[90] decided by the Supreme Court of Alaska in 1994, and *State v. French*, decided by the Supreme Court of Minnesota in 1990, although a few portions of the *French* opinion read as if it were written in 1890.[91] Following subsequent legislative clarification and judicial decisions in Minnesota, as well as the Supreme Court's decision in *Lawrence v. Texas*, it is likely that *State v. French* is no longer good law. Therefore, *Swanner* is the most helpful case for addressing potential conflicts between antidiscrimination laws and religious defenses to those laws in the housing context.

In *Swanner*, a landlord refused to rent apartments to three unmarried men who planned to live with women. The city of Anchorage prohibits discrimination based on "marital status" under its municipal code. Many states and localities have similar protections against discrimination based on marital status. The landlord did not dispute that he would have rented to the men if the women they planned to live with were their spouses. In fact, he was completely forthright and honest that he would not rent to unmarried couples because doing so would violate his religious values.

The men filed claims under the municipal code and won. The case wound its way up to the Alaska Supreme Court. The landlord made two arguments. First, he argued that refusing to rent to unmarried couples is not "marital discrimination" for purposes of the Anchorage municipal code; and second, even if it were "marital discrimination," enforcing that provision of the municipal code against him would violate his religious freedom under both the U.S. and Alaska constitutions. The Alaska Supreme Court held against the landlord on the first issue:

> Because Swanner would have rented the properties to the couples had they been married, and he refused to rent the property only after he learned they were not, Swanner unlawfully discriminated on the basis of marital status.[92]

This is consistent with the way in which a number of other states and localities have interpreted the term "marital status" in antidiscrimination laws, albeit in different contexts.

The court then turned to Swanner's argument that requiring him to rent to unmarried couples violates his free exercise rights. The court recognized that the law does place a burden on his religion, but following *Employment Division v. Smith*, the court held that the law applies the same to all landlords and is not targeted at religion. Therefore, there is no violation of the First Amendment to the United States Constitution. The court, however, found that the Alaska constitution gives greater free exercise rights. States are free to give greater rights under their constitutions than those given by the U.S. Constitution.

Therefore, the court applied the same test that would be applied under RFRA or RLUIPA. Does the government have an extremely strong interest in prohibiting discrimination based on marital status, and if so, is enforcing the antidiscrimination provision narrowly tailored to meet that interest? The court held that the answer to both questions is "yes."

As to the first issue, the court held as follows:

> The government views acts of discrimination as independent social evils even if the prospective tenants ultimately find housing. Allowing housing discrimination that degrades individuals, affronts human dignity, and limits one's opportunities results in harming the government's transactional interest in preventing such discrimination.[93]

As to the second question, the court held that the state's "most effective tool" for "combatting discrimination is to prohibit discrimination," and "these laws do exactly that."[94]

Interestingly, *Swanner* raised the very conflict mentioned earlier in this section that people of faith may be placed in if forced by state law to violate their religious tenets. The court's response, while written twenty years before *Hobby Lobby*, is an apt response to the *Hobby Lobby* Court's reasoning:

> Swanner complains that applying the antidiscrimination laws to his business activities presents him with a "Hobson's choice" – to give up his economic livelihood or act in contradiction to his religious beliefs . . .
>
> Swanner has made no showing of a religious belief which requires that he engage in the property-rental business. Additionally, the economic burden, or "Hobson's choice," of which he complains, is caused by his choice to enter into a commercial activity that is regulated by antidiscrimination laws. Swanner is voluntarily engaging in property management. The law and ordinance regulate unlawful practices in the rental of real property and provide that those who engage in those activities shall not discriminate on the basis of marital status. Voluntary commercial activity does not receive the same status accorded to directly religious activity.
>
> "As [James] Madison summarized the point, free exercise should prevail in every case where it does not trespass on private rights or the public peace." Michael W. McConnell, *Free Exercise Revisionism and the Smith Decision*, 57 Chi.L.Rev. 1109, 1145 (1990) (citation omitted). Because Swanner's religiously impelled actions trespass on the private right of unmarried couples to not be unfairly discriminated against in housing, he cannot be granted an exemption from the housing antidiscrimination laws. Therefore, we conclude that enforcement of [the municipal code] against Swanner does not violate his right to free exercise of religion under the Alaska Constitution.[95]

As I explained earlier, such sentiments are of little solace to those who must face such a harsh choice, but when core values in a pluralistic society conflict something has to give. Here it was Swanner's right to enforce his religious values on others in a commercial transaction in violation of an antidiscrimination law.

The other case, *State v. French*, involved the same questions in a similar context, but against a legal backdrop that was quite different. The majority opinion for the Minnesota Supreme Court relied heavily on the existence of a Minnesota "anti-fornication law" that, according to the court majority, could prohibit premarital sex both in its definition of "marital status" and in its determination of whether the government has a compelling interest in cohabitation. Thus, the court held that the antidiscrimination provision did not apply to the context of cohabitation between members of the opposite sex who are not married, and that the state had no compelling interest in protecting cohabitation.

As was explained in Chapter 3, these "anti-fornication laws" (such as anti-sodomy laws), whether applied to straight or same-sex couples are now unconstitutional based on the Supreme Court's decision in *Lawrence v. Texas*, which held that consenting adults have a right to engage in consensual sexual conduct in private. Moreover, in 1988 the Minnesota legislature redefined "marital status." The majority in *State v. French* held that this redefinition did not change it's conclusion that the law does not apply to unmarried, opposite-sex cohabitants. Yet, subsequent events demonstrate that the court's interpretation of that law is quite different from the way it is understood today.[96] Therefore, *State v. French* does not appear to be relevant outside of the time and limited context in which it was decided.

So what happens when RLUIPA or a state RFRA is raised as a defense to discrimination that violates the federal Fair Housing Act or state antidiscrimination provisions that prohibit discrimination based on sexual orientation or marital status? The latter is important because if a landlord is willing to rent to a straight married or unmarried couple, it certainly would violate a marital status provision if the landlord refused to rent to a same-sex married couple, post-*Obegefell*. This is where the rock, paper, scissors, lizard, Spock analogy comes into play.

The U.S. Constitution has a Supremacy Clause, which is quite important in this context. That clause says that the U.S. Constitution trumps all law and federal law trumps state law in areas where the federal government has power.[97] Thus, the following situations could arise based on the laws mentioned earlier:

A Federal religious freedom laws (RLUIPA or RFRA) versus federal antidiscrimination laws (Fair Housing Act). In this context, the analysis would be based on whether the antidiscrimination law provides a compelling interest and is narrowly tailored to meet that interest. As suggested earlier in this chapter and by the court in *Swanner*, the antidiscrimination laws should prevail.

B Federal religious freedom laws (RFRA or RLUIPA) versus state antidiscrimination laws. In this context, the federal law is likely to prevail over the state law as a result of the Supremacy Clause.

C State RFRAs versus state or local antidiscrimination laws. This is similar to *Swanner*, and the analysis from that case makes the most sense in this context.

Obergefell v. Hodges reinforces the argument that antidiscrimination provisions should prevail in these contexts. Since same-sex couples now have a constitutional right to marry, antidiscrimination provisions prohibiting discrimination by landlords not only promote general antidiscrimination principles, which are important in and of themselves, but also reinforce the constitutional right to marry. After all, once married, the home is the marital home.

Therefore, as a general matter when antidiscrimination laws that protect against housing discrimination based on sexual orientation or marital status are violated and a religious freedom defense is asserted, the antidiscrimination principle should win out legally. The fact that under *Hobby Lobby* large closely held commercial landlords are protected under RFRA and/or RLUIPA makes this essential. If one of those landlords were to discriminate and, against the weight of the legal reasoning, win based on a religious freedom defense, the backlash against religious freedom would rise to new levels, and rightly so.

Yet what about people who rent a room or apartment in a house in which they live and occupy the majority of the home? They may choose to rent a room to earn a bit of extra money. Is it right to force them to forgo income that might enable them to stay in their home rather then become complicit in a relationship they believe to be a sin? As should be clear by now, no duty exists to accommodate such a person, but should a permissive accommodation be granted in the limited context where people are renting out part of the home in which they live? By now, you can probably guess my answer: yes. I view this accommodation as a very limited compromise that need not be but *should* be granted to spare those who are not commercial landlords *and* who are renting a part of the home in which they live from having to choose between their religion and potentially saving their home.

Reasonable minds can disagree on this. One could easily argue that once you open the door to this sort of discrimination, it is only a small step to protect all landlords. From the other perspective, one might argue: why draw the line where people rent units within their own homes? Complicity in sin is an issue in other contexts as well. My answer to both of these positions is that compromise in a pluralistic society is a good thing, and that drawing the line at renting a room or apartment in one's own home is not arbitrary. It is the very fact that the homeowner lives in the majority of the home that creates a clear line of demarcation.

6   CONSCIENCE CLAIMS

Conscience claims can arise in many contexts. Perhaps the most famous is conscientious objection to military service, which has a history going back to the beginning of the nation when Quakers objected to military service on religious grounds. Of course the most famous conscientious objection cases occurred during the Vietnam War, when the issue came to the fore in public discourse. Several court cases arose from conscientious objector claims during that era.

Yet it is in the healthcare context that conscience claims have been most prevalent in recent years. In this context, even the term "conscience claim" is controversial. This is the language often used by those advocating for conscience based exemptions to healthcare requirements. Opponents refer to them as "refusal claims", because they allow healthcare providers to refuse to provide services that they would otherwise be legally required to provide.

I understand that the terminology one chooses to use is not just a matter of semantics, but I decided to use the term "conscience" rather than "refusal." Although I agree with those who focus on the significant concerns that arise for women's healthcare when certain forms of conscience claims are protected without consideration of the impact on third parties, the simple fact is that these "refusals" are indeed based on religious or moral "conscience." Therefore the term "conscience" is the better representation of the reasons why we have these exemptions, even if it is not the better representation of the effects that these exemptions may have when they are written in a way that does not consider patients' rights. By choosing to use the term "conscience," I am not picking sides on the broader issues relating to reproductive rights – as will be seen clearly in this chapter; rather, I am acknowledging that despite the power of words to define the nature of a phenomenon such as conscience or refusal, there are ways to protect interests on both sides regardless of which term one uses. So, to those of you who prefer the term "refusal," please do not assume that your position will be ignored or undervalued because I have chosen to use the term "conscience."

The healthcare context has provided a variety of examples, some good and some bad, of the sorts of compromises between religious and sexual freedom advocated in this book. A variety of conscience clauses at the state and federal levels exempt medical providers from engaging in practices that violate their conscience. These "clauses" are laws that use a variety of mechanisms to protect doctors, pharmacists, hospitals, and others who have religious or other conscientious objections to providing particular medical services. Some of these clauses do a good job of balancing the rights of patients with those of medical professionals, but as will be seen, others do not. This book advocates strong protections for conscience claims and strong protections for patient rights. Significantly, there are examples from several states of laws that protect both conscience claims and patients' rights. Federal laws such as the Weldon Amendment discussed in Chapter 3 tend to be more one-sided, but the federal Church Amendments also discussed in Chapter 3, include some interesting and useful compromise language, especially when merged with some of the better examples from the states.

Finally, conscience claims have been increasingly made in the same-sex marriage context. Some of these claims were addressed in Chapters 4 and 5. Others, such as Mandy Rodriguez's situation (introduced in Chapter 1), are addressed in this chapter. The healthcare context can be instructive here, but there are also significant differences between the healthcare context and the same-sex marriage context that need to be addressed.

I THE HEALTHCARE CONTEXT

Just as same-sex marriage and religious freedom can potentially conflict, so too can reproductive freedom and religious freedom. A major difference is the long history of legal and social responses relating to the potential conflicts between religious freedom and reproductive freedom. For many years, the federal government and states have had "conscience clauses" that protect the religious and moral convictions of healthcare providers in a variety of contexts. Moreover, religious freedom laws such as Religious Freedom Restoration Acts (RFRAs), along with these conscience clauses, have allowed healthcare providers to bring claims when their religious freedom is violated.

This is no panacea however, because some of these laws have had a detrimental (and sometimes Draconian) effect on women's access to healthcare. Other laws have done a much better job balancing protections for women's access to healthcare and religious freedom. It is these laws we look to for guidance. Before doing so, however, it is essential to understand more about conscience claims, and the nature of religious conscience in these contexts. It is also essential to get a glimpse of the vast array of laws that protect these interests around the country. To call these laws a patchwork would be an understatement. There are numerous variations among state conscience clauses.

Moreover, it is essential to address what are often called "mandatory contraception laws," which also take many forms. These laws frequently have exceptions for religious entities, but the protection of religious freedom claims raised by for-profit entities raises a number of interesting questions. Despite the religious exceptions, these laws sometimes conflict with conscience clauses. Legislatures and courts have often had to navigate these conflicts. A number of interesting developments have occurred recently in states as diverse as Washington and Georgia.

A What Is a Religious Conscience Claim?

When addressing religious conscience claims, one of the first points that needs to be mentioned is that not all conscience claims are "religious." Religious conscience claims are often a subset of broader conscience claims that may arise in reproductive rights, end of life issues, and many other morally charged contexts. As a practical reality, however, in the reproductive rights area the vast majority of conscience claims have some religious basis. Still, it is essential to note that many federal and state conscience clauses do not specifically mention religion, even if the majority of those using these clauses do so for religious reasons. In this sense, these clauses are different from RFRAs.

Conscience claims and conscience clauses in the healthcare context by their nature have the potential to affect patients' access to healthcare. Therefore, if these clauses were based purely in religion, serious potential problems would arise under federal and state constitutions' Establishment Clauses. These clauses prohibit government to one degree or another from favoring or promoting religion in a variety of contexts. Establishment of religion concerns may be especially powerful when government directly favors a religious objection over access to fundamental rights by others.

The U.S. Supreme Court has written that there is "play in the joints" between the Establishment Clause and the Free Exercise Clause of the U.S. Constitution. This means that the Establishment Clause of the First Amendment to the Constitution is not violated when government seeks to protect the free exercise of religion under statutes such as the Religious Land Use and Institutionalized Persons Act (RLUIPA) and RFRA. Yet, the cases asserting this "play in the joints" do not suggest that the state can favor one religion or religious view in a manner that leads to the denial of access to fundamentally protected care such as reproductive healthcare, or other fundamental rights such as same-sex marriage.[1] Healthcare-focused conscience clauses ostensibly avoid this problem by not being religion focused, but rather focused more broadly on any sort of objection to whatever procedures or activities they govern. For present purposes, we will put establishment of religion concerns aside and focus on the meaning of "religious conscience," accepting for purposes of the discussion that this is a subset, albeit a significant one, of conscience claims in the healthcare context.

What is "religious conscience"? Theologians and philosophers have debated this issue for centuries. It is also hotly debated in the legal context, where the very act of defining "religion" in the context of free exercise of religion has been fraught with difficulties. One common argument in the legal, philosophical, and theological contexts is that there is no coherent way to define "religious conscience." After all, how can we draw the line between religious conscience claims and conscience claims based on other philosophies or systems of belief about the world that may not be based in what is traditionally, or even nontraditionally, viewed as religion? This issue arose in the conscientious objector cases during the Vietnam War, but it now extends well beyond that context.

Volumes have been written on these issues, but luckily for us (although some might justifiably argue "unluckily" because these issues are so fascinating), we have a way around this hotly contested subject. This is good because it would be nearly impossible in this short volume to address the debates over the definition of "religious conscience" in a coherent manner. Our way around this debate is that many conscience claims arise from traditions that almost everyone would agree fit within the definition of religion. In fact, the vast majority of religious conscience claims in the healthcare context in the United States are brought by Christians of one denomination or other or by other theists. Claims brought by those with other strong commitments that may or may not be considered "religious" or that may be used to demonstrate the volatility and perhaps impossibility of finding a demarcation point between religion and other moral systems, are beyond the scope of this book.[2]

The prior discussion may be best understood as limiting the definition of "religious conscience" in the present context to conscience claims asserted by people that fit clearly within the concept of religion and are based in those individuals' religion. Yet, even this limited concept is not easy to define. So let's begin with the obvious.

A conscience claim is more than a simple assertion of a religious belief even if it may be related to religious beliefs. A person asserting a conscience claim is not just asserting that he or she believes that a given action is wrong. He or she is asserting that assisting the action directly and often also indirectly violates fundamental aspects of his or her being, thus making the person complicit in an action that goes to the core of what it means to be a good, just, and/or righteous person. This may be connected also to being a person who follows God's law, natural law as viewed by that person's faith, and/or basic humanity. It may involve concepts of justice in this life and/or one's eternal future.

For people of faith, these are not small concerns or odd superstitions. They are as real to people of faith as the things that many secularists take for granted, such as progressive values that are often based in what many call "natural rights." Natural rights have a connection, albeit an often uncomfortable one, to natural law because all such concepts rely on the existence of a higher set of values. Whether these values are based on systems such as those proposed by John Locke and John Rawls, where all people (or at least those raised in a particular political tradition) would agree to be governed by certain rules and rights if they were to determine those rules and rights without knowing what status they will occupy in society, or similar notions in natural law (or least the arguably secular versions of it) that certain moral values and rules are inherent and binding on any given society; they rely on the notion of higher values that can be known by humans. Of course in religious natural law, these values are ultimately attributable to God but are capable of being discovered and understood by humans.

The idea that certain actions or inactions are so wrong that they cannot be engaged in without sacrificing what it means to be a "good" person is somewhat universal, although what those actions and inactions are can vary by culture, era, and yes, religion. We can all agree that killing a person without justification is wrong. Yet what if we disagree on the meaning of "person" and "justification?" This is a common debate in moral philosophy, but one need not have a background in moral philosophy to understand the stakes for each side.

One problem I have seen repeatedly in the reproductive rights context and have increasingly seen in the LGBT rights context is a lack of empathy from those on both sides for those with opposing positions. This is certainly not universal, and perhaps it is understandable for both sides given the stakes involved, but it leads to the "all-or-nothing" positions that are destructive of compromise and may truly lead to all or nothing for one side. This is a risk that neither side should be willing to take. In this way, all-or-nothing approaches to conscience claims can be viewed as either a win-lose or lose-lose scenario. Who wins and who loses will vary by issue; since each side could lose totally on a given issue, the lose-lose scenario becomes more likely in the aggregate. The situations discussed later in this chapter demonstrate the risks for each side.

The lack of a possibility of compromise in the all-or-nothing scenario makes the stakes even higher. This, in turn, moves the possibility of compromise even further out of reach. Therefore, the all-or-nothing approach is self-reinforcing as it raises paranoia over losing and further entrenches each side in a high-stakes spiral away from compromise. With compromise, however, there is a chance for each side to maintain a greater level of freedom than either could maintain over the long run using the all-or-nothing approach.

Take for instance the hotly contested issue of when life begins and the role that medical professionals play in protecting this life in a variety of contexts. I am not Catholic, and although I am religious, I do not believe that life begins at conception. But does that mean that I should disregard and fail to understand or empathize with devout Catholics (or members of other faiths) who do believe that life begins at conception? If I fail to put myself in their shoes, why should they, or anyone else, empathize with my views that raise problems for both sides?

My religion is split between life beginning at live birth, viability, or quickening (when you can hear a heartbeat from the fetus). I subscribe to the belief that life begins at viability. Yet I also believe that government should not have the ability to interfere with a woman's medical choices made in consultation with medical professionals. Simply put, despite my faith I believe that government has no business in a woman's uterus.

I, a religious person who is pro-contraception and pro-choice, have no way to engage with people who devoutly believe that what I support is the taking of a life – *unless* I am willing to try to put myself in their shoes and they in turn also try to put themselves in the shoes of a woman who, for example, became pregnant because contraception failed. When I put myself in the shoes of a devout Catholic or other person who believes life begins at conception, I can see things that are often hard to see from my religious yet pro-choice vantage. These people are sincerely opposing what they view as murder.[3] Who wouldn't do that?

They define "life" and "justification" differently than I do, but that does not mean that I must reject the argument that their conscience claims should be accommodated whenever it is possible to do so without denying others reasonable access to healthcare. At the same time, it does not mean that I cannot still have legal, moral, and theological disagreements with these individuals whose views I respect. It does mean that I can engage with these individuals from a place of respect and that through dialogue we can try to persuade each other of whatever we choose to persuade each other of, while agreeing that the legal stance should be to maximize freedom on all sides. The reality is that many people on both sides will be unwilling to put themselves in the other side's shoes, or unwilling or unable to empathize even if they do, but I am openly appealing to the vast middle here.

Some have called this the "live and let live" position. I do not see it that way. I see it as the "maximizing freedom for all" position. It goes beyond live and let live, because as the Utah compromise demonstrates, it takes people of good faith on both sides to be willing to actively compromise.

The same is true for those who, like me, believe that life starts later in the process, but who unlike me do not believe that women should have the right to choose. Putting myself in their shoes as best I can opens my eyes to the pain and horror they must experience when abortions occur, even if they do not oppose contraception. They believe that a life is being taken and must experience it in the same way that most people experience and are repulsed by murder. Again, this does not mean I have to agree with them on reproductive rights.

What it does mean is that I see the value in accommodating the profound beliefs of people with whom I happen to disagree, unless accommodating those beliefs will cause harm to third parties. This is the point of conscience clauses: to keep people from causing or facilitating what they view as a profound sin. Of course, the question of what constitutes "harm to third parties" is still very much an issue and is addressed in the next section.

Some people on the pro-choice side object to conscience claims regardless of whether third parties would be affected. They are concerned that allowing anyone to refuse to perform what may be considered a medically necessary procedure or from dispensing contraception could start a slippery slope that will lead to denial of access that does harm third parties. On the other side, some have advocated for conscience protection regardless of the impact that a conscience claim may have on third parties. Let's explore the substance of some of these conscience clauses, as well as several conscience claims, to determine whether this all-or-nothing approach is warranted. In fact, I will give you a suggested answer now: no, the all-or-nothing approach is unwarranted on either side, and a more balanced approach can and has worked in several states. These states have passed laws that instantiate the reproductive rights version of the Utah compromise, and they protect both conscience claims and patient rights.

B Federal and State Conscience Clauses

Chapter 3 provided some background and insight into federal laws that protect conscience claims by doctors, hospitals, and others. Yet a wide array of state laws also protect conscience claims by medical professionals. Some of these are far more nuanced in their attempts to balance the rights of patients and healthcare providers than the federal laws. Federal laws tend to focus more on the provider than the patient. It would be impossible to engage in a detailed discussion of every state law that addresses these issues and maintain focus on the broader themes in this book. Fortunately, there are clear patterns and trends among state laws. We focus on those. This enables you to understand what is going on in many states as well as under federal law, without getting caught up in a thousand-page discussion of the details of every state law. This section first addresses the federal law and then focuses on state laws.

1 Federal Conscience Clauses
In Chapter 3, you learned a bit about the Church Amendments, The Weldon Amendment, and Section 245 of the Public Health Services Act. Other federal laws touch on the subject of conscience

claims by medical providers, but these three laws are the most relevant. Each of them protects conscience claims by medical professionals, such as doctors and/or medical facilities.

The Church Amendments were named for Senator Frank Church who proposed them shortly after the U.S. Supreme Court decided *Roe v. Wade*. The Church Amendments prevent all federal government officials and agencies from requiring any individual to violate his or her religious or moral convictions through performing or assisting in an abortion or sterilization. The amendments also provide the same protection to entities, such as hospitals or medical practices. In the latter context, the protections apply to making facilities available for performing abortions or sterilizations. The protections also apply to any individual or entity that receives federal grants, contracts, or loans. The Church Amendments also prohibit discrimination against medical professionals who refuse to perform or who do perform abortions or sterilization procedures.

The Weldon Amendment denies funding to any "Federal agency or program, or to a State or local government" that "subjects any institutional or individual healthcare entity to discrimination" because the healthcare provider "does not pay for, provide coverage for, or refer for abortions."[4] The Weldon Amendment is not a helpful example of a conscience clause because by its terms it imposes significant harm on patients. The Weldon Amendment prevents huge amounts of federal funds from going to agencies or states that "discriminate" against those healthcare providers.

It is this last provision that is troubling. Some of the best examples of state conscience clauses addressed later require doctors or hospitals that do not perform abortions or pharmacists who do not provide contraceptives to make the patient aware that they do not provide these services and either refer to someone or someplace nearby who does or at least make the patient aware that other providers are available who do provide these services. We address the benefits of these compromises, at least in areas where there are multiple providers available, in the "State Laws" section. The Weldon Amendment on its terms precludes this compromise since if a state or an agency discriminated against a healthcare provider because that provider refused to refer, the agency or state could lose a vast amount of revenue from the federal government, the loss of which could harm numerous patients.

Yet agencies with expertise in healthcare and states that license healthcare providers have good reasons to require providers to make referrals when the provider cannot provide medical care that a patient may want or need. Most of these providers are professionals or hospitals licensed by the state and are often subject to ethical guidelines from the American Medical Association or state medical associations or boards. Agencies and states have good reason to fine or otherwise challenge a provider who will not provide medical care to which the provider objects *and* who will not refer the patient for – or at least make the patient aware of the availability of – that care. This would be viewed as discrimination under the Weldon Amendment because it involves punishing a healthcare provider for failing to refer a patient.

In this sense, the Weldon Amendment goes beyond protecting conscience and potentially interferes with the federal agency and states' attempts to protect patients' access to healthcare. It is not that referrals do not raise conscience issues. Even referring a patient for a procedure that a healthcare provider objects to can raise concerns about being complicit in that procedure. Yet there is a point at which one's conscience can run roughshod over others' access to care. Not forcing someone to perform a procedure or prescribe a medication because of a conscience concern makes sense. Yet, leaving patients in the dark as to their options or failing to refer when requested, even when the refusal is based in conscience, raises significant questions that are addressed later.

Moreover, many states and localities require healthcare providers to provide informed consent – a legal term that essentially means clear notice – that they do not perform abortions or other procedures. If a state or local government enforced these informed consent laws against a healthcare entity that refuses to meet the requirements of the Weldon Amendment, the impact on funding for the state or local government could be extreme. As a practical matter, this could lead state or local governments not to enforce these informed consent laws in the reproductive rights context, thus leaving women without adequate information or access in areas dominated by hospitals affiliated with certain religions, such as the Catholic Church, or in areas where few healthcare providers are willing to provide these services even when a patient's health is at risk.

Section 245 of the Public Health Services Act requires any government entity (federal, state, or local) that receives federal funding not to discriminate against a healthcare entity that "refuses to undergo training in the performance of induced abortions, to require or provide such training, to perform such abortions, or to provide referrals for such training or such abortions." This is quite broad and raises many of the same problems as the Weldon Amendment, especially in the referral provision. In fact, the main difference between the two laws is that Section 245 applies not only to the refusal to perform abortions but also to the provision of training about abortions. Moreover, it applies to all federal funding rather than just the (still significant) funding at issue under the Weldon Amendment.

2 State Laws

A wide array of state laws address conscience claims. Moreover, some states have mandatory contraceptive coverage laws that provide conscience exemptions for religious entities, much as the Affordable Care Act has done under federal law. Yet when it comes to the specifics, there is wide variation among the states regarding what they protect and how they protect it.

One of the first questions that arises is which services are protected by a given state's conscience clause. Under federal law, the primary focus is abortion and sometimes sterilization. State laws are similar, but a number also address dispensing contraception and cover pharmacists as well as doctors, other medical staff, and hospitals. Moreover, even when state laws protect conscience claims for a particular practice or procedure, for example, abortions, there is wide variation in regard to who is protected. In some states, only private hospitals are covered; in other states, all hospitals are covered. In most states, individual providers are covered, but questions can arise as to whom that refers. Doctors performing the procedure? Nurses or other medical staff?

This section tries to give you a sense of these state laws. The primary focus is on state laws that provide the highest amount of protection in the aggregate for both conscience claims and patients' rights. As you will see, the states have created some interesting models. Some are good and some are bad depending on your perspective.

Forty-five states have laws protecting conscience claims. Most of these laws include more than just religious-based conscience objections. This has generally spared these laws from being successfully challenged under federal or state Establishment Clauses. As mentioned earlier, however, the vast majority of those who make such claims do so based on religion.

Forty-three states protect individual healthcare providers' conscience claims against performing or assisting in abortions. Forty-three states also protect institutions, such as hospitals, that assert conscience-based objections to allowing abortions at the hospital. Of these, fourteen states protect only private institutions. This includes the state of California, which only protects religious institutions. Yet, many distinctions exist among the large number of states that provide conscience-based protections in the abortion context.

For example, some states protect healthcare providers even from referring patients because of concerns about complicity in the ultimate procedure. Other states require referral as part of the duty of a professional. Some states require that patients be informed that alternatives exist for services that the provider will not provide, even if they do not require referrals. A few states also require hospitals that may ordinarily have a protected conscience claim to procedures in emergency situations where failure to do so could lead to the death of, or serious bodily harm to, the patient. These are just a few of the wide variations among the states. Some specific variations that are particularly helpful will be discussed later.

In addition to abortions, some healthcare providers have objected to performing sterilizations. As you saw, under federal law the Church Amendments specifically address these procedures as well. Fewer states protect conscience claims against performing sterilization procedures than those against abortions. Sixteen states protect conscience claims against performing sterilization procedures such as tubal ligations and vasectomies. It is important to note that if a state protected conscience claims only for sterilization procedures for women, it would be a clear violation of the Equal Protection Clause of the U.S. Constitution.

Perhaps the most controversial context for healthcare-related conscience clauses – and that is saying something given the other controversial contexts involved – is conscientious objection to providing contraception and, more often than not, objections to providing emergency contraception. As you saw in *Hobby Lobby*, some religious people view emergency contraception, also known by the brand names Plan B and Ella or the colloquial "morning after pill," as being an abortifacient. This assertion has some serious scientific problems, and recent scientific data suggests that these pills are not abortifacients.[5] Either way, objections to providing these drugs are covered under laws protecting conscience claims made by doctors who refuse to provide or pharmacists who refuse to dispense contraceptives.

Only six states directly protect pharmacists' rights to refuse to dispense contraceptives, but several other states have enacted broad conscience clauses that might be interpreted to protect pharmacists. Ten states protect doctors who have a conscientious objection to prescribing contraceptives. Recently, a countertrend has begun that, heavily supported by a case that arose in Washington state, is to require pharmacists and pharmacies to dispense contraception regardless of conscience concerns.

Under many of these state laws, as well as under the federal laws, there is an inherent tension between providers' conscience and access to healthcare. These concerns are not hypothetical; serious concerns do in fact exist on both sides.

As a general matter, healthcare providers have an ethical and professional duty to provide whatever services are necessary or helpful to their patients. In the reproductive rights context, we are also dealing with constitutionally protected rights. The Constitution dictates government actions since states license doctors and hospitals and also frequently (along with federal guidelines) provide rules that healthcare professionals and healthcare institutions must follow. Moreover, since government is involved in determining medical requirements, it is government that grants conscience-based exemptions either through conscience clauses or conscience claims decided by courts. The Supreme Court has held, however, that government need not provide doctors or facilities to perform abortions.[6] This creates a different set of concerns.

What if a state exempts healthcare professionals and institutions that have a conscience claim from performing abortions, and that state also does not allow or fund those procedures in state hospitals? Consider for a moment that in some parts of the country, the only options available may be a state hospital or religious hospital, such as a Catholic hospital, that does not allow abortions to be performed. In some cases, even a state hospital is not nearby, and some states have few abortion clinics. Where is a patient who seeks to exercise her constitutionally protected right to an abortion to go? In fact, where is a patient who needs an abortion for important medical reasons such as preserving her life, health, or ability to have children in the future to go?

In these situations, women, especially poorer women who have little or no access to transportation, may have no way to get an abortion, even though it is a constitutionally protected right. In this sense, conscience claims when taken in the aggregate can prevent access to healthcare. In states such as Texas, the situation is even more problematic. There, the potential for limited access due to conscience claims by healthcare facilities has combined with laws that have the effect of closing down abortion clinics to make abortions virtually unavailable in the state, even when medically necessary. These latter laws are not conscience clauses; however, when they are combined with conscience clauses, the impact on women's access to healthcare is huge. The Supreme Court is expected to decide the constitutionality of the Texas law in June 2016, but since the Court currently has only eight justices, a split opinion is quite possible. A split opinion would simply mean that the lower court decision is upheld and only binding on states within the lower court's jurisdiction.

Those who oppose abortion rights have therefore won some strong short-term victories on these issues. You might have noticed my use of the words "short-term victories." The situation in Texas, along with recent laws in Missouri, Indiana, and Oklahoma, and to a lesser extent laws in other states, made headlines and the backlash has focused not only on Texas's new facilities law but also on conscience claims. Rather than using reasonable state healthcare conscience clauses as proof in the same-sex marriage context that even in the most contested culture war arenas' concerns on both sides can be protected, state laws that do not seek to balance conscientious objection with patients' rights have increasingly called the entire enterprise of protecting conscience into question. This is especially true when conscience clauses are combined with other laws to make access to reproductive healthcare even more limited.

Social values are changing and, whether people like it or not, one state's overreaching can harm conscience protections elsewhere, especially when that overreaching is done by augmenting conscience-based objections with legislation that obviously has the purpose of preventing access to abortions regardless of conscience concerns. It is a classic case of winning the battle and losing the war, as we have already seen in the *Hobby Lobby* context. People have increasingly come to see conscience claims as being directly connected with other attempts to prevent access to reproductive healthcare.

Significantly, a number of states have conscience clauses that provide strong protection for conscience claims but also protect a woman's right to reproductive healthcare through required referrals and/or informed consent. Some require that conscience claims can only be protected when the patient has another reasonable option. For those who want to use government to make sure that no woman can have access to abortions, these sorts of compromises may be viewed as defeats. Yet in the long run, these individuals are fighting a losing social battle; and if their all-or-nothing approach leads to the rejection of conscience claims as a concept in the coming years, they will have lost everything, except perhaps in a few limited geographic areas where a large number of like-minded individuals reside.

Texas has done a potentially huge favor for pro-choice advocates in other states – although that does nothing to help the women directly affected by the law in Texas. Texas has thrown a ticking time bomb into the abortion debate at a time when society and demographics are shifting. There is a significant chance it will blow up on the pro-life side in the long run rather than the pro-choice side. Such is the nature of the all-or-nothing approach. Ironically, even if Texas loses the case currently before the Supreme Court, the damage is done. The Texas law has sunk into the public conscience as the media has increasingly covered the court case, and calls for the repeal of laws that interfere with access to healthcare, including conscience clauses, have increased.

After addressing conscience clauses that apply to pharmacists, we turn to a more moderate approach that attempts to protect rights on both sides.

In the pharmacy and pharmacist context, we see a variety of laws and some very interesting cases. One of the key factors that comes into play in the pharmacy context is whether the state has a mandatory contraceptive coverage law. More than twenty-five states do. These laws require insurance companies to cover FDA-approved contraceptives if they include prescription drug coverage. Of course, as you have already seen, the HHS Mandate under the federal Affordable Care Act also mandates contraceptive coverage. Most of the states that have these laws provide exemptions for religious entities such as churches and religious non-profits.

Conscience claims by pharmacists and pharmacies arise even in states that do not have mandatory contraceptive coverage laws; whether or not such coverage is mandatory, when a doctor prescribes medication for a patient, it is the duty of a pharmacist to fill that prescription unless the pharmacist has a legal basis for not doing so. In many situations such as Amy's from the beginning of this book, the doctor has prescribed the contraceptive for medical reasons other than contraception and a pharmacist cannot second-guess the doctor's reasons without a legal basis for doing so. Conscience clauses that cover pharmacists can provide such a legal basis.

Some states are more amenable than others to these sorts of conscience claims. I break down the current situation among the states into four groups: first, states that provide pharmacists with broad conscience protection; second, states that provide pharmacists with limited conscience protection; third, states that explicitly deny pharmacists conscience protection; and fourth, states that have no explicit protection for conscience claims by pharmacists, but which also have no rule of law denying pharmacists conscience protection (in this latter group the practical effect is that pharmacists will be bound by general state guidelines and therefore likely do not have conscience protection unless the state decides to give a permissive accommodation).

The majority of states fall into the fourth category. Yet twelve states fall into either category one or category two. What distinguishes these categories is an important factor. States in category two require that a pharmacist or pharmacy provide a referral to another pharmacy in the community for prescriptions they are unwilling to fill based on a conscience objection. Yet what if there is no other nearby pharmacy? Some of these states would then require the pharmacist to fill the prescription. There have been strong arguments that accommodating conscience claims by pharmacists creates a bigger problem than accommodating claims by doctors because of the time-sensitive nature of some prescriptions, as well as the significant inconvenience and dignitary harm that women endure when refused service by their pharmacist. These arguments came to a head in a recent case from Washington State and an earlier case in Wisconsin.

In *Stormans, Inc. v. Wiesman*,[7] a pharmacy and its pharmacists filed suit in federal court against the state to challenge a state law mandating that pharmacies provide "the timely delivery of all prescription medications by licensed pharmacists."[8] The pharmacy and pharmacists argued that the state law violated their conscience in contradiction to the Free Exercise Clause to the First Amendment to the U.S. Constitution by requiring them to prescribe the emergency contraceptives Plan B and Ella. The case made its way up to the U.S. Court of Appeals for the Ninth Circuit, which held in July 2015 that the First Amendment does not provide protection for conscience claims by pharmacists or pharmacies when those claims are raised in response to laws of general applicability (laws that apply regardless of religion). The state is free to accommodate conscience claims if it chooses to, but the Constitution does not mandate such protection.

Interestingly, the court addressed the plaintiffs' arguments that they could be accommodated through referrals. The court held that the state need not provide any accommodation to laws of general applicability, and the fact that the state allowed what were called "facilitated referrals" to other pharmacies when the pharmacy did not have a particular medication did not change this. Such referrals allow a pharmacy to refer a patient who needs medication not currently in stock to get that medication through a nearby pharmacy, but the court held that this did not mean that a pharmacy could refuse to stock or sell a given drug based on religious conscience when the state has a generally applicable requirement that pharmacists do so.

The court also acknowledged the inconvenience and harm that could arise for women in immediate need of emergency contraception, which is an exceptionally time-sensitive medication, if a pharmacy or pharmacist refused to provide it when that medication has been prescribed by a doctor. Thus, in Washington State pharmacists have a duty to provide emergency contraception regardless of conscience-based objections. Several other states have similar rules.

In a 2008 case decided by the Wisconsin Court of Appeals, *Noesen v. State Department of Regulation and Licensing*,[9] the court held that a pharmacist who refused to fill a prescription for contraception or refer that prescription breached the standard of care that pharmacists must meet. A breach of the standard of care is quite important because it can lead to tort liability in the form of malpractice suits, as well as to possible sanction by state licensing boards. Thus, in addition to states such as Washington that mandate pharmacists to provide contraception care, there are other states where failure to fill or refer prescriptions for contraception violates the standard of care for pharmacists.

This creates a double-edged sword that can be used against pharmacies or pharmacists who refuse to fill prescriptions based on religious objections. The Free Exercise Clause to the Constitution provides no protection because the laws that require these prescriptions to be filled are almost always generally applicable; without such a right, even in the absence of a mandatory coverage law, it is quite possible that failure to fill or refer a prescription could lead to a malpractice suit or negative action by state licensing boards.

The best way to avoid this is to provide conscience protection under state laws, but if these laws are not carefully drafted they may prevent patients' access to important prescriptions; this is especially problematic when those prescriptions are time-sensitive. Moreover, when one goes to one's pharmacy, one expects a prescription to be filled. This does not mean that an individual pharmacist could not be accommodated, but it does mean that when an entire pharmacy refuses to fill or refer a prescription, serious practical as well as dignitary harm can be imposed on the patient. Of course, as with the other contexts, a possible compromise will protect patients and many individual pharmacists.

3 A Possible Compromise

By now it should be clear that any approach to conscience claims in the reproductive rights context has benefits and drawbacks. An all-or-nothing approach may provide a win for one side in a given place and time, but it is not likely to lead to solutions that are successful over the long run. As each side further entrenches, backlash arises from the losing side of a given battle and sometimes from broader segments of society, and battle lines become stronger. In the end, a compromise is the best approach because it allows us to maximize freedom on both sides, even though neither side will be completely happy with the result. It may also lead to less conflict in the long run and perhaps even to increased dialogue outside of the legal context – although perhaps the latter is a bit of intrepid wishful thinking.

As you have seen throughout this book, accommodating religious freedom is permissible even when it is not mandatory. If a state wants to accommodate religious freedom claims, it may do so unless doing so conflicts with other laws (particularly federal laws). It is also possible that a RFRA might be used to support accommodation, even in a state that does not have a conscience law on the books. In this context, compromises that also protect patient rights, which are clearly a compelling government interest, could be the most narrowly tailored way to serve that interest. Of course, states need not accommodate religious freedom claims if they do not wish to do so by enacting conscience clauses, RFRAs, or through other means.

At the same time, states with conscience protection that extends to the healthcare context without regard to the impact on patients should amend those laws to account for this impact on patients. States are not required to do so under current law.[10] Yet, doing so may work to more effectively protect conscience over the long run, because not doing so may ultimately lead to a total lack of conscience protection as society changes. As I have advocated, compromise in these contested areas is immensely hard, but in the long run it is better for enabling both sides to live in relative peace and for maximizing freedom on all sides. Each side is still absolutely free to speak out and try to persuade people of its position, whether or not religiously based. This book simply proposes that neither side should be able to use government to impose its views on others who disagree and who would face significant and material harm were the other side to prevail without compromise.

The compromise in the healthcare context proposed here borrows from both federal and state laws. First, doctors and religiously affiliated hospitals would be afforded conscience protection with one important exception addressed later in this section. Moreover, doctors at non–religiously affiliated hospitals could not be discriminated against because they refuse to perform or do perform abortions or other procedures deemed objectionable based on conscience. Relatedly, doctors affiliated with state-licensed religious hospitals who perform abortions or other procedures at other locations may not be discriminated against by religiously affiliated hospitals, except that the hospital may deny the doctor access for performance of procedures to which the hospital has a conscience exception.

The important exception to this rule would arise when the only practitioners or facilities available in a given area have conscience objections such that patients would be denied access to complete reproductive healthcare were all conscience objections granted. In this scenario, we can borrow from state laws and from the county clerk context discussed in Chapter 4. Someone and someplace must be available to the patient so that he or she may receive reproductive healthcare. If every practitioner or facility in a community has a conscience-based objection to providing care, conscience claims would be invalid unless those objecting are able to find someone in the community and some facility in the community willing to do so or find an organization willing to subsidize travel – immediate if necessary – so that the patient can have access to reproductive healthcare.

In all cases, doctors must provide informed consent as to any treatments they are unwilling to provide or which a hospital with which they are affiliated is unwilling to allow. Robin Fretwell Wilson, one of the leading advocates for compromise between religious freedom and sexual freedom, has suggested that requiring objectors to disclose their objections and limitations in writing upon assuming their duties and before treating a patient is an easy way for objectors to let their employers — and patients — know if there are any services they are unwilling to perform.[11] In fact, doctors can post notice on the web and in their offices notifying patients of the services that they are unwilling to provide due to conscience objections. I would add that if medical professionals provide informed consent in this manner, they should require patients to sign forms acknowledging that the patient has read the notice. It would be good practice for professionals to verbally advise the patient to read the notices *and* inform the patient that if he or she cannot read or cannot read English, the information can be given verbally (this could even be done via a recording).

Moreover, in situations where what are known as "zombie hospitals" are the only facilities available in an area, any agreement imposing denial of particular services on the zombie hospital would be void as a matter of state law. Zombie hospitals are secular public or private hospitals or hospitals representing faiths that do not object to reproductive health procedures that have bought out a Catholic hospital or hospital of another denomination that objects to certain procedures and treatments on religious grounds and requires the party that buys them to maintain the refusal to provide those services. This requirement is important to the selling hospital because if that hospital believed that selling to the new entity would facilitate abortions or other procedures to which it has religious objections, the sale would not have been concluded.

The "zombie" clause in the sale allows the religious entity to assure itself that by selling it will not be complicit in any later action to which it objects. Thus, the suggested outcome here is limited to situations where no other facilities in the area can provide the services objected to. The rule that zombie clauses are unenforceable when there is no other facility in the area that can perform the needed services also provides notice to religious hospitals that are thinking about selling in communities where there are no other facilities that a zombie clause in the sales agreement could be invalid.

Finally, conscience claims by pharmacists would be protected so long as another pharmacist is immediately available to fill the prescription. This could include an on-call pharmacist at another pharmacy as long as it is legal in that state for a pharmacist to supervise a pharmacy tech filling prescription at a related pharmacy via telephone or video feed. This closely mirrors the county clerk solution in Chapter 4 as well as the limited protection of for-profit entities suggested in Chapter 5. It will allow patients to receive prescriptions with little to no delay and also allow pharmacists' conscience claims to be protected so long as someone else is available to fill the prescription.

A pharmacy could receive a conscience exemption to providing contraceptives so long as other nearby pharmacies can do so and accept the patient's insurance with the same or a lower co-pay. Moreover, the pharmacy claiming the exemption must immediately transfer the prescription to the nearest pharmacy and that pharmacy must be accessible to the patient. If the patient cannot easily access the pharmacy to which the prescription was referred, the pharmacy requesting the exemption could not receive it, although individual pharmacists might be accommodated as suggested earlier.

Needless to say, this compromise will cause serious concerns on both sides. Those who oppose conscience clauses in the healthcare context will argue that it goes too far in protecting religious objections because patients should be able to get all legal medical services from professionals licensed to provide those services. Therefore, in the opposition's eyes this approach allows doctors and hospitals to violate their duties to the public. Of course, this argument can be applied to any conscience claim brought in the healthcare context, and it represents an all-or-nothing approach. Either you are willing to provide all care in your area of expertise, even if you have profound religious objections to doing so, or you must find another area of practice or another profession, even if you are exceptionally good at what you do. I have some empathy for this position. It creates a nice clean line, but it does so at the expense of the profound religious commitments of doctors and hospitals that are very good at what they do and also care deeply for their patients. If there were no other way, maybe, but as demonstrated, there is another way.

Those who support unlimited conscience protections will argue that the presented approach still requires doctors, hospitals, and other healthcare providers to be complicit in activities that go against their very being and their core commitments. The alternative would be to grant every conscience claim regardless of the impact that these claims have alone, or in the aggregate, on patient rights. This is also an all-or-nothing solution; while I can empathize with this position as well, it leads to the denial of treatment for many women, and in some cases such as Amy's in Chapter 1 could lead to serious medical consequences. Moreover, given current social trends such an approach might work in one or two areas for a period of time; in the long run, it will lead to less conscience protection nationally and over time than the compromise approach will allow.

II THE SAME-SEX MARRIAGE CONTEXT

Conscience claims are not limited to the healthcare and conscientious objection to military service contexts. These claims increasingly come up in the same-sex marriage context as well. Chapter 4 addressed these sorts of claims when government employees, such as county clerks, seek a religious exemption to performing their duties. Chapter 5 addressed these sorts of claims when asserted by for-profit entities. Mandy Rodriguez's situation from Chapter 1, which is based in part on a real case, is another example. Section I.A of this chapter addressed the nature of religious conscience claims in the healthcare context. The nature of these claims in same-sex marriage situations is similar.

Those who assert a conscience-based objection to facilitating same-sex marriage are concerned about becoming complicit in something that they believe violates the core tenets of their being and perhaps their duties to family, religion, and God. Yet those who could be affected by these sorts of conscience claims may suffer infringement on a fundamental constitutional right and perhaps direct and meaningful dignitary harm. These latter two concerns are much stronger in situations involving government employees and for-profit entities than they are in a situation such as Mandy Rodriguez's or in cases involving churches or ministers.

A Conscience Claims in the Counseling Setting

The discussion in the previous sections of this chapter covered the vast majority of conscience claims besides those that are addressed in the next chapter, which focuses on religious non-profits other than "traditional" religious entities such as churches, synagogues, mosques, and temples. Conscience claims arise in a few other contexts, and Mandy Rodriguez's situation provides a great example.

In situations such as Mandy Rodriguez's, no direct harm to third parties occurs, and courts have recognized that the conscience concerns raised are significant. In situations involving churches and ministers, the answer is even easier because conscience claims by religious entities are automatically protected under the U.S. Constitution, as well as by a number of federal and state laws.

Mandy's hypothetical example was adapted from an actual case called *Ward v. Polite*.[12] A student was indeed expelled for refusing to counsel clients regarding a same-sex relationship because of her religious objections. She also refused to counsel clients involved in extramarital relationships for the same reason. The student had no objection to counseling gay and lesbian clients on matters unrelated to romantic relationships. Moreover, the counseling program's policies included exemptions that allowed for client referrals in other contexts, such as when clients with severe medical conditions sought advice on ending their lives or when "counselors determine an inability to be of professional assistance to clients."[13] The student in that case, Julea Ward, was expelled because the university asserted that she could not complete her practicum or meet the duties of a counselor because of her religious objection to counseling on same-sex relationships that could result in marriage.

The case was decided at what is called the "summary judgment" phase. A motion for summary judgment asks the court to decide the case based on the premise that the party asking for the motion – in this case the university – is entitled to win under the law because no set of facts could allow the other side to win under the law. If a court grants a summary judgment motion, the side that filed the motion wins the case or the specific issue about which the motion was filed without ever going to trial. In this case, the trial court granted the university's motion for summary judgment, but the court of appeals reversed the finding of the trial court and held that Julea Ward did have legal arguments, and facts to back those arguments up, that could allow her to win. Thus, the university was not entitled to have the case dismissed on summary judgment. The decision does not mean that Ward will ultimately win at trial, but the court of appeals' decision provided some pretty strong arguments as to why she might win.

Ward argued that her expulsion from the counseling program violated her free speech rights and her right to free exercise of religion. The court agreed that both of these arguments were potentially winners given the facts in her case. As for the free speech argument, this case is quite different from the for-profit cases discussed in Chapter 5. Evidence in this case showed that the university expelled Ward from the program because of her religious views and her expression of those views, not because she was incapable of meeting the duties of a counselor or because her refusal to serve clients on certain issues violated the school's legitimate educational concerns. In other words, there is evidence that the university expelled her because her religious views violated a sort of enforced political correctness rather than because she was not a capable counselor (in fact, her grades in the program and her overall academic performance were excellent).

The court also suggested that Ward might have a valid claim under the Free Exercise Clause because the school provided a variety of secular-based exceptions that allowed students to refer patients for a variety of reasons, while Ward was taken to task for her religious views. Therefore, the counseling program's policies may not have been generally applicable and in fact may have been enforced in a manner that discriminated against Ward's religious perspective. Such intentional targeting of religion – if a jury determined that it occurred in this case – would violate the Free Exercise Clause. As to impact on third parties, this case is quite different from the situations involving for-profit businesses. The case is similar in some ways to the ideal accommodations suggested earlier in this chapter, whereby the person seeking a marriage license or the patient seeking healthcare services is not even aware that someone in the office objects to providing services because someone else is immediately available to do so. As to third-party harm that could arise from accommodating Ward's religious concerns, the court wrote specifically:

"Nor did the referral request have a 'negative impact' on the client. Quite the opposite, as the client never knew about the referral and perhaps received better counseling than Ward could have provided [given her religious concerns]."[14]

So what does this mean for Mandy Rodriguez? Her case is even stronger than Julea Ward's because she has no objection to counseling gay or lesbian clients even about relationships so long as it is not about marriage. Yet, in the current climate in some (but not most) university programs, the simple fact that she has such religious commitments could make her a target. In some places, there is a sort of enforced political correctness on a wide range of issues that one eschews, whether based on religion or other reasons, at one's own expense. It is not all that different from some religious traditions that seek to impose their views on others without discussion or dissent. Of course, it is a caricature to suggest that all or even most university programs are this way.

Mandy's case is weaker than Julea Ward's in one respect, however. The professors in Julea Ward's case were a bit more blunt than the professors in Mandy Rodriguez's case. Regardless, the cases are similar enough to suggest that Mandy would have a potentially valid claim against the university under the Free Speech Clause and the Free Exercise Clause of the First Amendment to the United States Constitution for the negative action taken against her based on her conscience claim. She would also have a valid claim under a state RFRA if her state had one.

B The Possibility of Compromise

In situations such as Mandy's, compromise is far less painful than in the healthcare context because it is quite possible, if not probable, that third parties would not even be aware of the referral, or at least the reasons for the referral. When a counselor is already in practice and refuses to serve a client in relation to same-sex marriage, it is possible the client might be aware of the reasons: But as long as the counselor is respectful and refers the client elsewhere, little harm is done. In fact, under the ethics rules applicable to counselors, a counselor can turn down a client for a number of reasons if the counselor does not believe that he or she can serve the client adequately.[15] If a counselor is rude or openly discriminatory against a client or potential client based on that client's sexual orientation, then the counselor will likely have breached a duty to that client and might be subject to ethical sanctions, penalties under antidiscrimination laws, and/or a malpractice lawsuit. The same may be true if the counselor refused to refer a client who is unaware that he or she can go elsewhere.

Yet when a counselor simply refuses to serve a client because the counselor has a religious objection to counseling about same-sex marriage or relationships that may lead to same-sex marriage and politely refers the client elsewhere, the counselor should be accommodated. This ultimately serves the client better as well, because the nature of counseling is different from filling prescriptions. Counseling involves a lot of interaction at a close and personal level. If a counselor objects to the very relationship that is the focus of the counseling, it might be quite hard for the client to receive proper counseling. The *Ward v. Polite* court suggested this when it wrote that the client "perhaps received better counseling than Ward could have provided" as a result of the referral.

Therefore, the compromise here is a simple one. Psychologists and other counselors, including psychology or counseling students, who have a conscience objection to counseling on a certain matter may refer clients to other qualified professionals without penalty. If, however, the counselor acts in a discriminatory manner (other than through referral) or refuses to refer a client who is unaware of other options for counseling, then that counselor may be sanctioned under any relevant codes or antidiscrimination laws, or through malpractice claims. This seems to be the situation in many states and is certainly a compromise that would meet the legal concerns raised in *Ward v. Polite*. Under this compromise, Mandy Rodriguez could sue the university since she was expelled because of her conscience concerns and she would likely prevail. She could do so even if the state did not have a RFRA because she could assert valid claims under the First Amendment. Of course, if the state had a RFRA the case would be much simpler. Regardless, under this compromise she would win with or without a RFRA.

C Some Conscience Claim Nonissues

Some partisans in the same-sex marriage context have suggested clergy may be forced to perform same-sex marriage ceremonies even when doing so is forbidden by their faith or their conscience. Simply put, this is a nonissue. It will not happen. A compromise is not needed here because there is no legal basis, whether a state has a RFRA or not, for requiring clergy to officiate a same-sex wedding.

Moreover, there is no legal basis for requiring a church, synagogue, mosque, or other house of worship to accommodate same-sex marriages, except potentially in cases where they turn portions of their premises, such as a catering facility, into public accommodations by renting them to the public at large. If a house of worship chooses to celebrate same-sex marriages, as many have, it can do so. If it chooses not to do so, it cannot be forced to do so. If a house of worship rents its premises to a variety of groups for a variety of functions, and a state public accommodation law requires it to rent the premises for a same-sex marriage, it could be required to do so. Of course, if the state has a RFRA and a court determined that exempting houses of worship that rent their premises to the public at large from the state public accommodation law was a more narrowly tailored option than applying it to such houses of worship, the house of worship would prevail.

Significantly, the vast majority of situations involving church premises do not involve premises such as catering halls that have been rented to the public at large; therefore, in the vast majority of cases involving houses of worship, there is no way to force them to allow same-sex marriage ceremonies if their faith objects to accommodating those marriages. This too is a nonissue. Whatever you have heard to the contrary is just a smokescreen designed to rile people up.

Therefore, while questions about clergy being required to perform same-sex marriages have been raised in the media, as have questions about houses of worship being forced to accommodate same-sex marriages, these are nonissues because there is no legal basis for requiring clergy or houses of worship to do so. In fact, longstanding legal concepts prevent the government from requiring clergy and houses of worship to do so: the Ecclesiastical Abstention and Church Autonomy Doctrines, discussed in Chapter 2. These doctrines require that government not get involved in ecclesiastical matters. Forcing clergy to do something that violates their religion or forcing a house of worship to host a ceremony that violates the faith goes to the core of these doctrines. If the government tried to force a clergy member or house of worship to do so, it would be an obvious legal violation, and as a practical matter, it is exceedingly unlikely that any government entity would attempt to do so.

7 RELIGIOUS NON-PROFITS

Religious non-profits include a wide range of entities from soup kitchens to universities. This wide array of non-profits can raise a variety of different issues. In the sexual freedom context, there are four major areas where potential conflict arises. First are religiously affiliated healthcare entities, such as hospitals, which were addressed in Chapter 6. Second are religious charities, which have raised questions about tax-exempt status. Third are issues relating to conscience exemptions from mandatory contraception laws for religious non-profits that are not healthcare providers. Fourth are religious universities and adoption agencies, which raise some of the same questions as those that arise for religious charities more generally.

This chapter first addresses potential concerns over tax-exempt status if a religious non-profit discriminates based on sexual orientation (especially same-sex marriage status). These concerns can arise for any type of religious non-profit and thus are relevant to religious charities, religiously affiliated adoption agencies, and religiously affiliated universities. Next, the chapter focuses on religious charities and the question of conscience-based exemptions to mandatory contraceptive coverage laws, especially the HHS Mandate under the Affordable Care Act. Finally, this chapter addresses the variety of issues that arise when religious adoption agencies and universities experience conflicts between their religious tenets and sexual freedom concerns.

I THREATS TO TAX-EXEMPT STATUS

Many religious entities qualify for federal tax exemptions under Section 501(c)(3) of the Internal Revenue Code as non-profit charitable entities. Any organization exempt from federal taxes under Section 501(c)(3) is generally referred to as a Section 501(c)(3) organization. I use that term here.

Section 501(c)(3) organizations receive significant financial benefits both because the organization itself is tax exempt and because donations to the organization are tax deductible for those making the donations. A primary reason for providing these tax benefits is that Section 501(c)(3) charitable organizations are non-profit and provide substantial benefits to society. When a Section 501(c)(3) organization discriminates based on race or other protected characteristics, it can lose this status because the discrimination goes against societal interests. This is an important issue and is discussed after a brief overview of the requirements an organization must meet to receive a tax exemption under Section 501(c)(3).

The requirements for receiving Section 501(c)(3) tax status involve a number of criteria. First, a 501(c)(3) organization has to be "organized and operated exclusively" for a tax-exempt purpose.[1] Tax-exempt purposes include "religious, charitable, scientific, testing for public safety, literary, or educational purposes."[2] Second, none of a Section 501(c)(3) organization's net earnings can inure to the "benefit of any private shareholder or individual."[3] This is commonly referred to as the "private inurement" requirement, and it has led to a number of issues in the context of religious organizations that are beyond the scope of this chapter and do not relate to discrimination against third parties. Third, a Section 501(c)(3) organization may not carry out political activity. This means that exempt organizations may not financially support or devote a substantial part of their activities to "carrying on propaganda, or otherwise attempting, to influence legislation."[4] They also may not "participate in, or intervene in (including the publishing or distributing of statements), any political campaign on behalf of (or in opposition to) any candidate for public office."[5]

Significantly, the U.S. Supreme Court has clearly held that government should not and does not have to fund discrimination through tax exemptions, even for charitable organizations. In *Bob Jones University v. United States*,[6] the U.S. Supreme Court held that the IRS need not give Section 501(c)(3) status to religious schools that discriminate based on race.[7] This case involved two educational institutions.

Bob Jones University had a policy that denied admissions to anyone involved in interracial marriages or relationships or who advocated for interracial relationships. The university is a religious institution, and the Supreme Court noted that the university was a non-profit and that absent the discrimination it would qualify as a religious or educational institution under Section 501(c)(3). The university's policy at the time read:

There is to be no interracial dating

1 Students who are partners in an interracial marriage will be expelled.
2 Students who are members of or affiliated with any group or organization which holds as one of its goals or advocates interracial marriage will be expelled.
3 Students who date outside their own race will be expelled.
4 Students who espouse, promote, or encourage others to violate the University's dating rules and regulations will be expelled.[8]

The second institution involved in the case was Goldsboro Christian Schools. Goldsboro was a K–12 school. Based on its interpretation of the Bible, Goldsboro discriminated against African American students in its admissions. Goldsboro was a non-profit institution, and it would have qualified for Section 501(c)(3) status as a religious or educational institution if it had not discriminated.

The IRS revoked the tax-exempt status of both Bob Jones University and Goldsboro Christian Schools. The schools challenged the IRS's decision, in part, based on the argument that denial of Section 501(c)(3) status violated their religious freedom because the discrimination stemmed from their religious tenets. The Supreme Court held that the IRS could deny both institutions tax-exempt status. The Supreme Court explained:

Section 501(c)(3) therefore must be analyzed and construed within the framework of the Internal Revenue Code and against the background of the Congressional purposes. Such an examination reveals unmistakable evidence that, underlying all relevant parts of the Code, is the intent that entitlement to tax exemption depends on meeting certain common law standards of charity – namely, that an institution seeking tax-exempt status must serve a public purpose and not be contrary to established public policy.[9]

The Supreme Court held that when a non-profit entity discriminates, it violates public policy and does not confer the sort of public benefit required to be consistent with the Section 501(c)(3) requirement for "charitable" institutions.[10] The Supreme Court wrote:

> Whatever may be the rationale for such private schools' policies, and however sincere the rationale may be, racial discrimination in education is contrary to public policy. Racially discriminatory educational institutions cannot be viewed as conferring a public benefit within the "charitable" concept discussed earlier, or within the Congressional intent underlying ... § 501(c)(3).[11]

Thus, the schools were not entitled to the charitable exemption under Section 501(c)(3).

As for the school's arguments that they should not be subject to denial of Section 501(c)(3) status because their policies were based on religion, and therefore should be protected under the First Amendment to the U.S. Constitution (this case was decided before *Smith*, so the government had to have a compelling interest to deny the tax-exempt status and the denial had to be narrowly tailored to meet that interest, just as the Religious Freedom Restoration Act [RFRA] requires today), the Supreme Court held:

> Denial of tax benefits will inevitably have a substantial impact on the operation of private religious schools, but will not prevent those schools from observing their religious tenets.
>
> The governmental interest at stake here is compelling ... the Government has a fundamental, overriding interest in eradicating racial discrimination in education – discrimination that prevailed, with official approval, for the first 165 years of this Nation's history. That governmental interest substantially outweighs whatever burden denial of tax benefits places on petitioners' exercise of their religious beliefs. The interests asserted by petitioners cannot be accommodated with that compelling governmental interest, and no "less restrictive means," are available to achieve the governmental interest.[12]

If you have not already guessed, the *Bob Jones* case raises some interesting questions about tax-exempt status for religious non-profits that discriminate against same-sex couples in providing services or benefits, hiring, and retention. You may have heard concerns about this in the news after the Supreme Court upheld the constitutional right to same-sex marriage. Will religious non-profits lose federal tax-exempt status or similar state tax exemptions if the non-profit discriminates against same-sex couples based on its religious tenets?

While that decision is ultimately up to the IRS and state taxing authorities, it is still possible to make an educated guess. The answer in most contexts, at least at the federal level, is probably not. In a few contexts, however, revocation is more likely, such as when a religious non-profit discriminates broadly based on sexual orientation rather than just based on same-sex marriage. Also, the answer could change over time as social views on same-sex marriage evolve and influence the rule-making and enforcement processes at the IRS. The answer in regard to state taxing authorities will vary, but many will likely follow a similar path as the IRS.

Please understand that what I am about to suggest are the most likely set of outcomes. They are predictions based on a variety of legal and policy factors, but they are just that: predictions. No one should assume that what I am about to suggest will definitely occur. The IRS could go in a variety of directions. I do think, however, that the following are the most likely scenarios.

First, I think that at least in the immediate future the IRS will treat discrimination by religious non-profits based on same-sex marriage differently than it treats discrimination based on race. Second, I think it is quite possible that the IRS will treat discrimination based on sexual orientation, as opposed to discrimination based solely on same-sex marriage, more harshly. Third, I think that the absence of a federal anti-discrimination law protecting against discrimination based on sexual orientation will not be decisive in protecting religious non-profits that discriminate directly based on sexual orientation from IRS scrutiny. I do think, however, that even if an anti-discrimination law protecting against discrimination based on sexual orientation did pass, the IRS is unlikely to revoke tax-exempt status against religious non-profits that discriminate based solely on same-sex marriage, and not based on sexual orientation more generally. Finally, I think that the nature of the religious non-profit will make a difference. Churches, synagogues, mosques, temples, and other houses of worship will be far safer than large universities.

The IRS is likely to tread very carefully in regard to Section 501(c)(3) status of religious non-profits that discriminate based on same-sex marriage. As discussed earlier in this book, a number of analogies can be drawn between racial discrimination and discrimination against the LGBT community. There are also some differences, however. In twenty years perhaps these differences will be irrelevant; if such a shift occurs, it is quite possible that the IRS might revoke the tax-exempt status of religious non-profits that discriminate based on same-sex marriage. For now, however, it is more likely that the IRS will consider the differing contexts. And in this sense, the *Bob Jones* Court's discussion of the history of racial discrimination in the United States provides a good basis for the IRS and/or courts to treat the two contexts differently.

First, the Unites States has a unique history of racial discrimination. The nation began as one recognizing and affirming slavery, even at a time when many countries were rejecting it. After slavery ended, a period of formal and informal racial segregation began that lasted more than one hundred years (formal, and certainly informal, segregation continued, albeit unconstitutionally, well beyond the era of *Brown v. Board of Education*). Some segregationists based their views on religion, but many did not. Regardless, segregation – which included anti-miscegenation laws (laws that prohibited interracial marriage) – was an organized system for asserting racial inferiority. In the Bob Jones case, the Supreme Court recognized this when it wrote:

> The Government has a fundamental, overriding interest in eradicating racial discrimination in education – discrimination that prevailed, with official approval, for the first 165 years of this Nation's history.[13]

Discrimination has also long existed against members of the LGBT community. There is no history of formal segregation in this context, however; in most places, even informal segregation is rare. Undoubtedly, many members of the LGBT community have faced serious discrimination. Some of that discrimination is grounded in religion, while some stems from nonreligious homophobia.

You may recall that in *Obergefell v. Hodges*, the case holding that there is a constitutional right to same sex marriage, the Supreme Court relied in part on *Loving v. Virginia*, the case that held there is a constitutional right to interracial marriage. An analogy can be made on the basic rights involved in both of these cases. The *Obergefell* Court relied in part on *Loving* to support its holding that denying the right to same-sex marriage violates the Constitution. Yet, when addressing religious concerns over same-sex marriage, the *Obergefell* Court also used language suggesting that the nature and history of religious objections to interracial marriage and the nature and history of religious objection to same-sex marriage are quite different.

It would be unthinkable that the Supreme Court would write the following in regard to racial discrimination, either at the time that *Loving v. Virginia* was decided or today:

> Finally, it must be emphasized that religions, and those who adhere to religious doctrines, may continue to advocate with utmost, sincere conviction that, by divine precepts, same-sex marriage should not be condoned. The First Amendment ensures that religious organizations and persons are given proper protection as they seek to teach the principles that are so fulfilling and so central to their lives and faiths, and to their deep aspirations to continue the family structure they have long revered.[14]

Yet the majority of the Supreme Court wrote this in *Obergefell*. In Chapter 3, I contrasted this quote with language from *Loving* to demonstrate that the Supreme Court views religiously based discrimination against interracial marriages and against same-sex marriages differently. Chief Justice John Roberts's dissenting opinion in *Obergefell* makes this even more obvious.[15] In this chapter, we can contrast this quoted language with language from the *Bob Jones University* case, which directly addressed revocation of tax-exempt status because Bob Jones University had a policy, based in religious tenets, prohibiting interracial relationships:

> The governmental interest at stake here is compelling ... the Government has a fundamental, overriding interest in eradicating

racial discrimination in education – discrimination that prevailed, with official approval, for the first 165 years of this Nation's history. That governmental interest substantially outweighs whatever burden denial of tax benefits places on petitioners' exercise of their religious beliefs.[16]

The difference between the tone in these cases could just be based on the fact that the *Bob Jones* case was decided more than fifteen years after *Loving v. Virginia* and *Obergefell* were decided in 2015. It may simply be that we have not yet come to understand and contextualize the harm done by discrimination based on same-sex marriage, and this will change over time. Yet the tone of the language from *Obergefell* suggests that it may be that the Court sees value in specifically acknowledging the right of religions to exercise their freedom of religion and freedom of speech in the same-sex marriage context but did not see any benefit to doing so in the anti-miscegenation context. As Chapter 3 demonstrated, the tone regarding religious objections in the *Obergefell* and *Loving* cases is quite different. This may be, in part, because objections to interracial marriage were more directly connected to a broader system of racism, while religious objections to same-sex marriage are often limited to the issue of marriage.[17]

Another possible argument arises from the history of religiously based racism and religious denial of same-sex marriage. Rejection of same-sex marriage has a much longer tradition, as a well as a more direct theological pedigree, than does racism based in religion. Theological racism has a lineage connected to the African slave trade and especially the American use of race to support slavery and then segregation. It is deeply connected to a sense of racial superiority and inferiority. Theological notions that marriage is between a man and a woman go back thousands of years and have existed even in traditions that did not exhibit broader antigay ideals. This does not make the latter right, but it does denote a difference that could affect how the IRS responds to discrimination based on same-sex marriage, at least in the short run.

One might respond that same-sex marriage is a constitutional right; therefore, under the *Bob Jones* decision, the IRS has every right to try to revoke tax-exempt status of those who discriminate based on same-sex marriage status. That is absolutely correct. The question is not whether the IRS *can* revoke the tax-exempt status of religious non-profits; rather, the question is whether the IRS *will* do so.

Since the Supreme Court decided *Obergefell v. Hodges*, and in many locations before that, same-sex marriage has been affirmed as a fundamental right that the government may not deny, and in regard to which, the government may not discriminate. However, language from *Bob Jones* itself demonstrates that the Supreme Court viewed eliminating racial discrimination as an exceptionally "fundamental" and "overriding" interest:

> Few social or political issues in our history have been more vigorously debated and more extensively ventilated than the issue of racial discrimination, particularly in education. Given the stress and anguish of the history of efforts to escape from the shackles of the "separate but equal" doctrine of *Plessy v. Ferguson*, it cannot be said that educational institutions that, for whatever reasons, practice racial discrimination, are institutions exercising "beneficial and stabilizing influences in community life," *Walz v. Tax Comm'n*, 397 U.S. 664, 673, 90 S.Ct. 1409, 1413, 25 L.Ed.2d 697 (1970), or should be encouraged by having all taxpayers share in their support by way of special tax status.[18]

Moreover, in *Bob Jones* the Supreme Court held that revoking the tax-exempt status of a non-profit organization that may otherwise qualify for tax-exempt status should not be a common event. The reason for revoking that status must be weighed against the public benefit conferred by the non-profit organization in question:

> When the Government grants exemptions or allows deductions all taxpayers are affected; the very fact of the exemption or deduction for the donor means that other taxpayers can be said to be indirect and vicarious "donors." Charitable exemptions are justified on the basis that the exempt entity confers a public benefit – a benefit which the society or the community may not itself choose or be able to provide, or which supplements and advances the work of public institutions already supported by tax revenues. History buttresses logic to make clear that, to warrant exemption under §501(c)(3), an institution must fall within a category specified in that section and

must demonstrably serve and be in harmony with the public interest. *The institution's purpose must not be so at odds with the common community conscience as to undermine any public benefit that might otherwise be conferred.*

We are bound to approach these questions with full awareness that determinations of public benefit and public policy are sensitive matters with serious implications for the institutions affected; a declaration that a given institution is not "charitable" should be made only where there can be no doubt that the activity involved is contrary to a fundamental public policy. But there can no longer be any doubt that racial discrimination in education violates deeply and widely accepted views of elementary justice.[19]

These excerpts from *Bob Jones* demonstrate that the IRS must balance revocation of tax-exempt status against the benefits conferred by non-profits on the community. Moreover, the excerpts suggest that the long-standing and wide societal rejection of race discrimination made the IRS's decision an eminently proper call. In fact, while many racists certainly existed at the time that *Bob Jones* was decided and certainly still exist today, non-profit institutions with policies like Bob Jones University and Goldsboro Christian Schools were significant deviations from the norm, both religiously and in the broader societal context in terms of their segregationist and discriminatory policies.

Society's view of same-sex marriage, and the number of religious entities that object to it, are far different today than was the view of anti-miscegenation policies in the 1980s when the *Bob Jones* case was decided. One need not agree with those who reject same-sex marriage on religious grounds – and I certainly do not agree with them and would be happy to engage in theological debate over the topic – to see that the situation regarding religious objections to same-sex marriage is far different from the situation regarding interracial marriage was in the 1980s. Again, this does not mean that it is good for religious non-profits to discriminate based on same-sex marriage status. In fact, some people, myself included, would refuse to donate to such organizations. But it does mean that the IRS is unlikely to revoke these organizations' tax-exempt status.

A powerful argument that may be made to get the IRS to revoke the tax-exempt status of religious non-profits is that we should not wait until the discrimination has been allowed to remain for decades before acting to stop it. The idea here is that organizations that discriminate based on same-sex marriage are on the wrong side of justice and the wrong side of history, just as organizations that discriminated based on race were on the wrong side of justice and the wrong side of history. If these organizations want to continue with their discriminatory policies, taxpayers should not be helping foot the bill through tax exemptions. This argument has a lot of force, but the number of religious non-profits that have such policies is vast and the public benefits they provide are also vast. In some areas of the country, the homeless would have nowhere to go if local religious non-profits shut down or had to operate on vastly reduced budgets.

Many religious non-profits operate on tight budgets as it is, and loss of tax-exempt status under Section 501(c)(3) would not only remove their immediate tax benefits but would also limit the donations that keep many of these charities running because those donations would no longer be tax deductible. Of course, this is precisely the point of the earlier argument. If these charities lose their tax-exempt status, their donors may donate to other charities and at the very least the public would not be subsidizing the discrimination against same-sex couples.

Again, this is not to say that the IRS could not revoke the tax-exempt status of religious non-profits. It is, however, unlikely that the IRS will do so, at least in the near future. Additionally, as explained later, the IRS would almost certainly be sued under RFRA and the Free Exercise Clause of the First Amendment to the Constitution if it revoked a religious entity's tax-exempt status based on discrimination against same-sex couples. The *Bob Jones* case demonstrated that the IRS does have a compelling interest in revoking the tax-exempt status of schools that discriminate based on race, even when that revocation places a substantial burden on those schools. The *Bob Jones* case also held that there is no less restrictive way for the IRS to meet that compelling interest than revoking tax-exempt status. It is not, however, completely clear what the Supreme Court would do in the same-sex marriage context under RFRA in similar circumstances.

A final, yet important difference between the discrimination addressed in *Bob Jones* and discrimination by religious non-profits in the context of same-sex marriage is that the *Bob Jones* Court relied on a variety of laws and actions to support its holding that racial discrimination in education is "so at odds with the community conscience as to undermine any public benefit that might be conferred."[20] These included multiple decisions by the Supreme Court condemning racial segregation and discrimination, the existence of several federal laws passed by Congress – including the Civil Rights Act of 1964 – which condemn racial segregation and discrimination, and actions by presidents (called executive orders) condemning racial discrimination.[21]

The Supreme Court has condemned discrimination based on sexual orientation in a case called *Romer v. Evans*,[22] albeit in far less conclusive language than in cases involving racial discrimination. The Court also held in *United States v. Windsor*[23] that the federal Defense of Marriage Act is unconstitutional because it promoted discrimination under federal law against same-sex couples whose relationships were recognized by the states in which they lived. And, of course, the Court has recognized the fundamental right to same-sex marriage in *Obergefell*. Moreover, President Obama has issued executive orders preventing discrimination based on same-sex marital status in federal employment and other contexts.[24] Congress, however, has not passed any law prohibiting discrimination based on sexual orientation, let alone based on same-sex marital status. Therefore, while all three branches of government were strongly and unconditionally against racial discrimination well before the *Bob Jones* case was decided, the situation is different in regard to same-sex marriage. This may also cause the IRS to leave alone the tax-exempt status of religious non-profits that discriminate based on same-sex marriage.

What about religious non-profits that discriminate based on sexual orientation generally, rather than same-sex marriage specifically? This is much harder to predict. Will the IRS show deference to religious entities' decisions here, or will it revoke tax-exempt status? Society, including many religious people, is moving more quickly in the direction of rejecting this sort of discrimination.[25] This might suggest that non-profits that engage in this sort of discrimination are more outside of social norms and that these organizations are very much at odds with community standards, thus "undermining" the public benefits they provide. With the exception of houses of worship, it may not be possible to make a reasonable prediction of what the IRS will do. My guess – and that is all it is, an educated guess – is that the IRS will not act immediately to revoke tax-exempt status in these situations except perhaps in egregious cases, such as if a charity were to turn away homeless individuals based on sexual orientation. Eventually, however, I think it is quite possible the IRS will revoke tax-exempt status for organizations that discriminate in providing services to people based on sexual orientation.

What about religious universities that have policies against students or employees dating or engaging in sexual conduct with people of the same sex, as opposed to getting married? These are actually two very different situations. A number of religious universities have policies prohibiting premarital sexual conduct, at least on campus. If the university applied such a policy regardless of the sexual orientation of the students, there would not be any discrimination for the IRS to consider. If the school applied the policy only against gays and lesbians, it is possible that the IRS might revoke tax-exempt status, but that is an open question.

Dating is a different situation, however, because this sort of policy would be more likely targeted at same-sex relationships unless the university prohibits all students from dating regardless of sexual orientation. Unlike the premarital sex and sex on campus bans, which do exist at some universities, I am not aware of a university with a policy forbidding all romantic relationships between students. If a university has a policy banning just same-sex romantic relationships, its tax-exempt status may be more at risk, but again this is hypothetical at this point in time.

The discussion so far has focused on religious non-profits that are not churches. What about churches and other houses of worship? The concept of "church status" under Section 501(c)(3) makes situations involving houses of worship and other religious organizations a bit different.[26] The term "church status" is awkward because it applies not just to churches but also to synagogues, temples, mosques, and so on. The most significant advantages of church status are that churches are not required to receive a ruling from the IRS to have Section 501(c)(3) status, that churches need not file annual informational returns or Form

990 to maintain Section 501(c)(3) status (reports that other Section 501[c][3] entities are required to file), and that there are significant restrictions on the IRS's ability to investigate churches and specific procedures the IRS must follow if it does investigate a church. Of course, if the IRS chooses to investigate and finds that an entity claiming church status does not meet the requirements to hold that status, the IRS may revoke that entity's church status. If an entity loses church status, it may still remain a Section 501(c)(3) entity so long as it meets all of the requirements to qualify and maintain tax exempt status, including the filing of annual reports.

The IRS has revoked the church status of churches, and sometimes even Section 501(c)(3) status generally, when they have violated the requirements of Section 501(c)(3). Reasons for church status revocation include, for example, private individuals profiting from being affiliated with the church[27] or the church getting involved in politics.[28]

Yet it is far less likely that the IRS would revoke the church status or broader tax-exempt status of a church that was otherwise qualified for Section 501(c)(3) status because its doctrines prohibited it from performing same-sex marriages. Is it theoretically possible? Yes. Is it even remotely likely to happen? No. In fact, the chances of the IRS revoking tax-exempt status under these circumstances are beyond slim; as discussed later, even in the exceedingly unlikely event that the IRS was to do so, a church would have an even stronger claim under RFRA than would other religious non-profits. The same would likely be true even if the church denied membership based on sexual orientation in general. It is exceedingly unlikely that the IRS would revoke a church's tax-exempt status based on the church's religious doctrine.

If the IRS did decide to revoke the tax-exempt status of a religious non-profit, whether a church or not, the decision would likely be appealed under the Internal Revenue Code, and more relevant for our purposes, under RFRA. The IRS is a federal agency, and RFRA applies to actions taken by the federal government. State revocation of tax-exempt status may face similar challenges under state RFRAs.

Of course, in *Bob Jones* the Supreme Court held that while revocation of tax-exempt status does impose a substantial burden on a religious non-profit, the IRS had a compelling interest for revoking the schools' tax-exempt status, and revoking that status was the least restrictive means for meeting that compelling interest. In *Bob Jones*, the Supreme Court was applying the then-existent legal test under the Free Exercise Clause of the First Amendment to the Constitution. We learned in Chapter 2 that *Employment Division v. Smith* changed the legal test under the Free Exercise Clause, but the legal test used under *Bob Jones* is now the legal test used under RFRA. We also learned, however, that in the *Hobby Lobby* case, the Supreme Court held that RFRA provides even more stringent protection than does the earlier legal test under the Free Exercise Clause.

So would a religious non-profit that had its tax-exempt status revoked by the IRS because that non-profit discriminated in regard to same-sex marital status or sexual orientation be able to bring a successful claim under RFRA? It seems clear after *Obergefell v. Hodges* that the government, including the IRS, has a compelling interest in protecting the fundamental right to same-sex marriage. While earlier cases do not say so explicitly, it seems likely that the government would have a compelling interest in prohibiting discrimination based on sexual orientation generally, although that compelling interest would be on even sturdier footing if Congress passed a law protecting against discrimination based on sexual orientation.

The question would come down to whether revoking tax-exempt status is the most narrowly tailored way to serve the government's compelling interest in prohibiting discrimination based on same-sex marital status or sexual orientation more generally. On the one hand, revoking tax-exempt status does not preclude the religious entity from practicing its religion, as would an injunction by a court requiring the entity to stop discriminating. The entity would remain free to follow its tenets, but without taxpayer support through a tax exemption. It is quite possible then, that revocation of tax-exempt status could be viewed by a court as narrowly tailored.

On the other hand, it is possible that the religious entity could propose a more narrowly tailored measure such as a fine based on the number of people that it turns away, or revocation of only a percentage of its tax-exempt status based on the number of people it serves versus the number of people it turns away. This sort of approach may only make sense in charitable contexts involving the needy, rather than in educational contexts. It seems unlikely that a court would accept these alternatives because they may be unreasonably hard to implement, while denial of tax-exempt status seems narrowly tailored to the compelling governmental interest in not supporting discrimination.

It seems that the IRS would have a good chance of winning were its decision to revoke the tax-exempt status of a religious non-profit challenged under RFRA. Of course, as explained earlier, this is unlikely to become an issue precisely because the IRS is unlikely to revoke the tax-exempt status of a religious non-profit for discrimination based on same-sex marital status. It is possible that the IRS might do so to address and prevent more egregious forms of discrimination based on sexual orientation, and if in this instance the religious non-profit challenged the revocation of its tax-exempt status under RFRA, the IRS would most likely win.

II RELIGIOUS CHARITIES AND CONSCIENCE CLAIMS UNDER MANDATORY CONTRACEPTIVE COVERAGE LAWS

A number of situations in the news involve religious charities and the HHS Mandate under the Affordable Care Act, which requires that insurance plans cover contraceptive care. The Affordable Care Act has exceptions for religious entities. The first exception applies to "religious employers," which includes "churches, their integrated auxiliaries, and conventions or associations of churches."[29] These entities are completely exempt from providing contraceptive services under the Affordable Care Act. Please note that the term "church" used in this regulation is shorthand for any house of worship or religious order regardless of religious affiliation: so it would apply to synagogues, mosques, temples, and so on in addition to Christian churches. Most state mandatory contraceptive coverage laws have similar exceptions for religious employers. This category does not, however, include religious non-profits generally.

Religious non-profits are protected by another provision in the HHS regulations under the Affordable Care Act, but it is not a complete exemption because they must self-certify that they oppose contraceptive coverage to be exempted. The self-certification initiates a process whereby the insurer excludes contraceptive coverage from the protected entity's insurance plan and then must provide separate coverage for contraceptive services without charging anything to the employer, its insurance plan, or its employees for this coverage. The organizations protected by this provision are called "eligible organizations," and the following definition taken directly from the HHS regulations demonstrates that this provision would cover most religious non-profits that are not already protected as "religious employers":

> Eligible organizations. An eligible organization is an organization that satisfies all of the following requirements:
>
> (1) The organization opposes providing coverage for some or all of any contraceptive services required to be covered under §147.130(a)(1)(iv) on account of religious objections.
> (2) The organization is organized and operates as a nonprofit entity.
> (3) The organization holds itself out as a religious organization.
> (4) The organization self-certifies, in a form and manner specified by the Secretary, that it satisfies the criteria in paragraphs (b)(1) through (3) of this section, and makes such self-certification available for examination upon request by the first day of the first plan year to which the accommodation in paragraph (c) of this section applies. The self-certification must be executed by a person authorized to make the certification on behalf of the organization, and must be maintained in a manner consistent with the record retention requirements under section 107 of the Employee Retirement Income Security Act of 1974.[30]

At first glance, it appears that this accommodation for religious non-profits that object to providing contraceptive coverage under their insurance plans would make everyone happy. The religious non-profit need not provide the coverage or pay for it in any way. The employees are still able to receive the coverage and do not have to pay anything extra for it. Third-party insurers who provide the coverage when the religious non-profit is self-insured receive an in-kind offset for the expenses through a reduction in the fees they must pay the government under the Affordable Care Act. Finally, according to the HHS other insurers will not lose any money and may come out ahead for providing contraceptive services because if the services were not provided, the insurer's costs would be much higher. In other words, the cost of not providing contraceptives for the insurer is equal to or higher than the cost of providing them.

So everyone should be happy, right? Not exactly. A group of religious non-profits sued the HHS challenging the requirement that they must self-certify that they oppose providing contraceptive care. Their argument is that this self-certification triggers the process that provides the contraceptive coverage to their employees. They argue this makes them complicit in the ultimate use of contraception, which violates the tenets of their faith. They seek a complete exemption such as the one "religious employers" enjoy, or perhaps a system whereby the employees themselves would apply for the contraceptive coverage without requiring the employer to self-certify.

These cases made their way all the way to the Supreme Court, and on May 16, 2016 – perhaps as a result of the Court having a vacancy – it urged the parties to work the situation out and find a compromise. In the meantime, the lawsuits filed by the parties can serve as notice that those employers object to providing contraceptive coverage. Other religious non-profits will still be required to follow the HHS notice requirements and therefore the challenges are likely to continue.[31] Of course, these non-profits filing suit are the exception rather than the rule, because many religious non-profits have no serious issues with providing contraceptive coverage since doing so does not conflict with their faith.

Among the entities that sued to challenge the HHS self-certification requirement, the most famous, at least from a media perspective, is Little Sisters of the Poor. [32] Let's explore the claims made by Little Sisters of the Poor and the other organizations that sued the government in these cases, and see how they may be decided under RFRA if the Supreme Court ever decides the issue. After that explication, I suggest an accommodation that should be provided no matter how the Supreme Court decides the issue. Finally, I explain why this accommodation should not be available to for-profit entities.

Chapter 6 addressed conscience claims in the healthcare and same-sex marriage contexts. Yet when religious entities assert an objection to being involved in mandatory contraceptive coverage because of concerns that being involved would make them complicit in the use of contraception, they also assert a conscience claim. The concern is that when they self-certify that they object to providing contraceptive care, these entities set into motion a process that leads to the very use of contraceptives that violates their faith. It is their employees who receive the coverage, and even if it is not directly paid for by the non-profits, the coverage is only provided because the non-profit fills out the form. If there were a way to cover employees without requiring the religious non-profit to certify anything or fill out a form, the complicity concerns would be minimal or even nonexistent.

Of course, if the government completely exempted these organizations as it does churches, there would also be no complicity concern, but the employees of these entities would lose coverage for contraceptives entirely. This would create a significant gap in contraceptive coverage, given the number of Catholic and certain other religious non-profits that could be involved. That gap would significantly undermine the government's interest in providing contraceptive coverage. Completely exempting other religious entities such as churches, which primarily serve their own flocks rather than the general public, and which often employ only people who share the faith of the church, is an exemption that makes sense as a matter of public policy. In fact, once the issue was brought to the attention of the Obama administration, the exemption for what are now called "religious employers," such as churches, was quickly recognized.

Even if religious non-profits such as charities and universities are carrying out the mission of the faith, as a practical matter they often employ and serve more people outside of the faith than do most churches. Yet providing a complete exemption for these entities in the aggregate would deny contraceptive coverage for a large number of women; make no mistake, the negative impact of the denial of contraceptive coverage falls almost exclusively on women. Yet what if there were a way to ensure that every one of these employees who wants contraceptive coverage could get it at no additional expense, and without requiring the religious non-profit to provide the coverage or subsidize it? This is the underlying basis for the current system requiring self-certification by these organizations. It would be easy for someone who does not understand the concept of complicity in sin to argue essentially, "You have already been accommodated. Stop the complaining and just be happy you aren't being forced to provide the coverage directly."

The response to this requires that often hard-to-find quality in these hotly contested spaces: the ability to put oneself in the other side's shoes. Imagine for a moment that you oppose the use of certain pesticides because of the harm they can cause to children and animals. Your community has experienced an outbreak of a nonnative species of insect, which is harming native populations and crops, and potentially also carries diseases that can infect cattle. The state has determined that if 90 percent of the property in your community (and nearby communities) is treated with a particular pesticide, the invading species will either die out or be overcome by native species that are not affected by this particular pesticide. You are a chemist and you believe that your research demonstrates this pesticide is harmful, but the government did not agree with your testimony on the issue when you opposed the measure. You think the government might be overreacting to the situation or perhaps is even being influenced by the farmers who are most affected by the invasive species.

You have refused to allow the spraying on your property, which consists of several acres. The government has told you that you have two options. You can pay massive daily fines until you agree to have your property sprayed or you can certify that you oppose the spraying and therefore other properties will be sprayed instead. At this point, only you and ten other landowners are refusing to allow the spraying, but the government has decided not to spray schools or hospitals out of an abundance of caution (they do plan to spray other government buildings and parks). If you certify that you oppose having your property sprayed, it is most likely that some property at a school or hospital will have to be sprayed to reach the 90 percent needed to drive out the invasive species. Your research tells you that this could dramatically harm children at the school or patients in the hospital. Extrapolating from the evidence based on your research, you believe the harm could pose serious issues for the children or patients in the future. The government does not agree and rejects your use of the evidence and your methodology. What should you do?

This is similar to the position facing religious non-profits like Little Sisters of the Poor. They are placed in a Hobson's Choice: certify to something that they believe would make them complicit in serious harm to others, pay hefty fines that will bankrupt them, or stop serving the community that they have served and needs their help. Some might argue that in the hypothetical example, the objecting person has scientific evidence to back up his or her concerns, but the religious non-profits take on faith the idea that life begins at conception and therefore contraception is sinful. But in the hypothetical scenario, the government rejected the individual objector's scientific arguments as being inaccurate, so the situations are analogous: Government is forcing you to certify to something that will set a process in place that you, but not the government or public at large, are certain will cause harm. By certifying you become complicit in that harm. Let me be clear: This situation is not related to the debate between some religions and science in which, as I have written elsewhere, science should win when the public schools are involved.[33]

As you may recall from Chapter 2, individuals and entities must prove three things to win under RFRA. First, they must prove that whatever it is the government is doing places a substantial burden on the objecting parties' religion. I think it is fairly certain that this element will be met by Little Sisters of the Poor and the other religious non-profits involved in the case. Even with the accommodation provided under the Affordable Care Act, these entities are arguing that either they must be complicit in something they believe to be morally and religiously repugnant and sinful or they must pay massive fines or close down entirely. Given the ease with which the Supreme Court found in *Hobby Lobby* that for-profit entities were substantially burdened by the choice between paying the fines under the Affordable Care Act and providing the coverage, it seems likely that the Court will agree there is a substantial burden imposed on Little Sisters of the Poor and the other non-profits in the case. The primary difference between the situation in *Hobby Lobby* and that in the *Little Sisters of the Poor* case is that the self-certification system is designed to accommodate religious entities. This difference might be relevant for the third requirement under RFRA, but it is unlikely to prevent the Supreme Court from finding a substantial burden on religion in the case.

Next it must be determined whether the government has a compelling interest (an exceptionally important interest) in whatever it is doing that imposes the substantial burden. In *Hobby Lobby*, the Supreme Court simply assumed for the sake of argument that the government had a compelling interest in requiring contraceptive coverage under the Affordable Care Act. As was explained in Chapter 2, there are compelling interests supporting the contraceptive coverage requirement under the Affordable Care Act that have been recognized by courts in other contexts, such as protecting women's health, saving the government substantial money (contraceptive coverage is substantially cheaper than covering unwanted or accidental pregnancies), and perhaps most obvious, protecting the constitutional right to contraception and reproductive freedom in government-mandated programs. So if the Court were to address this issue, it is likely that it would find a compelling interest on the merits.

Finally, if the government has a compelling interest for imposing the requirement, is the manner in which it implemented the exemption for religious non-profits the most narrowly tailored way to serve that interest, or are there less restrictive ways for the government to serve its interest? The government has gone quite far in accommodating religious non-profits. The charities will likely argue that the government could have completely exempted them as it did churches and similar religious employers. That, however, could greatly undermine the government's compelling interest in making sure that women have access to contraceptive coverage. The non-profits in the case are wide-ranging entities from small charitable organizations to large universities. If all of these entities were exempt tens of thousands of employees could be affected, and, of course, even larger universities and charities might be able to claim exemptions.

Even more problematic is that for-profit entities that object to providing contraceptive coverage are now covered by an identical self-certification system. If the religious non-profits are exempted because the self-certification process is not narrowly tailored, then the religious for-profits, which the Supreme Court analogized to religious non-profits in the *Hobby Lobby* decision, might also have to be completely exempted. The impact on the government interest in providing women with adequate contraceptive care would be dramatically undermined.

Another option might be to require female employees to certify that they want the coverage rather than asking the employer to do it, but this also raises serious problems. It places the burden on female employees who want coverage to learn that they must certify (and it seems unlikely that many of the entities involved would be willing to provide notification directly to their employees), and then to do so simply to receive benefits that the government has determined they should be entitled to. More problematic is the fact that even if the certification system is confidential, female employees may fear that their certification could be found out and that they might be retaliated against or otherwise negatively affected at work, or even in the community at large. It is possible that the Supreme Court might accept this as a more narrowly tailored alternative, but it would appear to place a significant burden and risk on the female employees. While two or three justices of the Supreme Court might not see a problem with this alternative, I think at least five would find it problematic, especially in light of Justice Kennedy's concurring opinion in *Hobby Lobby*, where he clearly asserted that accommodating religious freedom claims should not place burdens on third parties.

However, yet another potential alternative could work were it not for the *Hobby Lobby* decision. The government could keep the bulk of the system used for religious non-profits under the Affordable Care Act, but not require self-certification. Therefore, all religious non-profits would be covered (not solely houses of worship). The government could then allow those religious non-profits that want to opt into direct coverage to "opt in." The government could even provide an incentive for these entities, and many religious entities would opt in because they support contraceptive care for their employees. If the religious non-profit does not opt in, contraceptive care would be covered by the same system as exists now to accommodate religious non-profits; so either way the employees would receive coverage without being inconvenienced or harmed.

Of course, this accommodation raises its own problems. First, what constitutes a religious non-profit as opposed to a charitable or educational non-profit could become an issue since religious non-profits would be automatically exempt. However, this issue can be resolved by borrowing from the IRS's approach, which recognizes that a non-profit can serve more than one charitable function. Therefore, there would be no problem as long as religious non-profits could be identified regardless of what other functions they might serve. Yet, how could government do that without getting into the tricky business of determining which organizations are truly "religious" (a business that the IRS has long been in without being challenged successfully under the First Amendment to the U.S. Constitution)? In most cases, it will be obvious which entities are religious non-profits and which are not based on their tax filings, articles of incorporation, charters, and so on. When in doubt, however, the government could ask for certification that the entity is a religious non-profit. This would not make the entity complicit in contraceptive coverage because the employees would be covered regardless. The certification in this scenario simply allows the religious non-profit to be recognized as such.

Second, there is *Hobby Lobby*. This proposed accommodation works well so long as we are only dealing with religious non-profits, but now that closely held for-profits are covered under RFRA, and the same sort of accommodation has been applied to them under the Affordable Care Act, this accommodation may not be workable. This would be ironic because it would mean that traditional religious entities such as Little Sisters of the Poor could be denied a workable accommodation and lose their case because the protection of for-profit entities would make that accommodation unworkable and no longer a viable alternative in the eyes of the courts. The practical reality is that it would be almost impossible for government to know which for-profit companies have religious objections to providing contraceptive coverage, and it is more likely that for-profit entities might claim objector status for financial rather than religious reasons, even though some would do so strictly for deeply rooted religious reasons. The system would be unworkable if closely held for-profit entities were covered.

As a result, no option may be more narrowly tailored than the current system; under that system, Little Sisters of the Poor and the other religious non-profits would lose. I would recommend that government cover them anyway as a permissive accommodation, but there is a risk that religious for-profits might challenge such an approach for excluding them. They might lose that challenge, but even the possibility could make the HHS wary. It is ironic that Little Sisters of the Poor would have a much better alternative accommodation if *Hobby Lobby* had not been decided the way it was. I think that Little Sisters of the Poor should win given the nature of RFRA, while Hobby Lobby should have lost, but of course that is not what happened.

III RELIGIOUS UNIVERSITIES AND ADOPTION AGENCIES

Religious universities also pose some special problems. Many religious universities serve a wide range of students and employ a diverse array of faculty and staff who may or may not share the faith of the institution. Think about large religious universities such as Notre Dame, Brigham Young University, Yeshiva University, and so forth. Not all religious universities would have a problem with providing contraceptive coverage, providing benefits to same-sex couples, or hiring faculty or staff or admitting students who are in same-sex relationships. But some of these institutions do have problems with these issues.

For example, Notre Dame University filed suit over the same issue as Little Sisters of the Poor. The university ultimately was forced to self-certify or pay hefty fines that would have had a negative impact on its students, faculty, and staff, as well as on its broader religious and educational mission. If the *Zubik* case, which involves Little Sisters of the Poor, but also involves three smaller colleges, is resolved in favor of the religious non-profits, Notre Dame might consider seeking whatever accommodation is given the non-profits in the case. Of course, as was explained earlier, for now the *Zubik* case is on hold under an order from the Supreme Court requesting that the parties find a compromise.

Another concern for religious universities is the potential revocation of tax-exempt status. The analysis of threats to tax-exempt status discussed in Section I is relevant in the university context. I think it unlikely that the IRS will threaten the tax-exempt status of a religious university if that university denies benefits to or refuses to recognize the same-sex marriages of faculty or students. But if the university discriminates based on sexual orientation generally, or perhaps if it refused to hire faculty or admit students in same-sex marriages, it becomes more likely that the IRS or a state taxing authority might attempt to revoke tax-exempt status. With that said, as the discussion in Section I of this chapter explains, any attempt to discern what the IRS or state taxing authorities might do is simply an educated guess at this point.

Government grants, funding, and contracts raise other important questions for religious universities. These can come from a variety of government agencies at both the federal and state levels. What if one or more of these agencies decided to deny funding, grants, or contracts to entities that refuse to hire, admit, or provide spousal insurance coverage for those in same-sex marriages? I do not think this is likely to happen on a large-scale basis, but given the wide array of agencies that are involved in funding, grants, and contracts, it certainly could happen. There is basically nothing that the university could do other than file a challenge under RFRA or argue that the denial violates the terms of the government program that supports the funding, grant, or contract. RFRA would not likely be helpful here because the compelling interest in fostering nondiscrimination in government programs is clear after *Obergefell*, and because denying specific funding, grants, or contracts is likely to be viewed as far more narrowly tailored than levying fines, denying all funding, or even revoking tax-exempt status.

Adoption agencies raise an additional set of questions. Many, but not all, adoption agencies are religious. Some religious adoption agencies object to placing children with same-sex couples on religious grounds. This creates a catch-22 for state officials who regulate adoption agencies. There is no scientific basis for denying placement to same-sex couples. In fact, the studies to date demonstrate that children thrive as well in same-sex parented households as in other households.[34]

State authorities, especially in states with anti-discrimination laws prohibiting discrimination based on sexual orientation and/or marital status, are concerned that allowing these agencies to continue to discriminate while licensed by the state would violate state anti-discrimination laws, and in states without such laws would violate the rights and interests of same-sex couples. On the other hand, if the state requires these religious adoption agencies to place children with same-sex couples or levies hefty fines on the agencies, the agencies might shut down rather than violate their religious missions. This would have a negative impact on the number of children placed for adoption in the state, and therefore on the children themselves. This is exactly what happened in Massachusetts. The state went after religious adoption agencies, including a large Catholic adoption agency, because those agencies would not place children with same-sex couples. The Catholic adoption agency shut down in the state rather than violate its religious tenets.[35] In fact, Massachusetts is not alone; adoption and foster care agencies in Washington, D.C. and Illinois have closed rather than allow same-sex couples to adopt.[36]

Yet accommodations are possible in many of these cases. If there are secular adoption agencies or other religious adoption agencies that do place children with same-sex couples in the same or nearby areas, it would make sense to accommodate a religious adoption agency that does not place children with same-sex couples unless a state anti-discrimination law would not allow it (many of these laws have exemptions for religious entities). This provides the maximum placement for children while not preventing same-sex parents from being able to adopt. This is not an ideal solution because the adoption agency would still be discriminating, but it is a religious entity rather than a for-profit public accommodation, which may create less dignitary harm in a pluralistic society for any couple that is denied placement as long as they can go elsewhere without significant inconvenience. Therefore, while not ideal this solution balances the interests of the state and the children in placement with the interests of same-sex parents to be able to adopt.

Yet what if the religious adoption agency that refuses to place children with same-sex couples is the only one in the area, and the state cannot supply or facilitate an alternative? For wealthier couples, this may be less of an issue because they could go elsewhere, but for many people this is not an option. Moreover, the lack of a local option may create more of a meaningful harm since the state licenses these agencies and thus has at least implicitly condoned a situation where same-sex couples who are not wealthy enough to travel far away to adopt now have no access to adoption. The problem is that, as we saw in Massachusetts, it is entirely possible that if the state levied heavy fines on the religious agency or required it to allow same-sex couples to adopt, the agency might stop operating in that state if it is part of a larger religious entity.

This is a very tough question. I am torn on how to answer it because of the potentially negative impact on the children involved if the agency were to shut down. Yet under such circumstances, if a claim were filed against the agency, the state should require the agency to allow same-sex couples to adopt or at least to find some alternative way to allow the couples to adopt that imposes no cost on the couples. This could lead to a terrible outcome for orphaned children if the agency shut down, but if the state were able to provide or facilitate a secular alternative, there would be no need for the agency to close.

8   SOME CONCLUDING THOUGHTS

At this point, you should have a decent understanding of the law that determines outcomes when there is conflict between religious freedom and sexual freedom. You should also know that in most situations, there need not be any conflict between religious freedom and sexual freedom. Most religious freedom claims have little or no impact on anyone other than the individual or entity seeking a religious accommodation. Most importantly, you should know that even where conflict exists, it is possible to compromise, and thus maximize freedoms on both sides. You may not agree that such compromise is necessary, or even that it is beneficial, but you know that it is possible under the law.

Of course, the law is not everything. Issues of religious freedom and sexual freedom raise important social questions. The culture wars have perhaps deafened too many people's ears to the concerns of the other side, or to the concerns of either side. Hopefully you have at least gotten a sense for the deep commitments and important impacts that these issues have for religious people, members of the LGBT community, and women whose reproductive freedom hangs in the balance. In Chapter 1, I wrote that these issues all involve what it means to be a human being and how we define ourselves, and perhaps how we are defined by others.

The rights involved on both sides go to the core of human freedom; without compromise, we will tip in one direction or the other and lose part of what it means to be free. You have met many people in this book, including real people whose cases have defined the law that applies to all of us, and fictional people from the four hypotheticals at the beginning of the book, each of which was drawn from either a real case or a real scenario. If you did not feel for these people or for any of those from the real cases in the chapters that followed, I have failed you – and for that I am sorry. Yet I hope that most readers have been able to feel for some of those involved in these scenarios; perhaps it is too much of a dream, but I hope most readers were able to empathize with people on both sides.

There are winners and losers, but they ebb and flow depending on the issue. One side wins and then it loses, before winning again and then losing. It is the nature of legal battles in the culture wars. Yet if we talk to each other and seek compromise, perhaps the wins will not be complete because the losers will be accommodated to the greatest extent possible. If such is the case, then everyone, including society and the American value of freedom, wins. That is, unless that value is just puffery used by one side or the other to represent only its own freedom.

Freedom is easy when you are the one getting it. It is much harder when it allows someone whose beliefs or lifestyle you oppose to have freedom. But this is the beauty of real freedom: It is not just for one side. It is for everyone – or at least that is the idea.

This chapter provides some concluding thoughts, as well as addressing two final issues. First, I address how the four hypotheticals at the beginning of this book would be decided today, how they would most likely be decided if we let the extremes on each side define the outcome, and how they would most likely be decided if we are able to find common ground on these issues.

Second, I explain and make some observations about a phenomenon that I have observed over the past few years. I understand that what I assert is controversial and certainly may ruffle some feathers – feathers that do not take much to ruffle. Moreover, I do not have a solution for the concern, but I need to mention it because I fear that if it continues it could cause a chasm too deep to cross, or at least pose a long-term threat to compromise. The phenomenon I am referring to is the double-edged sword of extreme social conservatism and extreme political correctness. These two heads seem to most people to be miles apart, one on the "right" and one on the "left," but the problem is that they are more alike than you might think. Both try to squelch discourse with which they disagree and impose their will on dissent. If we cannot speak about things and try to treat the other side with a modicum of respect, we are doomed to a cycle of self-radicalization that will spiral further and further from any chance at finding common ground. The section addressing this concern contains just a few observations, but I would be remiss if I did not discuss these issues at all.

I WHAT WILL HAPPEN TO MICHELLE AND JANET, JONATHAN, AMY, AND MANDY?

We explore each of these scenarios in three stages. First, we look at what the results would be today under the current law. Second, we predict what the results would be if we let the extremes on either side determine the outcome. Third, we imagine what the results would be if some of the compromises suggested in this book were implemented.

A What Would Happen under Current Law?

1 Michelle and Janet
Many things have changed since 2010, when this hypothetical is set. Since that time, the U.S. Supreme Court has held that there is a fundamental right to same-sex marriage. Therefore, today Michelle and Janet could be legally married and Michelle would be able to qualify as a spouse on Janet's insurance policy.

It is possible that Janet's employer might claim, based on *Hobby Lobby*, that it should not have to cover same-sex couples, but this is exceedingly unlikely unless it happens to be a closely held company run by people who have a religious objection to same-sex marriage *and* who decide to deny benefits. If this did occur, the employer would most likely lose any lawsuit filed against it because if it provides spousal benefits it would have a hard time justifying any discrimination even under a RFRA, especially now that the right to marry has received constitutional protection.

Assuming that a federal benefits law, such as the ACA, was involved, the employer could assert a defense under the federal

RFRA. If state law were involved and the state had a RFRA that protects for-profit entities, it is possible that the employer might assert a RFRA defense. If they had to sue, and the employer defended under a RFRA, Michelle and Janet would most likely win because the federal or state government would have a compelling interest in mandating equal access to benefits. Moreover, requiring coverage would most likely be narrowly tailored to meet that interest.

Still, *Hobby Lobby* leaves the possibility that a court would find that requiring coverage is not narrowly tailored and the government might have to step in to accommodate. This could be a crapshoot because of the politics involved in any remedy created or funded by the government. Of course, if we take the *Hobby Lobby* Court's word at face value, the harm here would certainly be more than zero, and therefore a court is likely to find that requiring coverage is narrowly tailored. Additionally, if the state has an antidiscrimination provision in its insurance coverage law or a state antidiscrimination law that protects based on marital status or sexual orientation, Michelle and Janet would almost certainly win, even if the employer asserted a claim under a state RFRA, because requiring non-discrimination is narrowly tailored to meet the compelling interest in enforcing a non-discrimination law.

2 *Mandy*

Mandy's situation may be the easiest to answer under today's law. The plaintiff in the actual case on which Mandy's hypothetical is based, Julea Ward, won her case. She won under the First Amendment to the U.S. Constitution. Therefore, Mandy would likely win her case (if she sued the university) today. Still, the Supreme Court has not addressed the issue directly, and it is possible that a different federal court from the one that decided Julea Ward's case could decide differently under the Constitution.

If Mandy lost her claims under the U.S. Constitution, whether she ultimately wins or loses would be decided by whether or not her state has a RFRA. If it does, she would most likely win. If it does not, she would most likely lose unless that state's courts interpret the state constitution to apply a standard similar to RFRA.

3 *Amy*

Amy may have a glimmer of hope, or rather two glimmers. First, the Department of Health and Human Services has provided an accommodation for for-profit employers such as Hobby Lobby and Amy's employer, which allows those employers to certify that they will not provide coverage for certain contraceptives and therefore receive the same sort of accommodation that religious non-profits do. A third-party policy will cover the contraceptives since Amy's employer is self-insured. The federal government will offset the cost for the third-party insurer through lower fees under the Affordable Care Act. Thus, for now at least, Amy could be covered.

This, of course, could change when a new president is elected if the Executive Branch – through the secretary of Health and Human Services – decides not to support this accommodation because it increases costs related to the Affordable Care Act, or for other reasons. This would put Amy in the position of having to sue her employer for denying her benefits and thus violating the HHS Mandate under the Affordable Care Act, unless the government was willing to sue on her behalf. Assuming she was willing to do this (which is not an easy decision for anyone), and assuming she had standing (this is a legal term meaning that she would have a right to bring a personal lawsuit under the Affordable Care Act), her employer would defend under RFRA citing *Hobby Lobby*. Amy would have a better chance at winning than the employees in *Hobby Lobby* would have had because under this scenario the very accommodation that the Supreme Court suggested in Hobby Lobby would have been rejected by the new secretary of Health and Human Services. Therefore, there may be no more narrowly tailored alternative than requiring her employer to cover her. She also might have a claim under her state's mandatory contraceptive coverage law, depending on how that law and defenses based on religious objections by a for-profit entity would be interpreted by her state's courts.

Amy could face another possible issue. As mentioned earlier, currently for-profit employers with religious objections to providing contraceptive coverage are protected by the same accommodation as religious non-profits under the Affordable Care Act, which requires that they certify they have a religious objection to providing coverage. As Chapter 7 explained, the Supreme Court has not issued a final decision in a case challenging the accommodation given to religious non-profits under the HHS Mandate. If that challenge is successful, the accommodation will be found to violate RFRA for religious non-profits. At that point, for-profit entities with religious objections to providing contraceptive coverage might use the Supreme Court's decision in that case, combined with *Hobby Lobby*, to argue that the accommodation is also invalid as to for-profit entities. This might be a harder argument because the Supreme Court specifically suggested this accommodation as a possible one for for-profit entities in *Hobby Lobby*. If somehow her employer won on such a claim, Amy would not have coverage unless the government paid for it, her state's law was interpreted differently, or some other acceptable accommodation was found.

4 Jonathan

Jonathan has one of the tougher situations under today's law, which is ironic because his case is a classic religious freedom scenario. It reflects the many claims brought by people whose religion was not considered when general rules were made because they are not as well represented in society as mainline Christianity and do not have enough power or are too far out of the mainstream to easily get accommodation. One question will determine Jonathan's fate: Does his state have a RFRA or interpret its constitution to provide protections similar to those provided by a RFRA? We already know the answer to that question. His state has no such law; therefore, under today's law he loses.

The injustice of this situation should be palpable to many of you. Here is a kid who just wants to take off from school for holidays central to his faith without suffering punishment or negative repercussions. His requested accommodation does not harm anyone else. Yet unless his state has a RFRA, he loses. Of course, the principal could try to give him a permissive accommodation, but the principal already explained to Jonathan's parents that he cannot do so under the school's policies without the consent of the coach and teacher involved.

B What Would Happen if Either Extreme Had Its Way?

1 Michelle and Janet

Scenario 1: Those who support unlimited religious freedom and oppose sexual freedom win

Under this scenario, legislation would likely be passed trying to minimize any protections or benefits, or at least government funding for them, that could help same-sex couples. These laws would most likely be unconstitutional under *Obergefell v. Hodges* (the same-sex marriage case). If any of these laws interfered with Janet's insurance plan, it could create problems in the short term while the law is challenged in court, which is long enough to cause Michelle serious health concerns. Moreover, a law would be likely to expand RFRA-type coverage to for-profit entities and the insurance context generally. Therefore, if Janet's employer did assert a religious freedom claim to not have to provide coverage, it may be able to do so under one of these laws unless the law was found to be unconstitutional. Finally, no antidiscrimination law based on sexual orientation would protect Janet and Michelle. Currently there is no federal statute protecting against discrimination based on sexual orientation, but at present there is some chance for such a law. If those who oppose any protection for sexual freedom prevail, that chance would be gone.

Scenario 2: Those who oppose religious freedom win

This would not change the outcome from today's law much, assuming that Janet's employer did not assert a religious freedom claim. Michelle would be covered under Janet's policy. If the employer did assert a religious freedom claim, it would likely lose because RFRA would be repealed so the employer would have to rely on the Free Exercise Clause of the First Amendment to the Constitution. Since the HHS contraceptive coverage mandate under the Affordable Care Act applies to all employers providing coverage under the act, whether or not religious, the employer would lose. As mentioned earlier, however, even with RFRA the employer would likely lose in this case.

2 Mandy

Scenario 1: Those who support unlimited religious freedom and oppose sexual freedom win

Mandy wins because every state would have a RFRA, and because she would also have claims under the Free Speech and Free Exercise Clauses of the First Amendment.

Scenario 2: The opponents of religious freedom win

Mandy might still prevail on claims under the Free Speech and Free Exercise Clauses, assuming whatever court she filed suit in agreed with the court that decided Julea Ward's case. If not, Mandy's expulsion would go into effect. Her only hope in this instance would be prevailing on one of her constitutional claims. No RFRA would protect her and if she lost her constitutional claims, she would have no other right to assert.

3 Amy

Scenario 1: Those who support unlimited religious freedom and oppose sexual freedom win

Amy could be in trouble and her health could be at risk. First, the HHS mandatory contraceptive coverage mandate would be gone, as would her state's mandatory contraceptive coverage law. Unless Slangtontech agreed to cover her contraceptives, she would not have coverage. In the hypothetical, Slangtontech had a religious objection to providing contraceptive care, so it could deny coverage. Slangtontech would be protected by RFRA, which in this scenario would be amended to clearly protect for-profit employers more broadly than under current law. In fact, if those who oppose protecting sexual freedom win, it might be possible that any kind of objection to providing contraceptive coverage – including financial objections – would be adequate to deny coverage.

Scenario 2: Those who oppose religious freedom win

Amy would have coverage under the current system. Amy's employer would have no basis to prevent paying for the coverage because RFRA would have been repealed.

4 Jonathan

Scenario 1: Those who support unlimited religious freedom and oppose sexual freedom win

Jonathan's state would have a RFRA so he would be accommodated. The coach and teacher would be required not to take any negative action against Jonathan because he exercised his religious freedom to attend synagogue for these important holidays.

Scenario 2: Those who oppose religious freedom win

Jonathan would not be accommodated. There would be no RFRA, and permissive accommodation would be discouraged. Jonathan's chances of getting a scholarship would be reduced, and he could be punished every year in high school and in college for following his faith if he happened to encounter intolerant, unsympathetic, or ignorant teachers or administrators. This could have a profound impact on his future.

C What Would Happen if the Compromise Approach Advocated in This Book Were Used?

1 Janet and Michelle

Michelle would be covered under Janet's policy based on the current law. If Janet's employer had a religious objection to covering Michelle because Janet and Michelle are a same-sex couple, it would lose its claim under RFRA because it would be asserting a right that negatively affects third parties, namely its female employees. Moreover, there would be an antidiscrimination law protecting against discrimination by for-profit employers based on sexual orientation, as well as an exemption to the antidiscrimination law for religious entities. The government would, however, be expected to provide an accommodation for the employer, if reasonably feasible, to allow it to avoid being complicit in the coverage, and the system and culture in place would encourage permissive accommodations. Regardless, Michelle would be covered because RFRA would be amended to preclude for-profit entities from RFRA protection (but not from permissive accommodations) and RFRA would not protect a religious accommodation that directly harms third parties. Any amendment to RFRA, however, would also encourage government to provide accommodations when it is reasonably feasible to do so.

2 Mandy

RFRAs would exist in every state, but they would not allow harm to third parties as a result of a religious accommodation. Mandy would win under her state's RFRA. All states and the federal government would also have antidiscrimination laws protecting against discrimination aimed at members of the LGBT community by employers and public accommodations, but since Mandy did not refuse to serve the client based on raw animus because of sexual orientation, but rather because of her religious objection to same-sex marriage, she would prevail. The religious freedom protections under RFRA would need to be balanced against the antidiscrimination principles under the state antidiscrimination law. Since the counseling field allows a number of exceptions in situations where counselors do not believe they can adequately serve the client, Mandy's exemption would be an easy one to provide and the university could not expel her based on her religious objection.

Further helping her case would be the fact that the client never even knew that Mandy objected. Even if Mandy were in private practice and respectfully rejected the client because of her religious concerns, she could be accommodated as long as she referred the client elsewhere or advised the client that he or she could seek counseling elsewhere. If Mandy demonstrated hatred or general dislike for members of the gay and lesbian community unconnected to her religious objections, and refused to serve them regardless of their relationship or marital status, the school could decide that she did not belong in its counseling program since this sort of discrimination would not be based in religion. If, however, she did not want to serve any gay or lesbian clients based on sincerely held religious concerns that she could unexpectedly end up needing to counsel the client about a romantic relationship, thus violating either her religious tenets or her duties to counsel clients she has agreed to see – the university could not expel her without violating her state's RFRA.

3 Amy

Reproductive Freedom would be protected and neither the federal or state RFRAs would protect for-profit entities like Slangontech, Inc. Therefore, Amy could not be denied benefits. Slangontech might assert a claim under the U.S. Constitution, but contraceptive coverage laws are generally applicable so Slangontech would lose its constitutional challenge. Moreover, protections under the state constitution, even if it provided protection similar to RFRA, would not help Slangontech because for-profit entities would not be protected.

4 Jonathan

Under the compromise approach, Jonathan would win. His state would have a RFRA and the school would be required to accommodate him. He could be required to make up any work he missed, and the coach could require him to do extra practice to make up for any practice time lost. Jonathan could not be benched for taking off school for the Jewish High Holidays, nor could his grade be lowered because he needed to take the test at a different time. Also, the teacher could simply decide to administer the test on a different day, but that would be up to the teacher's discretion. Either way, Jonathan would be accommodated.

II SOME OBSERVATIONS AND CONCERNS
ABOUT THE CURRENT POLITICAL CLIMATE

I am neither a sociologist nor a political scientist. As a law and religion scholar, I do, however, have a good sense of the climate on both sides of the current political chasm. What I see are people on both sides digging in their heels and sometimes disparaging people on the other side. This should come as no surprise in regard to culture war issues. I wish that these people, especially those in government, would strive for compromise rather than stoking conflict. The best scenario involves protecting rights on both sides: instituting both RFRAs and antidiscrimination laws protecting members of the LGBT community.

If I had my way, for-profit entities would not be protected by RFRAs, but all religious entities would be; religious entities that are carrying out religious functions and not serving the public at large would also receive exemptions under antidiscrimination laws. Even the people digging in their heels may be able to engage in this sort of compromise over time. Yet simply for expressing what I just wrote, I open myself to attacks from both sides. Such is the risk for those who seek compromise in the culture wars, but millions of other people also want compromise and are simply not in the public spotlight. Moderate positions are not sexy and are certainly not easy to spell out in twenty-second sound bites. I hope you too will be willing to seek compromise and willing to stand up for rights on both sides.

There are the general partisans in the culture wars, and then there is a group that worries me far more. Most people would view what I call "a" group here to actually be two groups. To me, however, they are simply two sides of the same coin: authoritarianism. They go beyond arguing for their position. They try to silence and shame those who do not agree with them – or those who simply seek open discourse. I am, of course, referring to the extreme social conservatives, as well as their relatives on the other side, the extreme warriors for political correctness. Both try to silence and demean those who do not agree with them, or even those who do agree with them but remain willing to entertain discourse on issues central to each side's agenda.

Please do not misunderstand me. Not all social conservatives are incapable of listening. Moreover, many within the political correctness movement do not oppose discourse on the issues that drive them. Yet, with increasing frequency we see people attacked or silenced by both sides for simply trying to discuss an issue rather than assuming that one answer or the other is inherently correct. In fact, in the politically correct context, people who call for dialogue with those who disagree with the politically correct norm about an issue have been attacked for wanting discourse even though they agree with the politically correct ideals asserted by those attacking them. Not to be outdone, some social conservatives attack other conservatives for not being "truly conservative" and try to shut down any attempts by their more thoughtful colleagues to engage on issues. Some conservative radio talk show hosts have used this tactic.

I do not mean to end on such a negative note, but my observation is that these groups are gaining more power within their realms, and thus are further adding to the spiral away from finding common ground. You may be able to negotiate with a culture warrior who will listen; but as these extremes gain in power at the fringes, their attempts to silence and attack reverberate inward, affecting more and more people who may not even realize they are being affected: people who become afraid to speak for fear of reprisal or harsh responses.

It is easy to destroy bridges and much harder to build them. The danger from those who want to silence discourse is that they prevent people from daring to build, and they allow what has been built to rot by making people afraid to step out of the shadows and repair things. This is just a slower form of destruction.

I beseech you, the reader, regardless of what side you are on, to talk, to discuss, and to try to identify as best you can with those who have different backgrounds or ideas from yours. Do not be afraid to build bridges. After all, the process of building is rewarding and the ability to cross chasms is as well. Freedom's edge can be seen as a cliff or as the entrance to a bridge. However you view it, we must make sure that we do not fall off and lose the freedom to be who we are.

NOTES

1   A VIEW FROM THREE PLACES

1. This question can raise issues in the area of religiously affiliated employ-ers such as churches, religious charities, religious schools, and so on. As will be seen in Chapter 5, religious employers have a ministerial exception to anti-discrimination laws.
2. Ward v. Polite, 667 F.3d 727 (6th Cir. 2012).
3. Roe v. Wade, 410 U.S. 113 (1973); *see also* Griswold v. Connecticut, 381 U.S. 479 (1965); Planned Parenthood v. Casey, 505 U.S. 833 (1992).
4. Some of the drugs at issue in the *Hobby Lobby* case discussed throughout this book are believed to be abortifacients by those seeking religious exemp-tions, but the scientific evidence shows that they are not abortifacients. See Caroline Mala Corbin, *Abortion Distortions*, 71 Wash. & Lee L. Rev. 1175, 1197–1205 (2014). Later chapters will address what should happen when a religious exemption claim is factually inconsistent with scientific under-standings of the underlying concern objected to by the religious person or entity.
5. A recent Pew Research Center Survey showed that 59 percent of the gay community identified as being religiously affiliated. Interestingly, 11 per-cent of the gay community identified as being members of non-Christian religions, while only 6 percent of the straight community did. Conversely, 48 percent of the gay community (which is still a large number) identified as being affiliated with a Christian denomination, as opposed to 72 percent of the straight community. Overall the level of religiously unaffiliated people in the gay community was 41 percent, which was higher than in the straight community (22 percent). Still, 59 percent of the gay community constitutes a lot of people of faith. Pew Research Center, *America's Changing Religious Landscape*, Chapter 4, May 2015 at p. 87, www.pewforum.org/2015/05/12/chapter-4-the-shifting-religious-identity-of-demographic-groups/

6.   573 U.S. ___, 134 S. Ct. 2751 (2014). The *Hobby Lobby* Court claimed that there was no imposition on the rights of female employees as a result of accommodating the employers' religious concerns, but as we will see in Chapter 2, this seems to go against the facts.

7.   *Jim Daly Statement on Supreme Court Ruling on Marriage*, June 26, 2015 (Focus on the Family website and press release).

8.   Elliot Mincberg, "The Right's Slimy New Scheme: The Made-Up "Religious Freedom" Protection Designed To Gut Same-Sex Marriage," *Salon*, June 9, 2015.

9.   Mincberg is almost certainly correct, however, about some religious marriage exemption bills. Those will be addressed in later chapters. As will be seen, there may be ways to accommodate religious objections by county clerks when others can perform the duties with no harm or delay to the rights of applicants for marriage licenses, but not when those objections lead to denial or delay of licenses.

10.   Jeremy Diamond, "Chief Alabama Judge Would Defy the Supreme Court in Gay Marriage Ruling," CNN (Feb. 12, 2015), www.cnn.com/2015/02/12/politics/ray-moore-alabama-gay-marraige-supreme-court-slavery/. To be clear Moore had told state probate judges at the time that they need not follow a federal district court order and the U.S. Supreme Court had not yet decided the case, but even the refusal to follow the federal district court order should and did raise serious legal concerns.

11.   The Alabama Court of the Judiciary will hear the charges and determine whether to remove or sanction Moore. Kent Faulk, "What Now for Suspended Chief Justice Roy Moore," Al.com (May 10, 2016), www.al.com/news/birmingham/index.ssf/2016/05/suspended_alabama_chief_justic.html. It is a distinct possibility that Moore will be removed from the bench.

2   RELIGIOUS FREEDOM

1.   Academic arguments against religious freedom, especially those based in the notion that no line of demarcation allows one to separate religion from other comprehensive philosophies, are far more nuanced and are discussed in a different section of this chapter.

2.   For some, faith may be the central basis for all of this. For others, practice is more central than faith, although practice may be based on deeply held beliefs.

3.   494 U.S. 872 (1990).

4.   374 U.S. 398 (1963).

5. Frank S. Ravitch, *Be Careful What You Wish For: Why Hobby Lobby Weakens Religious Freedom*, 2015 BYU L. REV. 55, at 58–59 (forthcoming 2016).

6. 42 U.S.C. §2000bb et seq. (1993).

7. Scott C. Idleman, The Religious Freedom Restoration Act: Pushing the Limits of Legislative Power, 73 TEX. L. REV. 247, 248 (1994); President William J. Clinton, Remarks on Signing the Religious Freedom Restoration Act of 1993, 29 WEEKLY COMP. PRES. DOC. 2377 (Nov. 16, 1993).

8. City of Boerne v. Flores, 521 U.S. 507 (1997).

9. Ravitch, *supra* note 5 at 59.

10. *Id.*

11. Holt v. Hobbs, ___ U.S. ___ (2015); Gonzales v. O'Centro Espirita Beneficente Uniao Do Vegetal, 546 U.S. 418 (2005).

12. As will be seen in Chapter 7, accommodations for some religious institutions such as religious universities and adoption agencies can have significant impact on third parties, but even then the dynamic is different from that for for-profit entity situations.

13. Significant scientific evidence supports the argument that the drugs are not abortifacients.Carolyn Mala Corbin, *Abortion Distortions*, 71 WASH. & LEE L. REV. 1175 (2014).

14. Corporation of Presiding Bishops v. Amos, 483 U.S. 327, 342 (1987) (Brennan, J., Concurring) (addressing this under Free Exercise Clause); Gonzales v. O Centro Espirita Beneficiente Uniao do Vegetal, 546 U.S. 418 (2006) (applying RFRA to such an entity).

15. 366 U.S. 599 (1961).

16. 455 U.S. 252 (1982).

17. Ravitch, *supra* note 5 at 68–69, 111–112.

18. See, for example, Scott W. Gaylord, For Profit Corporation, Free Exercise, and the HHS Mandate, 91 WASH. U. L. REV. 589 (2014); Alan J. Meese and Nathan B. Oman, Hobby Lobby, Corporate Law, and the Theory of the Firm: Why For-Profit Corporations are RFRA Persons 127 HARV. L. REV. 273 (2014); Ronald J. Colombo, The Naked Private Square, 51 HOUS. L. REV. 1 (2013); Michael A. Helfand and Mark L. Rienzi, God and Profits: Is There Religious Liberty for Money Makers?, 21 GEO. MASON L. REV. 59 (2013); Jonathan T. Tan, Nonprofit Organizations, For-Profit Corporation, and the HHS Mandate: Why the Mandate Does Not Satisfy RFRA's Requirements, 47 U. RICH. L. REV. 1301 (2013); Robert K. Vischer, Do For-Profit Businesses Have Free Exercise Rights? 21 J. CONTEMP. LEGAL ISSUES 369 (2014) 2014).

19. See, for example, Amicus Curiae Brief of Corporate and Criminal Law Professors in Support of Petitioners, Hobby Lobby, 134 S. Ct. 2751 (Nos. 13-354, 13-356) (amicus brief by law professors urging the Court to, among other things, reject protection for for-profit entities under RFRA), 2014 WL 333889; *see also*, Caroline Mala Corbin, The Contraception Mandate, 107

Nw. U.L. Rev. Colloquy 151 (2012); Alan E. Garfield, The Contraceptive Mandate Debate: Achieving a Sensible Balance, 114 Colum. L. Rev. Sidebar 1 (2014); Thomas E. Rutledge, A Corporation Has No Soul – The Business Entity Law Response to the PPACA Contraceptive Mandate, 5 Wm. & Mary Bus. L. Rev. 1 (2014).

20. Citizens United v. Federal Election Commission, 588 U.S. 310 (2010).
21. *Id.*
22. See generally, Ravitch, *supra* note 5.
23. *Hobby Lobby* at 2785 (Kennedy, J., Concurring).
24. *Hobby Lobby* at 2802 (Ginsburg, J., Dissenting).
25. 80 U.S. 679 (1871).
26. Hosanna Tabor Evangelical Lutheran Church and School v. EEOC, 565 U.S. ___, 132 S.Ct. 694 (2012).
27. This exemption is not adequate in the view of some of these entities, because it requires that they file notice of their objection to providing contraceptive coverage. Several religious entities have objected to filing the notice because doing so starts the process of third-party coverage and therefore, in the view of these entities, makes them complicit in the ultimate provision of contraceptives. A number of lawsuits have been filed. Geneva College v. Secretary of Health and Human Services, No. 13–3536, 2015 WL 543067 (3rd Cir. Feb. 11, 2015); Michigan Catholic Conference v. Burwell, 755 F.3d 372 (6th Cir. 2014); Priests for Life v. Department of Health and Human Services, 773 F.3d 229 (D.C. Cir. 2014); Wheaton Coll. v. Sebelius, 703 F.3d 551 (D.C. Cir. 2012); Colorado Christian University v. Sebelius, No. 13-cv-02105-REB-MJW, 2014 WL 2804038 (D.Colo. June 20, 2014); Catholic Benefits Ass'n v. Burwell, No. CIV-14–685-R, 2014 WL 7399195 (W.D. Okla. Dec. 29, 2014); University of Notre Dame v. Sebelius, 988 F.Supp.2d 912 (N.D. IN 2013). In November 2015, the Supreme Court consolidated several of these cases in Zubik v. Burwell, and on May 16, 2016, 578 U.S. ____ (2016)(slip opinion), the Court issued a short *per curiam* opinion in that case, which essentially suggests that the parties work the situation out and find a compromise. In the meantime, the lawsuits filed by the parties can serve as notice that those employers object to providing contraceptive coverage. It seems that other employers may still be required to follow the HHS notice requirements.
28. Bob Jones University v. United States, 461 U.S. 574 (1983).

3 SEXUAL FREEDOM

1. __ U.S. ___, 135 S.Ct. 2584 (2015).
2. 478 U.S. 186 (1986).

3. 539 U.S. 558 (2003).

4. *Id.* at 2484.

5. 517 U.S. 620 (1996).

6. Loving v. Virginia, 388 U.S. 1 (1967); Turner v. Safley, 482 U.S. 78 (1987).

7. 570 U.S. ___, 133 S.Ct. 2675 (2013).

8. 381 U.S. 479 (1965).

9. 410 U.S. 113 (1973).

10. Centers for Disease Control, Abortion Surveillance – U. S., Surveillance Summaries, Nov. 27, 2015/64(SS10); 1–40: www.cdc.gov/mmwr/preview/mmwrhtml/ss6410a1.htm?s_cid=ss6410a1_e.

11. Frank S. Ravitch, *Be Careful What You Wish For: Why Hobby Lobby Weakens Religious Freedom*, 2015 Byu L. Rev. 55 (2016).

12. In November 2015, the Supreme Court consolidated several of these cases in Zubik v. Burwell, and on May 16, 2016, 578 U.S. ____ (2016)(slip opinion), the Court issued a short *per curiam* opinion in that case, which essentially suggests that the parties work the situation out and find a compromise. In the meantime, the lawsuits filed by the parties can serve as notice that those employers object to providing contraceptive coverage. It seems that other employers may still be required to follow the HHS notice requirements and the challenges will continue.

13. Weldon Amendment, Consolidated Appropriations Act, 2009, Pub. L. No. 11–117, 123 Stat. 3034 (2009).

14. Planned Parenthood v. Casey, 505 U.S. 833, 872–73 (1992).

15. Planned Parenthood League of Massachuchusetts v. Bellotti, 641 F.2d 1006, 1021-22 (1st Cir. 1981); Charles v. Carey, supra, 627 F.2d at 772, 784-86 (7th Cir. 1980); Leigh v. Olson, 497 F.Supp. 1340 (D.N.D.1980); Planned Parenthood Ass'n v. Ashcroft, 483 F.Supp. 679 (W.D.Mo.1980).

16. Hodgson v. Minnesota, 497 U.S. 417, 450-55 (1990); L. v. Matheson, 450 U.S. 398, 412–13 (1981); Bellotti v. Baird, 443 U.S. 622, 641 (1979).

17. Planned Parenthood v. Casey, 505 U.S. 833, 896–99 (1992); Planned Parenthood v. Danforth, 428 U.S. 52, 69–72 (1976).

18. Planned Parenthood v. Casey, 505 U.S. 833, 835–37 (1992); Hodgson v. Minnesota, 497 U.S. 417, 448–50 (1990).

19. The case is called Whole Woman's Health v. Hellerstedt, Case No. 15-274 (2015 Term). Oral arguments before the Supreme Court were heard on March 2, 2016.

20. www.cdc.gov/mmwr/preview/mmwrhtml/ss6311a1.htm; M. LeRoy Sprang, MD & Mark G. Neerhof, DO, *Rationale for Banning Abortions Late in Pregnancy*, 280 J. Am. Med. Assn. 744, 746 (1998).

21. Ala. Code 1975, § 26-23B-2 (2011); Ark. Code § 20–16-1104 (2005); Idaho Code § 18–503 (2011); Minn. Stat. § 145.4242 (2006); Neb. Rev. Stat. § 28–3,104 (2010); Okla. Stat. §1–738.9 (2006).

22. Planned Parenthood v. Casey, 505 U.S. 833, 879 (1992) ("[A] state may not prohibit any woman from making the ultimate decision to terminate her pregnancy before viability.")

4 COUNTY CLERKS AND OTHER GOVERNMENT EMPLOYEES

1. Obergefell v. Hodges, ___ U.S. ___, 135 S. Ct. 2584 (2015).
2. Dominic Holden, *Kim Davis's Lawyers Have Said Things that are Literally Unbelievable*, BuzzFeed News, www.buzzfeed.com/dominicholden/kim-daviss-lawyers-have-said-things-that-are-literally-unbel#.vcmdAkxE4.
3. *Id.*
4. *See* Employment Division v. Smith, 494 U.S. 872, 890 (1990) (exemptions to generally applicable laws are not required by the Free Exercise Clause, but government entities are free to give accommodations to generally applicable laws if they choose to do so).
5. 388 U.S. 1 (1967).
6. Douglas Laycock et al. eds. *Same-Sex Marriage and Religious Liberty: Emerging Conflicts* (Rowman and Littlefield Publishers, 2008); Kent Greenawalt, Religious Toleration and Claims of Conscience, 28 J.L. & Pol. 91, 114 (2013); Douglas Laycock, Sex, Atheism, and the Free Exercise of Religion, 88 U. Det. Mercy L. Rev. 407 (2011); *but see,* James M. Oleske, Jr., The Evolution of Accommodation: Comparing the Unequal Treatment of Religious Objections to Interracial and Same-Sex Marriages, 50 Harv. Civ. Rts.-Civ. Lib. L. Rev. 99 (2015) (arguing that the differences between religious objections to same-sex marriage and interracial marriage have been overblown).
7. Kent Greenawalt, Religious Toleration and Claims of Conscience, 28 J.L. & Pol. 91, 111–14 (2013).
8. *Id.* at 11.
9. ___ U.S. ___, 135 S. Ct. 2584 (2015).
10. *Id.* at 2607.
11. *See, for example,* United States v. Windsor, 570 U.S. ___, 133 S. Ct. 2675 (2013) (holding DOMA unconstitutional in part because it disparaged same-sex couples who could legally marry in one state from affirming "their commitment to one another before their... community"); Romer v. Evans, 517 U.S. 620 (invalidating Colorado constitutional amendment that prevented any government entity within the state from protecting people from discrimination based on sexual orientation because the basis for the proposed amendment was discriminatory).

12. Frederick Mark Gedicks & Rebecca G. Van Tassell, RFRA Exemptions from the Contraception Mandate: An Unconstitutional Accommodation of Religion, 49 HARV. C.R.-C.L. L. REV. 343 (2014).

13. 494 U.S. 872 (1990).

14. 544 U.S. 709 (2005).

15. This has not happened in any state, though legislation has been proposed in Alabama that would eliminate the requirement for marriage licenses – but this bill would change the process so that couples would submit a marriage contract that would then be recorded rather than the probate judge issuing a marriage license. Mike Carson, *Bill to Eliminate Marriage Licenses Moves Closer to Passing*, Alabama.com, www.al.com/news/index.ssf/2015/09/bill_to_eliminate_marriage_lic.html (Sept. 14, 2015). While the law raises numerous practical and legal problems, there is no reason to believe that this would lead to a requirement of a marriage ceremony that could only be performed by a religious entity.

16. N.C. Gen. Stat. §51–5.5, §7A-292(b) (2015); Utah Code §17–20-4, §30–1-6, §63G-20–101, *et seq* (2015).

17. Miller v. Davis, ___ F.Supp.3d ___, 2015 WL 4866729; *Same Sex Couple Confronts Kentucky Clerk*, NY TIMES VIDEO, www.nytimes.com/video/us/100000003885415/same-sex-couple-confronts-kentucky-clerk.html (Davis says clearly that she is denying the license based on "God's authority").

18. Miller v. Davis, Civil Action # 15–44-DLB, Order Filed on 9/8/2015 at fn. 1 (United States District Court, Eastern District of Kentucky) ("Plaintiff's marriage licenses have been altered so that "Rowan County" rather than "Kim Davis" appears on the line reserved for the name of the county clerk, Plaintiffs have not argued that the alterations affect the validity of the licenses").

19. Utah Code §17–20-4 (2), §30–1-6 (requiring that a county clerk or designee be available during business hours to solemnize a legal marriage, thus adding this to the list of those who may solemnize marriages).

20. N.C. Gen. Stat. §51–5.5 (a)-(c), §7A-292(b).

21. 494 U.S. 872 (1990).

22. U.S. CONST. Art. VI, Cl. 2.

23. Eliana Dockterman, *Kim Davis' Lawyers Argue Altered Marriage Licenses Are Valid, Time* (Oct. 13, 2015) (noting state attorney general and governor have approved the altered licenses as valid).

24. Ky. Rev. Stat. Ann. §402.100 (1)(c) (West 2006), requiring use of a form prescribed by the state Department of Libraries and Archives, but only requiring the signature of the "county clerk *or deputy county clerk* issuing the license" [emphasis added]. Therefore, if the state Department of Libraries and Archives does not require the name of the clerk to be on the form, removal of the name should not be a problem.

25. Ky. Rev. Stat. Ann. §402.080 (West 2006), requiring that the license be issued by "the clerk of the county." §402.100 (1)(c) suggests that this might include deputy clerks, but one might argue that it must be the county clerk him- or herself. Moreover §402.100 (3)(a) requires that after the ceremony is performed, the person performing the ceremony must deliver a certificate and that certificate must include "the name of the county clerk under whose authority the license was issued." Again, this could be interpreted to include deputy clerks when the county clerk refuses to issue licenses or have his or her name on the licenses, a position with which the former governor and former state attorney general seemed to agree, *see supra* note 23, and accompanying text, but one could argue against this interpretation under the statute.

26. Miller v. Davis, ___ F.Supp.3d ___, 2015 WL 4866729; *Same Sex Couple Confronts Kentucky Clerk*, NY Times Video (Davis says clearly that she is denying the license based on "God's authority").

5   FOR-PROFIT COMPANIES, SHOPS, AND COMMERCIAL LANDLORDS

1. 309 P.3d 53 (N.M. 2013).
2. See, for example, Bob Jones Univ. v. U.S., 461 U.S. 574 (1983) (discussed in greater detail in Chapter 7); Fiedler v. Marumsco Christian School, 631 F.2d 1144 (4th Cir. 1980).
3. *Elane Photography*, 309 P.3d at 61
4. *Id.*
5. *Id.* at 62.
6. *Id.*
7. As the New Mexico Supreme Court explains, this formula comes from the Supreme Court's decision in Rumsfeld v. Forum for Academic & Institutional Rights Inc., 547 U.S. 47 (2006).
8. West Virginia Bd. of Education v. Barnette, 319 U.S. 624 (1943) (at the time this case was decided, the words "under God" were not part of the pledge).
9. Wooley v. Maynard, 430 U.S. 705 (1977).
10. *Elane Photography*, 309 P.3d at 65.
11. *Id.* at 65–66.
12. See, for example, Craig v. Masterpiece Cakeshop, ___ P.3d ___ (2015), 2015 WL 47604530 (rejecting similar free speech arguments in a case involving a bakery that refused to bake a wedding cake for a same-sex couple).
13. United States v. Lee, 455 U.S. 252 (1982).

14. *Elane Photography*, 309 P.3d at 76.
15. *Id.* at 79–80 (Bosson, J., specially concurring).
16. Craig v. Masterpiece Cakeshop, ___ P.3d ___ (2015), 2015 WL 47604530.
17. *Id.* at 6.
18. *Id.* at 7.
19. *Id.* at 10–12.
20. *Id.* at 18.
21. Shaw v. Reno, 509 U.S. 630, 654 (1993) ("The States certainly have a very strong interest in complying with federal antidiscrimination laws that are constitutionally valid as interpreted and applied").
22. Presley v. Etowah County Com'n, 502 U.S. 491, 509–10 (1992).
23. Bankers Life and Cas. Co. v. Crenshaw, 486 U.S. 71, 82–85 (1988).
24. The *Hobby Lobby* decision does not provide such reasons, but the work of some legal scholars has done so. See, for example, Scott W. Gaylord, For Profit Corporation, Free Exercise, and the HHS Mandate, 91 WASH. U. L. REV. 589 (2014); Alan J. Meese and Nathan B. Oman, Hobby Lobby, Corporate Law, and the Theory of the Firm: Why For-Profit Corporations are RFRA Persons 127 HARV. L. REV. 273 (2014); Ronald J. Colombo, *The Naked Private Square*, 51 HOUS. L. REV. 1 (2013); Michael A. Helfand and Mark L. Rienzi, *God and Profits: Is There Religious Liberty for MoneyMakers?*, 21 GEO. MASON L. REV. 59 (2013); Jonathan T. Tan, *Nonprofit Organizations, For-Profit Corporation, and the HHS Mandate: Why the Mandate Does Not Satisfy RFRA's Requirements*, 47 U. RICH. L. REV. 1301 (2013); Robert K. Vischer, *Do For-Profit Businesses Have Free Exercise Rights?*, 21 J. CONTEMP. LEGAL ISSUES 369 (2014) 2014).
25. 565 U.S. ___, 132 S.Ct. 694 (2012).
26. Philip Hamburger, *More Is Less*, 90 VA. L. REV. 835 (2004) (addressing this phenomenon under the First Amendment); Vincent Blasi, *The Pathological Perspective and the First Amendment*, 85 COLUM. L. REV. 449 (1985) (addressing this phenomenon under the First Amendment with a significant focus on free speech issues).
27. Hamburger, *supra* note 26 at 837–38.
28. Vincent Blasi, *The Pathological Perspective and the First Amendment*, 85 COLUM. L. REV. 449 (1985) (addressing this phenomenon under the First Amendment with a significant focus on free speech issues).
29. Henry L. Chambers, The Supreme Court Chipping Away at Title VII: Strengthening or Killing It? 74 LA. L. REV. 1161 (2014).
30. Frank S. Ravitch and Marsha B. Freeman, The Americans with "Certain" Disabilities Act: Title I of the ADA and the Supreme Court's Result Oriented Jurisprudence, 77 DENV. U. L. REV. 119 (1999).
31. Sheldon Nahmod, *Section 1983 Discourse: The Move from Constitution to Tort*, 77 GEO. L. J. 1719 (1989).
32. 477 U.S. 57 (1986).

33. *Id.* at 64.

34. *Id.*

35. *Id.* at 67.

36. *Id.*

37. Sarah E. Burns, Evidence of a Sexually Hostile Workplace: What Is It and How Should It Be Assessed after Harris v. Forklift Systems, Inc, 21 N.Y.U. REV. L. & SOC. CHANGE 357 (1995).

38. Judith L. Johnson, *License to Harass Women: Requiring Hostile Environment Sexual Harassment to Be "Severe or Pervasive" Discriminates among "Terms and Conditions" of Employment*, 62 MD. L. REV. 85 (2003).

39. *Id.*

40. 42 U.S.C. §12101 (purpose and findings sections, including the statement that the goals of the ADA include "to provide a clear and comprehensive national mandate for the elimination of discrimination against individuals with disabilities").

41. *Id.* at 144–47.

42. 527 U.S. 471 (1999).

43. 527 U.S. 516 (1999).

44. *Id.* at 122–23.

45. *Id.* at 146–47.

46. *Id.* at 124–33.

47. *Id.* at 147–50.

48. *Id.* at 150.

49. 42 U.S.C. §12101.

50. *Id.* at 147–50.

51. 98 U.S. 145 (1879).

52. 374 U.S. 398 (1963).

53. *Employment Div.* v. *Smith*, 494 U.S. 872 (1990).

54. Frank S. Ravitch, *Masters of Illusion: The Supreme Court and the Religion Clauses* (NYU Press, 2007).

55. Stephen M. Feldman, *Please Don't Wish Me a Merry Christmas: A Critical History of Separation of Church and State* 218–54 (NYU Press 1997).

56. *Id.*

57. Hamburger, supra note 26.

58. 406 U.S. 205 (1972).

59. Feldman, *Please Don't Wish Me a Merry Christmas, supra* note 55.

60. In fact, no non-Christian has ever won a Free Exercise Clause exemption case before the Supreme Court and even most Christians have lost such cases. Mark Tushnet, *Of Church and State and the Supreme Court: Kurland Revisited*, S. CT. REV. 373, 381 (1989).

61. Lower court cases went both ways after *Sherbert* and *Yoder*, while many denied the claimant's exemptions, a number did not. *See*, for example, Dayton Christian Schs., Inc. v. Ohio Civil Rights Comm'n, 766 F.2d 932

(6th Cir. 1985) (school's free exercise rights violated by application of civil rights laws); McCurry v. Tesch, 738 F.2d 271 (8th Cir. 1984) (enforcement of state order against operation of church school in violation of state law infringed church's free exercise rights); *Warner v. Graham*, 675 F. Supp. 1171 (D.N.D. 1987) (Free Exercise Clause violated where plaintiff lost her job because of sacramental peyote use); United States v. Lewis, 638 F. Supp. 573 (W.D. Mich. 1986) (rule requiring government to consent to waiver of a jury trial violated defendants' free exercise rights); United States v. Abeyta, 632 F. Supp. 1301 (D.N.M. 1986) (Bald Eagle Protection Act violated defendant's free exercise rights); Equal Employment Opportunity Comm'n v. Fremont Christian Sch., 609 F. Supp. 344 (N.D. Calif. 1984) (same); Congregation Beth Yitzchok of Rockland, Inc. v. Town of Ramapo, 593 F. Supp. 655 (S.D.N.Y. 1984) (regulations interfering with congregation's operation of its nursery school violated free exercise rights); Chapman v. Pickett, 491 F. Supp. 967 (C.D. Ill. 1980) (free exercise rights of Black Muslim prisoner were violated by his punishment for refusal to follow order to handle pork); Geller v. Sec'y of Def., 423 F. Supp. 16 (D.D. C. 1976) (regulation denying Jewish chaplain right to wear facial hair violated his free exercise rights); Lincoln v. True, 408 F. Supp. 22 (W.D. Ky. 1975) (denial of unemployment compensation to claimant who terminated employment for religious reasons infringed her free exercise rights); Am. Friends Serv. Comm. v. United States, 368 F. Supp. 1176 (E.D. Pa. 1973) (tax withholding statute violates plaintiffs' free exercise rights); Nicholson v. Bd of Comm'rs, 338 F. Supp. 48 (N.D. Ala. 1972) (statutory oath required of applicant for admission to state bar infringed on applicant's free exercise rights).

62. Michael W. McConnell, *Free Exercise Revisionism and the Smith Decision*, 57 U. Chi. L. Rev. 1109, 1121 (1990); Ira C. Lupu, *Employment Division v. Smith and the Decline of Supreme Court Centrism*, Byu L. Rev. 259, 267 (1993); Maxine Eichner, *Who Should Control Children's Education?: Parents, Children, and the State*, 75 U. Cin. L. Rev. 1339, 1384 (2007).

63. McConnell, *supra* note 62.

64. Hamburger, *supra* note 26.

65. Kathleen Gray, Michigan Religious Freedom Bill Stalls in Lame-Duck Session, Detroit Free Press (December 17, 2014).

66. *See infra* notes 76–77, and accompanying text.

67. Christopher Cousins, Controversial Maine 'Religious Freedom' Bill Rejected by Legislative Committee, Bangor Daily News, Jan. 23, 2014; Mario Moretto, "Religious Freedom" Bill in Maine Would Lead to Legalized Discrimination, Opponents Say, Bangor Daily News, Jan. 16, 2014.

68. April Hunt, Georgia Equality Spokesman Correct on Claim, The Atlanta Journal-Constitution, Jan. 21, 2015, at B1; Peter Berg and David Key Sr.,

Law, Religion: Keeping Balance, THE ATLANTA JOURNAL-CONSTITUTION, Jan. 16, 2015, at A12; Jeff Graham, No Threat to Religious Liberty, The Atlanta Journal-Constitution, April 10, 2014, at A10.

69. Tony Cook, Religious Freedom Bill Gets Hearing, INDIANAPOLIS STAR, Feb. 9, 2015, at A1; Abdul-Hakim Shabazz, No Service, INDIANAPOLIS STAR, Jan. 18, 2015, at A16; Tony Cook and Marisa Kwiatkowski, Religious Freedom Bill Is Drafted, INDIANAPOLIS STAR, Dec. 27. 2014, at A1; Editorial, Freedom to Discriminate, Kokomo Tribune, Feb. 22, 2015.

70. Cal. Health & Safety Code § 1367(i) (West 2014) (requiring all health-care service providers to provide "all of the basic healthcare services provided in subdivision (b) of Section 1345."); Cal. Health & Safety Code § 1345(b) (West 2003) (defining "basic health services"); Letter from Michelle Rouillard, director, Dep't of Managed Health Care of Cal., to Mark Morgan, Cal. president of Anthem Blue Cross (Aug. 22, 2014) (*available at* www.dmhc.ca.gov/Portals/0/082214letters/abc082214.pdf).

71. Brian Dowling, Health Care Ruling Studied for Its Effect on Connecticut; Democratic Officials Decry Decision; Family Institute, Archdiocese Encouraged, THE HARTFORD COURIER, June 30, 2014.

72. Justin A. Hinkley, Report Slams Michigan for Inequality, Lansing State Journal, Jan. 24, 2015, at A8; Teresa Wiltz, Michigan Religious Freedom Act May Open Door to Discrimination, Critics Say, SUN-SENTINEL (Florida), Dec. 21, 2014, at A16; Kathleen Gray, Religious Freedom Legislation Stalls in Lansing, DETROIT FREE PRESS, Dec. 18, 2014, at A13; Editorial, Kendall Stanley – Lame Duck Is Right, PETOSKY NEWS-REVIEW, Dec. 15, 2014; Nathan Triplett, Passing Religious Freedom Bill Spells Trouble for Michigan, THE ARGUS-PRESS, Dec. 14, 2014; Editorial, Religious Freedom Bill Wrong for State, LIVINGSTON COUNTY PRESS, Dec. 14, 2014, at A14; Olivia Lewis, Some Local Clergy Not Sold on Bill, BATTLE CREEK ENQUIRER, Dec. 11, 2014, at A2; John Matuszak, Protestors Say GOP Bill Is a "License to Discriminate," THE HERALD PALLADIUM, Dec. 9, 2014, at local 1; WJBK Detroit, Pending State Religious Freedom Act a "License to Discriminate," Dec. 9, 2014; Kathleen Gray, Religious Freedom Bill Passes Out of Michigan House, DETROIT FREE PRESS, Dec. 7, 2014.

73. Chrissie Thompson, Sponsors Kill Religious Freedom Bill, LANCASTER EAGLE GAZETTE, Feb. 27, 2014, at A1 (Ohio); Tom Loftus, Gov. Steve Beshear Vetoes Religious Freedom Bill, Says It Threatens Public Safety, Civil Rights, The Courier-Journal, March 22, 2013 (Kentucky); Joseph Gerth, Religious Freedom Act: Fischer Adds His Voice in Opposition, THE COURIER-JOURNAL, March 20, 2013, at A1.

74. Christopher Cousins, Controversial Maine "Religious Freedom" Bill Rejected by Legislative Committee, BANGOR DAILY NEWS, Jan. 23, 2014;

Mario Moretto, "Religious Freedom" Bill in Maine Would Lead to Legalized Discrimination, Opponents Say, Bangor Daily News, Jan. 16, 2014.

75. Tony Cook, Religious Freedom Bill Gets Hearing, Indianapolis Star, Feb. 9, 2015, at A1; Abdul-Hakim Shabazz, No Service, Indianapolis Strar, Jan. 18, 2015, at A16; Tony Cook and Marisa Kwiatkowski, Religious Freedom Bill Is Drafted, Indianapolis Star, Dec. 27. 2014, at A1; Editorial, Freedom to Discriminate, Kokomo Tribune, Feb. 22, 2015.

76. April Hunt, Georgia Equality Spokesman Correct on Claim, The Atlanta Journal-Constitution, Jan. 21, 2015, at B1; Peter Berg and David Key Sr., Law, Religion: Keeping Balance, The Atlanta Journal-Constitution, Jan. 16, 2015, at A12.

77. State of Georgia, Office of the Governor, *Transcript: Deal HB 757 Remarks*, March 28, 2016, gov.georgia.gov/press-releases/2016-03-28/ transcript-deal-hb-757-remarks-0 (this is a link to the veto statement by Governor Nathan Deal); Sandhya Somashekhar, *Georgia governor vetoes religious freedom bill criticized as anti-gay*, Washington Post, March 28, 2016, www.washingtonpost.com/news/post-nation/wp/ 2016/03/28/georgia-governor-to-veto-religious-freedom-bill-criticized-as-anti-gay/.

78. One of the worst examples of this is a law recently passed in Mississippi known as HB 1523, or the "Protecting Freedom of Conscience from Government Discrimination Act," which seems aimed directly at same-sex marriage and LGBT rights, but has language that spans even further. It covers public accommodations, for-profit entities, government workers, and even foster care. The Act was signed into law on April 4, 2016. The law goes far beyond the protection already afforded under a RFRA Mississippi already had in place. A Federal District Court found the law to be unconstitutional on June 30, 2016 and an appeal is likely.

79. Cal. Health & Safety Code § 1367(i) (West 2014) (requiring all health care service providers to provide "all of the basic health care services provided in subdivision (b) of Section 1345."); Cal. Health & Safety Code § 1345(b) (West 2003) (defining 'basic health services"); Letter from Michelle Rouillard, Director, Dep't of Managed Health Care of Cal., to Mark Morgan, Cal. President of Anthem Blue Cross (Aug. 22, 2014) (*available at* www.dmhc.ca.gov/Portals/0/082214letters/abc082214.pdf).

80. J. Thomas Sullivan, Requiem for RFRA: A Philosophical and Political Response, 20 U. Ark. Little Rock L.J. 295 (1998); See also, Douglas Laycock, *Religious Liberty and the Culture Wars*, 2014 U. Ill. L. Rev 839, 845-46 (2014)(noting that religious accommodations and RFRA have "become far more controversial than [they] used to be"); Scott C. Idleman, The Religious Freedom Restoration Act: Pushing the Limits of Legislative Power, 73 Tex. L. Rev. 247, 248 (1994) (explaining that RFRA was widely supported when passed).

81.	Alan E. Garfield, *The Contraception Mandate: Achieving a Sensible Balance*, 114 COLUM. L. REV. SIDEBAR 1 (2014).

82.	Mike McKinnon, Calls to End Gay Renter Discrimination, Global News, March 28, 2014.

83.	Douglas Laycock, *Religious Liberty and the Culture Wars*, U. ILL. L. REV 839, 879(2014).

84.	*Id.* at 879–80.

85.	Corporation of Presiding Bishops v. Amos, 483 U.S. 327, 342 (1987) (Brennan, J., Concurring) (addressing this under Free Exercise Clause); Gonzales v. O Centro Espirita Beneficiente Uniao do Vegetal, 546 U.S. 418 (2006) (applying RFRA to such an entity).

86.	Western Presbyterian Church v. Bd. of Zoning and Adjustment, 862 F. Supp. 538 (D.D.C. 1994); Jesus Ctr. v. Farmington Hills Zoning Bd. of Appeals, 544 N.W.2d 698 (Mich. Ct. App. 1996). Of course, just because an entity has free exercise rights or is protected by RFRA does not mean that it will win its claim. Daytona Rescue Mission, Inc. v. City of Daytona Beach, 885 F.Supp. 1554 (M.D. Fla. 1995).

87.	Jimmy Swaggart Ministries v. Bd. of Equalization of California, 493 U.S. 378, 381 (1990); Note, When Rights Collide: In A Battle Between Pharmacists' Right of Free Exercise and Patients' Right to Access Contraception, Who Wins? – A Possible Solution for Nevada, 7 NEV. L.J. 212, 230 (2006).

88.	Holt v. Hobbs, 574 U.S. ___ (2015); Cutter v. Wilkinson, 544 U.S. 709 (2005).

89.	Department of Housing and Urban Development, *Equal Access to Housing in HUD Programs Regardless of Sexual Orientation or Gender Identity*, 24 CFR Parts 5, 200, 203, 236, 400, 570, 574, 882, 891, 982 (2012), 77 Fed. Reg. 5662 (Feb. 3, 2012) (protecting LGBT rights in HUD programs under the Fair Housing Act); *cf.* Smith v. Fair Employment & Housing Commission, 913 P.2d 909 (Calif. 1996) (protecting against marital status discrimination under state law); Swanner v. Anchorage Equal Rights Commission, 874 P.2d 274, (Alaska 1994) (same).

90.	874 P.2d 272 (Alaska 1994).

91.	460 N.W.2d 2 (Minn. 1990).

92.	Swanner, 874 P.2d at 278.

93.	*Id.* at 283.

94.	*Id.* at 280 fn.9.

95.	*Id.* at 283–84.

96.	Most relevant is the decision in Lawrence v. Texas, 539 U.S. 558 (2003), but the dissenting opinion in *French* also suggests that it may have been an improper reading in 1990 as well. 460 N.W.2d at 11 (Popovich, C. J., Dissenting).

97.	U.S. Const. Art. IV, Par. 2.

6   CONSCIENCE CLAIMS

1. Cutter v. Wilkinson, 544 U.S. 709 (2005); Locke v. Davey, 540 U.S. 712 (2004).
2. For an excellent discussion of the possibility that it is impossible to find a demarcation point between religious and secular moral systems see Winnifred Fallers Sullivan, *The Impossibility of Religious Freedom* (Princeton Univ. Press 2007).
3. To be clear, I am speaking here of the majority of pro-life individuals and not the more radical individuals who use violence and intimidation to achieve their goals.
4. Weldon Amendment, Consolidated Appropriations Act, 2009, Pub. L. No. 11–117, 123 Stat. 3034 (2009).
5. See Carolyn Mala Corbin, Abortion Distortions, 71 Wash. & Lee L. Rev. 1175 (2014).
6. Webster v. Reproductive Health Services, 492 U.S. 490 (1989).
7. 794 F.3d 1064 (9th Cir. 2015), *Pet. for Cert.* filed *in*, Stormans, Inc., Dba Ralph's Thirftway, *et al.* v. John Wiesman, Secretary, Washington State Department of Health, *et al.*, U.S., Jan. 6, 2016.
8. *Id.* at 1071.
9. 752 N.W.2d 385 (Wis. Ct. App. 2008).
10. Employment Div. v. Smith, 474 U.S. 872 (1990) (religious exemption to generally applicable laws not required by the Constitution).
11. Robin Fretwell Wilson, The Calculus of Accommodation: Contraception, Abortion, Same-Sex Marriage, and Other Clashes between Religion and the State, 53 Boston Coll. L. Rev. 1417, 1470 (2012).
12. 667 F.3d 727 (6th Cir. 2012).
13. *Id.* at 735.
14. *Id.* (bracketed material added).
15. 667 F.3d 727 (6th Cir. 2012).

7   RELIGIOUS NON-PROFITS

1. I.R.C. §501(c)(3).
2. *Id.*
3. *Id.*
4. I.R.C. §501(c)(3); Treas. Reg. § 501(c)(3)-1 (detailing the requirements for organizations to be organized and operated "exclusively" for an exempt purpose); see, for example, Better Bus. Bureau of Washington, D.C., v. United States, 326 U.S. 279, 283 (1945) (establishing the meaning of

"exclusively" by deciding "that the presence of a single [non-exempt] purpose, if substantial in nature, will destroy the exemption regardless of the number or importance of truly [exempt] purposes"); *Living Faith, Inc.*, 950 F.2d at 367; Church in Boston v. Comm'r, 71 T.C. 102, 107 (1978) (discussing the Section 501(c)(3) requirement of exclusivity: "The term exclusively, however, has been construed not to mean 'solely' or 'absolutely without exception.' An organization which engages in nonexempt activities can obtain and maintain exempt status so long as such activities are only incidental and less than substantial.").

5.   I.R.C. §501(c)(3); Treas. Reg. § 501(c)(3)-1(d) (2008) (explaining "exempt purpose" for Section 501(c)(3) qualification); see, for example, Bob Jones Univ. v. United States, 461 U.S. 574, 598 (U.S.S.C. 1983) (holding that an organization whose practices "violate fundamental public policy" cannot be found to be operating for an exempt purpose); *IHC Health Plans, Inc.*, 325 F.3d at 1200; *St. David's Health Care Sys.*, 349 F.3d at 237–39; *Bethel Conservative Mennonite Church*, 746 F.2d at 392; *Presbyterian & Reformed Pub. Co.*, 743 F.2d at 156.

6.   461 U.S. 574 (1983).

7.   *Bob Jones Univ,*. 461 U.S. at 595 ("It would be wholly incompatible with the concepts underlying tax exemption to grant the benefit of tax-exempt status to racially discriminatory educational entities").

8.   *Id.* at 580–81.

9.   *Id.* at 586.

10.   *Bob Jones Univ,*. 461 U.S. at 595 ("Racially discriminatory educational institutions cannot be viewed as conferring a public benefit within the 'charitable' concept").

11.   *Id.* at 595–96.

12.   *Id.* at 603–4.

13.   *Id.*

14.   *Id.* at 2607.

15.   *Obergefell,* 135 S.Ct. at 2611 (Roberts, C.J., Dissenting).

16.   *Bob Jones University,* 461 U.S. at 604.

17.   Kent Greenawalt, Religious Toleration and Claims of Conscience, 28 J.L. & Pol. 91, 111–14 (2013).

18.   *Id.* at 595 (citations omitted).

19.   *Id.* at 591–92 (footnotes omitted and emphasis added).

20.   *Id.* at 592.

21.   *Id.* at 593–96.

22.   517 U.S. 620 (1996).

23.   570 U.S. ___, 133 S.Ct 2675 (2013).

24.   *Cf.* Executive Order 13672 (signed by President Obama on July 21, 2014) (prohibits discrimination in employment for federal workers and in hiring by federal contractors based on sexual orientation and gender identity).

25. Caryle Murphy, *Most U.S. Christian Groups Grow More Accepting of Homosexuality*, Pew Research Center, FactTank, December 18, 2015, www.pewresearch.org/fact-tank/2015/12/18/most-u-s-christian-groups-grow-more-accepting-of-homosexuality/ (an increasing number of American Christians, 54 percent, across a variety of denominations, as well as 83 percent of religious Americans who are not Christian, think homosexuality should be accepted by society).

26. 26 I.R.C. § 501(c)(3) (West 2010).

27. *See* Hall v. Comm'r, 729 F.2d 632, 634 (9th Cir. 1984) (affirming the denial of tax-exempt status to a religious organization that serves "almost exclusively to funnel a rental allowance to its officers"); Church of the Chosen People v. United States, 548 F. Supp. 1247, 1253 (D. Minn. 1982) (finding private inurement of church leaders when their "entire rent" was paid for by the church); Unitary Mission Church of Long Island v. Comm'r, 74 T.C. 507, 514 (1980) *aff'd without published opinion*, 647 F.2d 163 (2d Cir. 1981) (finding parsonage allowances of unexplained amounts to be excessive); Church of Living Tree v. Comm'r, 71 T.C.M. (CCH) 3210, at *3 (T.C.1996) (finding that provision of rent-free housing to the organization leader – who deeded the property to the church – is private inurement); *See also*, Page v. Comm'r, 58 F.3d 1342, 1348–49 (8th Cir. 1995) (finding private inurement when a church leader's "food, utilities, airplane maintenance, [and] provision of transportation" is paid for by the church account to which he is the primary contributor); Basic Unit Ministry of Alma Karl Schurig v. Comm'r, 670 F.2d 1210, 1212 (D.C. Cir. 1982) (finding private inurement when 70% of the organization's expenses was used to pay the living expenses of members); S. Church of Universal Bhd. Assembled, Inc. v. Comm'r, 74 T.C. 1223, 1224–25 (1980) (finding that payment of minister's "utilities, fuel, maintenance, and repair expenses of the parsonage ... food, postage, stationery, pots and pans, dishes, glassware, sheets, blankets, towels, and curtains," with church funds almost entirely contributed by the minister is private inurement); Church of Modern Enlightenment v. Comm'r, 55 T.C.M. (CCH) 1304 (T.C. 1988) *aff'd without published opinion*, 875 F.2d 307 (2d Cir. 1989) (finding payment of church leader's "food, clothing, shelter and other necessities of life" when he is the sole contributor to the church and only employed part-time with the church is private inurement); New Life Tabernacle v. Comm'r, 44 T.C.M. (CCH) 309 (T.C. 1982) (finding that payment of church member living expenses without quantification of the services performed in return is private inurement).

28. Branch Ministries v. Rossotti, 211 F.3d 137, 141–42 (D.C. Cir. 2000) (holding that a church's placement of political ads in newspapers violates the ban on political activity in §501[c][3]); Christian Echoes Nat. Ministry,

Inc. v. United States, 470 F.2d 849, 854 (10th Cir. 1972) (holding that substantial political activity by a religious organization disqualifies it from tax-exemption).

29.   45 C.F.R. §147.131(a).

30.   45 C.F.R. §147.131(b).

31.   In November 2015, the Supreme Court consolidated several of these cases in Zubik v. Burwell, and on May 16, 2016, 578 U.S. ____ (2016)(slip opinion), the Court issued a short per curiam opinion in that case urging the parties to find a compromise.

32.   Little Sisters of the Poor Home for the Aged v. Burwell, No. 15–105 (Petition for Writ of Certiorari Granted, Nov. 2015).

33.   Frank S. Ravitch, *Marketing Intelligent Design: Law and the Creationist Agenda* (Cambridge University Press, 2011).

34.   Kate C. Prickett, Alexa Martin-Storey, & Robert Crosnoe, A Research Note on Time with Children in Different- and Same-Sex Two-Parent Families, 52 DEMOGRAPHY 905, 908–912 (2015) (finding few differences between same-sex and heterosexual parent-child relationships); Abbie E. Goldberg, April M. Moyer, & Lori A. Kinkler, Lesbian, Gay, and Heterosexual Adoptive Parents' Perceptions of Parental Bonding During Early Parenthood, 1 COUPLE & FAM. PSYCH.: RES. & PRAC. 14–15 (2013) ("Our findings suggest that practitioners should be mindful that the bonding process for same-sex couples to their adopted children appears to be more similar to than different from that of heterosexual parents"); Rachel H. Farr & Charlotte J. Patterson, Coparenting Among Lesbian, Gay, and Heterosexual Couples: Associations With Adopted Children's Outcomes, 84 CHILD DEVEL. 1226, 1238–39 (2013) ("Results suggested that parental sexual orientation was linked more with qualitative differences in family experiences than with differences in outcomes for children"); Wendy D. Manning, Marshal Neal Fettro, & Esther Lamidi, Child Well-Being in Same-Sex Parent Families: Review of Research Prepared for American Sociological Association Amicus Brief, 33 POPULATION RES. & POL'Y REV. 485, 491–94 (2014) (examining social and behavioral data on children of same-sex and different-sex parents and finding few differences between the two); Alicia Crowl, Soyeon Ahn, & Jean Baker, *A Meta-Analysis of Developmental Outcomes for Children of Same-Sex and Heterosexual Parents*, 4 J. LGBT FAM. STUDIES 385, 398 (2008) ("For the outcome of parent-child relationship, same-sex parents reported having significantly better relationships with their children than did heterosexual parents").

35.   Robin Fretwell Wilson, Matters of Conscience: Lessons for Same-Sex Marriage from the Healthcare Context, *in Same Sex Marriage and Religious Liberty: Emerging Conflicts* (Douglas Laycock, Anthony Picarello Jr., & Robin Fretwell Wilson, eds., The Becket Fund for Religious Liberty and Rowman and Littlefield Publishers 2008).

36.   Robin Fretwell Wilson, The Calculus of Accommodation: Contraception.
      Abortion, Same-Sex Marriage, and Other Clashes Between Religion and
      the State, 53 BOS. COLL. L. REV. 1417 1446-47 (2012). The Illinois situa-
      tion led to closures but also to transfers of some services to other non-profit
      organizations outside the church. *Id.*

INDEX